ATLAS
of MAN
and RELIGION

Designed and compiled by:
GORDON K. HAWES M.A., B.D.

(signature)

Layout and maps by:
STANLEY KNIGHT F.R.G.S.
General Manager, The Cartographic Department, Pergamon Press Ltd.

(signature)

THE RELIGIOUS EDUCATION PRESS   A member of the Pergamon Group of Companies

We acknowledge with grateful thanks the loan and use of many photographs from:

World Council of Churches.
United Nations Agencies:
WMO,
UNESCO,
FAO,
ILO.
Oxfam.
Israel Government Tourist Office.
The British and Foreign Bible Society.

Maps Edited and Drawn by:
Gordon O. Bell, M.A. Edinburgh.
R.W. Anson, M.A. (Oxon)
George F. Humby.
William Thompson.
David A. Cox.

First published 1970

08 006999 1   Library of Congress Catalog Number
78-653717

THE RELIGIOUS EDUCATION PRESS
A Member of the Pergamon Group
OXFORD   NEW YORK   TORONTO
SYDNEY   BRAUNSCHWEIG

Printed in Great Britain by A. Wheaton & Co., Exeter

CONTENTS

CONTENTS

The responsibility of the spread of Christianity for the basic characteristics of the pattern of the human scene is clearly established. The dating of the calendar from the birth of Jesus Christ is sufficiently widespread to warrant such a conclusion. The marks of its Christian origin are to be seen throughout our civilization. This requires a closer inspection of the origins and development of the Christian religion.

Such an enquiry takes us far back beyond the beginning of the Christian era. Christianity claims its origins in the Old Testament story of the birth and history of the Chosen Nation. The Atlas will therefore include maps giving an indication of the broad sweep of history which accompanied the emergence of the Hebrew people as well as those containing the more detailed references involved in the biblical records. The ground covered is parallel to that in most biblical atlases but the approach is rather different. The maps are designed to illuminate spheres of influence rather than scenes of episodes. The missionary journeys of Paul will not be found here, but the route of the Exodus will be. This is because the actual journeys and the serial order by which Paul went from place to place are relatively unimportant: the places where he established Christian churches are the paramount concern. In the case of the Exodus, however, we are dealing with a journey which dominated succeeding history; to which the Hebrews looked back as the most important factor in their sense of providence; to which prophets and psalmists made constant reference as the outstanding guarantee of God's care for His people.

The twentieth century has witnessed more change in more fields during the first three-quarters of its existence than the previous thousand years. The speed of technological advance has opened up the prospect of human achievements beyond the imagination of the most brilliant science fiction writers. Such a prospect involves both hopes and fears, and conjures up the possible alternatives of an earthly paradise and a cataclysmic hell. The threat of annihilation in a third world war no longer belongs to the world of fantasy: it hangs over the world like a mushroom-shaped cloud.

The undying hope for the future lies in man's basic optimism. Increase in the knowledge of the world's problems is accompanied by an increase in the determination to co-operate for humanitarian purposes. This is seen in the fact that the twentieth century has produced organization on a world-wide scale concerned with almost every aspect of human welfare. Most of the bodies involved in this humanitarian enterprise are associated directly or indirectly with the United Nations Organization.

The importance of this section of the Atlas cannot be over-emphasized. The maps associated with it indicate visually the world-wide character of international co-operation. They also illustrate the very considerable influence that the United Nations has exercised in keeping peace and preventing war. The fact that wars have not been entirely prevented is a cause for considerable disappointment and shame; but it must not be forgotten that the United Nations has done much to settle disputes and prevent bloodshed. Places where the United Nations has intervened with varying effectiveness are indicated in this section, as well as the locations of the various headquarters of the United Nations agencies.

4

CONTENTS

The most outstanding features of the twentieth century in the field of the Christian religion is the enormous impetus that has been given to the movement towards Church unity. The preoccupation of this Atlas with Christian civilization and its traditions demands that we should give special attention to this movement.

For the first thousand years of its existence the Christian Church enjoyed unity of organization as well as of spirit. The division into Eastern and Western churches continued for a further five centuries, or thereabouts, when the Reformation split the Western churches into Roman Catholic and Protestant wings. Further fragmentation followed within the Protestant churches and the twentieth century inherited a multitude of organized communities all claiming Christian allegiance but often denying each other's right to the name of Christian. It goes without saying that this disunity hampered the spread of the Gospel and impaired the Christian image.

The patient attempts over many years to repair this fragmentation has borne fruit over the past sixty years at an increasing rate. The scrutiny of the maps in this final section of the Atlas will give some idea as to how this movement has gathered momentum.

The Greek word OIKUMENE, which means 'world wide', has been adopted as the 'watchword' of the World Council of Churches, and the movement towards unity has become known as the 'ecumenical' movement. The emergence and development of the World Council of Churches leading to dialogue between Catholic and Protestant, and even between Christian and Communist, is here described. The issues concerned are highlighted by recent events, and the reader of this Atlas is left at the last to assess the values and defects of the traditions and standards of the world in which we live today.

5

CONTENTS

INTRODUCTION

THE planet Earth is the home of man.

It can be described in many other ways, according to the interest and approach of the observer. It is part of the Solar system, of the galactic stellar mass, of the whole physical universe. It is an object of geological, zoological, botanical and other such studies.

But, first and foremost, it is the home of man.

'Astronomically speaking', said the scientist, 'man is insignificant!' 'Not so', replied his more perceptive friend, 'even astronomically speaking, man is the astronomer!' It is man alone, so far as we know, who has the power and the interest to assess his place in the universe and to exploit to his own advantage the resources of the natural world. In the course of evolution man has emerged as the master of his environment.

This is the basic assumption behind the pattern of this atlas. It is a human document designed to give an accurate account of the human factors by which the world we live in has been affected and shaped. It aims to be objective and 'open-ended', by which we mean that it is not intended to press a claim, even though it does inevitably betray a point of view on the part of the author.

In view of this contention some justification is needed for the particular interest shown in the Christian religion and its impact on the world in the course of history. Two sections are devoted specifically to the background and expansion of Christianity and one to the activities of the World Council of Churches. This is very easily

OUTER SPACE. A view of the earth from a satellite, 540 miles above India. The space age has far-reaching implications for education, communications, meteorology and many other aspects of life on earth. The UN works to ensure that the exploration of outer space is carried out for the benefit and in the interests of all mankind.

Blowing the ram-horn (during the New Year holiday, Israel)

explained. The atlas is being produced in the area of so-called Western civilization, which owes its standards and values to the influence and impact of Christianity. The indisputable evidence of this fact is seen in the dating of our calendar from the birth of Jesus Christ. We cannot fully understand the character of our particular part of the world without reference to the claims of the Christian Gospel and the historical facts which led to the rise of Christian culture and civilization. This demands the inclusion of those maps which illustrate the developments represented in the history of the Old and New Testaments.

Although the facts are presented as objectively as possible, the very attempt to be faithful to the truth must be affected by the author's conviction that in the Christian faith lies the clue to an understanding of man's nature and destiny, and of his place in the world. Nevertheless, he is well aware, as will be apparent, that the impact of Christianity has not always been true to its founder's principles, and it has not only condoned, but sometimes caused and encouraged bloodshed and suffering to mankind. The history of Christendom has some very dark patches, but its general influence has been progressive and life-giving.

It might be expected that an atlas entitled 'Man and Religion' would present the view of man and his world from the standpoint of other contemporary faiths and trace their historical influences.

However desirable this might be, the difficulties in producing such a book are considerable. The gathering of sufficient acceptable material would present a formidable task, and even if accomplished it would remove the unity of approach which is an advantage, so long as it is consciously 'open-ended'.

The phrase 'Man and Religion', which is applied not only to this atlas but to a comprehensive series of books for school use published by the R.E.P., needs some explanation.

We have moved away from the narrow connotation of the word 'Religion' as applied only to the faith and practice of those committed to particular systems of belief. Etymologically, it can be understood in a much wider context, and we have come to use the word to embrace, beyond the narrower definition, the whole conception of man as a responsible person. The Latin root of the word encourages the thought that men are 'bound together'—to one another, and perhaps also to God. They have mutual responsibilities which can be met only in terms of mankind as a unity, or as a brotherhood.

It is hoped that the facts set out and discussed in this atlas will lead to an understanding of the essential unity of the world and the implications involved in making the brotherhood of man a reality.

The five sections of this atlas follow a logical sequence.

In *Section I* an attempt is made to give an accurate and objective picture of the world in relation to the human race, with particular reference to the rise of western civilization which has since dominated world history.
Notice is drawn to the paramount influence of the spread of Christianity in this continuing process.

Section II goes on to describe in more detail this predominant influence and its impact first upon the western world and thence to all parts of the globe.

Section III still further isolates this particular influence and describes the background from which the Christian Gospel arose and the atmosphere in which it was nurtured. In other words, this section illustrates, in a rather unusual way, the worlds of the Old and New Testaments.

The *excursus*, in Sections II and III into the origins of our civilization is not altogether reassuring. The values and virtues of the Christian religion have not been unmixed with a sense of frustration and failure, and the twentieth century of the Christian era finds us by no means as confident nor as optimistic as our forefathers were in the latter part of the nineteenth.

Nevertheless, faith in the ultimate triumph of good over evil persists and human nature will not allow it to die. In *Section IV* we return to the contemporary world and record the current attempt to establish brotherhood and peace in the world, particularly through the agencies and activities of the United Nations Organisation.

TRADE. Fruit being loaded in Budapest for air shipment to Western European markets. Meetings on regional economic problems are helping countries to overcome some of the obstacles to regional and world trade.

9

A superficial scanning of the history of the past two thousand years offers a chaotic mixture of good and evil, of triumph and disaster; and it sometimes seems that 'Ichabod' is written over the structure of Christendom. The glory has departed. But this judgment would indeed be superficial.

In the span of the world's history, the two thousand years in which the Christian Gospel has flourished is but a brief moment. The Church has persisted in spite of the frailty of its human form. Bruised and broken by the errors and the crass stupidity of its own supporters it has proved an 'anvil which has worn out many hammers'. Moreover, the twentieth century, in which the human race has come near to committing suicide, in two world wars, has seen also the emergence of what Archbishop William Temple once called 'the great new fact of our era'—the modern movement towards Christian unity, known as the Ecumenical Movement and given concrete expression in the World Council of Churches.

Section V is devoted to a description of this phenomenon, showing how it came into being, how it has grown, what it is trying to do, and where it is succeeding in the Christian task of reconciliation.

Thus we end on a note of genuine optimism and well-founded hope for the future of this little planet called Earth. As man travels further into Space, we are conscious of a double process going on: The Earth becomes smaller and smaller in relation to the vast reaches of the modern astronaut, but at the same time it becomes more and more desirable to return to from the inhospitable alternatives such as the Moon and the planet Venus now within reach.

The planet Earth is still, indeed, the home of man.

Recent developments in UN-aided projects throughout Asia have been recorded on film by a travelling motion-picture unit sponsored by the United Office of Public Information. In Afghanistan, the unit visited various Government projects which are receiving UN technical assistance, including villages participating in the community development scheme. In this scene, Afghan Public Health Nurse calls on an expectant mother in a rural village

SECTION ONE

THE WORLD WE LIVE IN

At an international voluntary work camp organised in Nysted by the World Council of Churches and UNESCO. A group of young volunteers from Germany, USA, Denmark, Sweden, UK. Switzerland and India recently joined forces to transform a garage into a gymnasium for handicapped children.

IT GOES without saying that you who are using this atlas can read, and there is no doubt that you can write as well. We take these things for granted. There are other things which we may equally assume. If you are ill or injured in an accident, a doctor will take care of you or you will be quickly taken by ambulance to a hospital. You expect to enjoy three good meals a day, to say nothing of a snack or two between meals. Every now and then you will be provided with new shoes, shirts, dresses, suits and other necessary clothing. You no doubt live with other members of your family in a house, flat or apartment, and you think of this as 'home'.

To most of us all these things are regarded as the normal ingredients of our way of life, and it comes as a considerable shock to realise for the first time that we who regard such amenities as normal are exceptional. The majority of our fellow-members in the human race do not know what it means to live like this.

Most people in the world today can neither read nor write.

Most people do not have enough to eat. From the time they are born their bodies are under-nourished. They suffer from 'deficiency diseases'—which means that they gradually starve to death.

Most people have no trained doctor within reach, and have never received expert medical treatment when they are ill. They have never known what a hospital looks like.

Many have no adequate clothing to protect them from the elements, nor proper houses to live in. Many, indeed, have no homes, and even no country, to call their own; they are refugees—victims of war, plague, earthquake, flood, political persecution and other causes of misery and distress.

Within every nation distinction is often made between the 'haves' and the 'have nots'. This distinction, however, where it is applied within the so-called 'developed' nations, is dwarfed in comparison with the distinction between them and the under-developed nations. The least privileged members of the 'richer' nations are infinitely better off than the majority of those living in the under-developed parts of the world.

The maps in this section of the atlas are designed to give evidence on which to base a true picture of the world we live in, emphasizing both the unity by which we are held together, and the characteristic differences which distinguish areas of the world and the conditions under which people, of differing colour and race, live.

The world we live in is both more united and more divided than ever before. It is

SHE'S LEARNING FAST   A seven-year-old Arab refugee learns to read and write at a school in Lebanon.

THIS IS HOME.   200,000 people in Calcutta live and die on the pavement. This man eats his daily meal of rice. The animal is better fed.

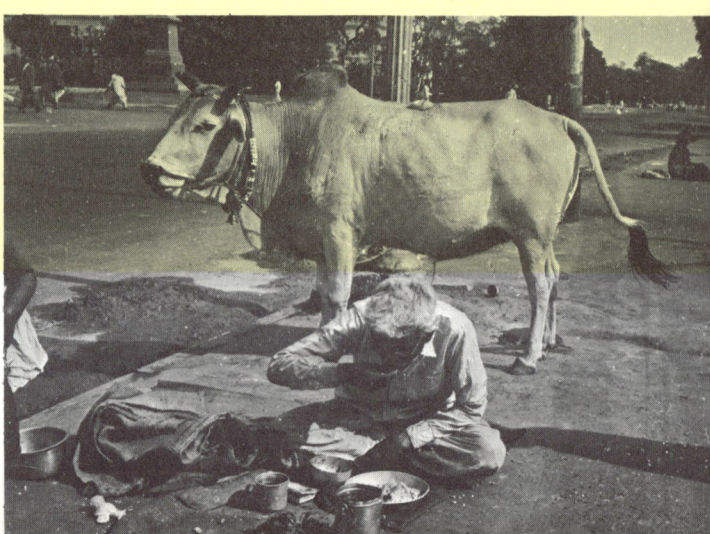

more united because we are more involved with one another than ever before; it is more divided because we are more aware of the inequalities and differences which separate us from one another, and of the friction which they can cause.

Fifty years ago Maxim Litvinoff, a Russian diplomat, made the then startling assertion 'Peace is indivisible'. He meant that, so long as there was fighting in any part of the world, the world was at war. It is no longer possible to cut oneself off from the consequences of what is happening elsewhere. More than three hundred years ago John Donne, a poet who was also dean of St. Paul's cathedral, expressed the same thought in an oft-quoted sermon:

> 'No man is an Island, entire of itself, every man is a piece of the Continent, a part of the main. Any man's death diminishes me, because I am involved in Mankind; And therefore never send to know for whom the bell tolls, it tolls for thee.'

We all belong together, and the joy or suffering of one man enriches or impoverishes humanity. This has always been

CHILD WELFARE. Lunchtime in Guatemala. The developing countries are trying to improve the lot of their children, many of whom are undernourished and very susceptible to disease. The UN and its agencies assist these efforts by providing technical advice and assistance.

true, but we are more aware of this truth than ever before in history because of our immediate practical involvement with each other. The speed of travel has brought the most remote parts of the world within less than 24 hours distance of each other, while telecommunications, by cable, radio and television, make it possible to join in conversation, take part in celebrations, and watch events of all sorts while they are actually taking place, almost anywhere in the world. We have seen in the daily newspapers, on the news-reels in the cinema and on TV, the actual devastation, bestiality and suffering involved in Viet-nam, in Africa, in America. We have become

BEFORE AND AFTER
Starvation in Vietnam is aggravated by war conditions. These children are lucky to receive new life in an orphanage helped by Oxfam.

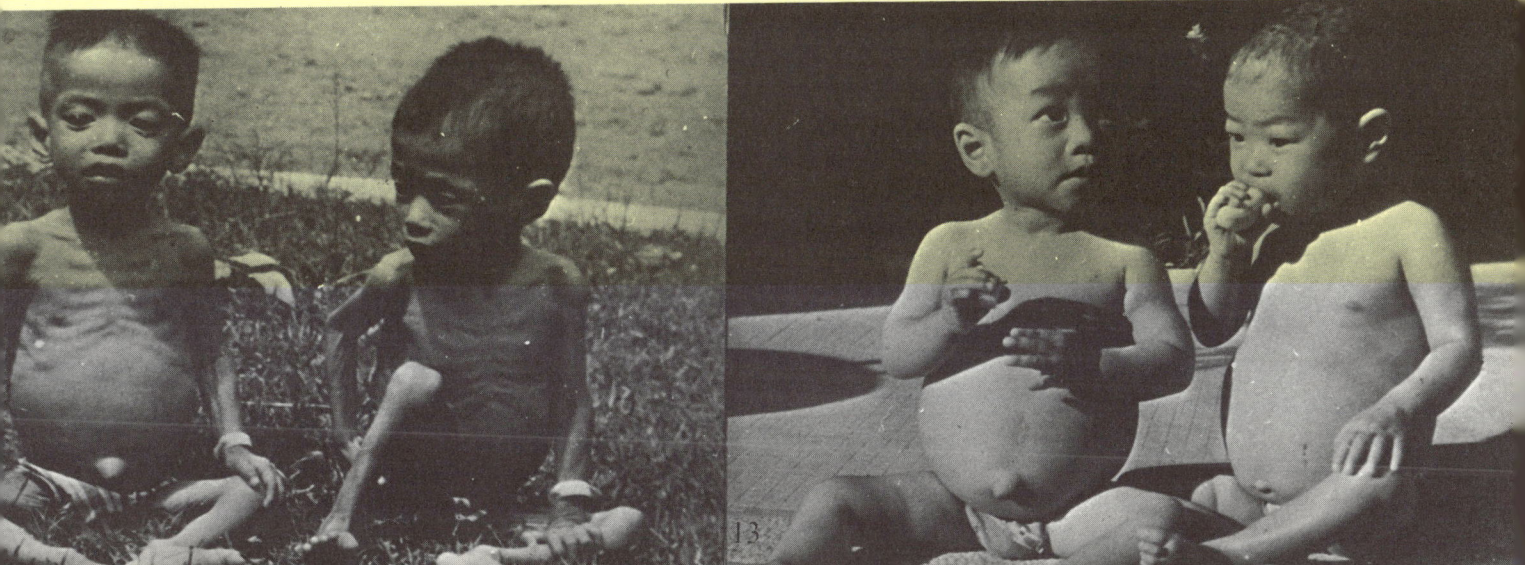

HEALTH. *An Ethiopian father and his sick child in a village where there is a health centre helping to control disease.*

spectators of demonstrations, protest marches, riots and hooliganism at football matches and elsewhere, while they are actually taking place, in our own country as well as abroad. Poverty, disease, illiteracy and the problems of race and colour, are no longer academic problems or mere statistics. They affect our everyday lives in a thousand different ways.

The first map is the only one in which the frontiers dividing nation from nation are emphasized. Our world is artificially divided up into nation states, each with its own laws, currency, standard of living, language, military forces and loyalties. Jealousy and prejudice together with commercial interests combine to create political problems which lead to friction and ultimately to war. The other maps emphasize the unity of the world and illustrate the inequalities which exist in terms of world significance rather than national.

SOMETHING TO SHOUT ABOUT *These happy laughing African children do not know what it means to be 'under-privileged'.*

14

The number of people in the world is difficult to determine accurately because there are parts of the world where reliable records are not kept. However, from what records there are, together with intelligent calculation, it is estimated that in 1968 the world population was about 3,490 million people. During the last 63 years the population has doubled and it is expected to double again in the next 40 years. In 1967 it is reckoned that 13,000 babies were born every hour, while 6,100 people died every hour. By the year 2000 there are likely to be between 6,000 and 7,000 million people in the world. The densest concentration of population is in Asia and 21% of the world population (722 million) live in China.

The distribution of races and of officially recognized languages gives some idea of the problems of communication and how they are being overcome. The spread of literacy is, of course, related to the understanding of a language and also to the facility of travelling. As these factors increase, literacy becomes more widespread. It is estimated that fewer than 40% of the people in the world can read or write, and in Africa the proportion rises to 81% of illiterates. Among the vast population of China there are 300 million who can neither read nor write.

These are frightening figures but modern methods of education have been shown to be capable of reducing them drastically. This becomes easier when only a few languages are necessary for communication and although it would be a pity if the multifarious minority languages were to die out, the advantages of having at least a second language which is known over a wide area of the earth are very great.

With the increase of communication, both physical and mental, the distinctions between nationalities and races will tend

NOT UNWILLINGLY TO SCHOOL   Palestine refugees go to school in Lebanon, built and staffed with the help of United Nations Relief and Works Agency.

HOPE FOR THE FUTURE   Refugee children at the Dikwaneh Camp School, near Beirut, are given school uniform and the chance to be educated.

SITTING ON THE WHEEL-SHAFT WITH NO GRAIN TO GRIND
Famine in Mysore is no unfamiliar experience.

to become less. Radio and television make it possible for us to share experiences and to watch what is going on at the same time in all parts of the world. Moreover, as we have already noticed, we now understand what poverty, disease, race prejudice and war mean in terms of human life and suffering in a way that has never been possible hitherto.

The people of the world are being increasingly brought together by the demands of world trade and communications and in the process they are learning to adopt habits and customs unknown to their forefathers. Moreover, the commonplace and hitherto immutable distinctions between, say, night and day, summer and winter, are wearing thin. The spaceman travelling in orbit round the earth at 18,000 miles per hour, passes from day to night and night to day many times in 24 hours, and the cricket enthusiast with money to burn can fly from the cold of an English winter to the scorching heat of an Australian summer to spend a few days watching a Test Match.

These factors make it quite inevitable that the people of the world will intermix, in spite of all the political, social and national barriers which may seek to discourage this process. So long as the means of communication are so easily available, to try and prevent these consequences is like

trying to stem the tide. Sooner or later, and the sooner the better, we must face the fact of multi-racial societies and come to terms with the problems which they pose.

It is against the background of such facts that these maps become significant. The maps depicting Climatic Zones and Vegetation no longer indicate simply the local availability of certain kinds of food at certain times of the year. In the world context they represent conditions in various parts of the globe which can be exploited to the advantage of the whole family of mankind. The differences in climatic conditions in different areas make possible the mutual enrichment of the peoples of the world. They make it possible, given the will, to plan the abolition of hunger, poverty and disease, wherever they are to be found. This represents a new approach to an understanding of the geographical features of the world.

The map of the changes in animal distribution indicates two important factors. Firstly, that the animal world has had to adapt itself to the demands of man. This demonstrates that man is, under his creator, lord of creation. Secondly, it makes us

A WOMAN MAKING FUEL FROM COW-DUNG AND STRAW
For millions in India this is their only source of fuel; coal is unobtainable and wood far too precious.

acutely aware of the responsibility of man towards the animal creation. Man can cause the extinction of an animal species or he can ensure its preservation and development. He can push back the jungle, but in doing so he must realize what a difference he is making to the animal life which depends on the jungle for its survival.

The responsibility of weighing the possible practical alternatives involved in these problems cannot be avoided as the human race advances and increases in numbers.

There is an important fact which is illustrated by these maps which must not be overlooked, but which must be seen in its proper perspective. The division of the nations of the world into the 'haves' and

INDUSTRIALIZATION. A fibre factory in Ghana. Many countries, as a first priority, seek assistance in improving existing industries and setting up new ones. The UN Industrial Development Organization, set up in 1966 to promote and assist them in speeding up industrialization, makes available a broad range of technical assistance services.

TYPICAL OF MANY IN BIHAR, INDIA This boy's chances of survival are slim. After the drought few of his generation have escaped the mark of hunger.

SHARING SKILLS (U.N. TECHNICAL ASSISTANCE) *Rice is the staple food of seventy per cent of Asia's people. But while the population has increased, the rice output is still below the pre-war level. Indian agriculture experts with assistance from Food and Agriculture Organization of the United Nations (FAO) are working to develop a hybrid of Japanese and Indian rice which might greatly increase the yield.*
HERE; One of the special activities of the International Rice Commission of FAO is the Rice Hybridization Project at Cuttak, in India.

UPPER VOLTA *Backward agriculture and long dry seasons each year join together to bring hunger and malnutrition to the villages of many African countries. Upper Volta is one of the countries where United Nations help has been sought to fight the problem. In this country the Food and Agriculture Organization, backed by the United Nations Special Fund, is helping to train a new generation of farmers who can grow more, who can better conserve what they grow and thus escape from their slavery to the soil and climate.*
Veteran cattle farmer gives students practical demonstrations in ploughing with oxen, a practice rare in sub-Saharan Africa, where generally puny hand instruments are the only means of cultivation. Before the actual demonstration, FAO expert Philippe Augusta of Haiti (in white shirt, centre) instructs trainees in the theory and practical advantages of ploughing with oxen.

TRAINING *These young students at a training institute in Ceylon are learning to become skilled metalworkers. An aim of the World Employment Programme, launched in 1969 by ILO, is to help governments set up and extend programmes leading to productive employment for everyone.*

'have nots', the 'developed' and the 'under-developed' corresponds closely with 'western' civilization which derives largely from the influence of Christianity. It is no accident that it is in Christendom that modern science has flourished and its results have percolated down to affect the lives of the most humble people. In the ancient civilizations science never became integrated into the way of life of the people because the context of belief did not encourage it. Christianity had the effect of breaking down these inhibitions and has encouraged the pursuit of truth and its practical expression.

Christianity has had a liberating influence, and literacy, education, medical services, schools and hospitals were all first developed in the areas where the Christian gospel was proclaimed.

We must not, however, jump too hastily to the conclusion that the higher standards of living enjoyed in 'the more affluent and cultured areas of the world are entirely due to Christian influences. A study of the maps in sections II and III will make it clear that the spread of Christianity was made possible by the coincidence of several important factors—the fact of the Roman Empire, with its unifying administration; the consequent existence of a network of roads, along which travel was encouraged and news travelled fast; and the adoption of a common language, 'koine' Greek (an everyday adaptation of 'classical' Greek), so that ideas could be discussed and points of view exchanged more readily. The Christian gospel was proclaimed just at the time and place when and where it could most easily be disseminated through this part of the world.

These factors would have favoured any new movement sufficiently imaginative and ready to take advantage of them, and they encouraged the breakdown of superstitious beliefs and of the accompaniments of privilege which characterize a static society.

Nevertheless, granting all this, the fact that Christianity was prepared for such an expansion, and indeed demanded it for its very survival, adds an element sufficiently significant to be taken seriously. A short period of reflection may well lead to the conclusion that the very nature of Christianity has made possible, as no other force could do, the fullest exploitation of the advantages. It has led to the rise of what we call 'western' civilization, which survived

ECONOMIC DEVELOPMENT. One of several roads under construction which will permit Gabon to develop rich untapped hardwood forests, now inaccessible to logging companies. The investment money needed for such projects is often more than than 'a country can manage alone and some funds are provided by UN financial agencies.

FUNDAMENTAL EDUCATION IN CAMBODIA. Villagers in and around Tonle Bati are being helped to improve their living conditions by students of the National Fundamental Education Centre which was set up with the help of UNESCO Experts from the United Nations and from WHO and FAO are also assisting in the training programme.
Here, Miss Francoise Cornet (France), a World Health Organization public health nurse from the Centre, demonstrates the proper way to bathe a baby to some of the villagers in Damrey Slap.

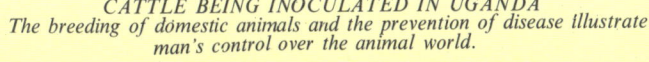

CATTLE BEING INOCULATED IN UGANDA
The breeding of domestic animals and the prevention of disease illustrate man's control over the animal world.

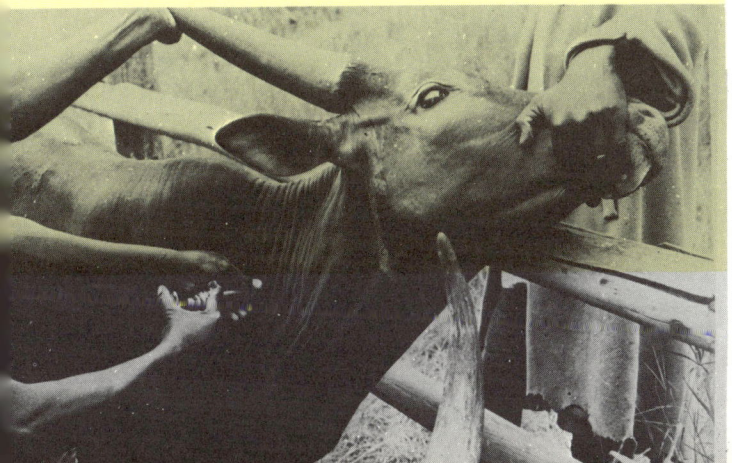

the inevitable fall of the Roman Empire and became the dominant influence in changing the pattern of the whole world in which men dwell.

And so, the line drawn between the 'haves' and 'have nots', the literate and the illiterate, the healthy and the chronically sick, corresponds very closely to that between those who have and those who have not come under the influence of Christianity.

This has, of course, been reflected in the realms of industrial and commercial enterprise, and it leads on to the second tendency, referred to above.

In the interests of commercial development, the need for raw materials and cheap labour has induced industrialists and others to exploit resources and people in parts of the world which have not yet enjoyed the advantages of 'western' civilization. In general, this exploitation has been carried out in the interests of the economy of the industrial countries rather than for the benefit of the native population. This has meant that the rich countries have become richer and the poor countries have been

EDUCATION.
An elementary class in the Philippines. Many nations are building and improving existing schools and training teachers to help the young explore and develop their capabilities to the fullest extent.

COMMUNICATIONS.
A telecommunications training centre in Thailand.

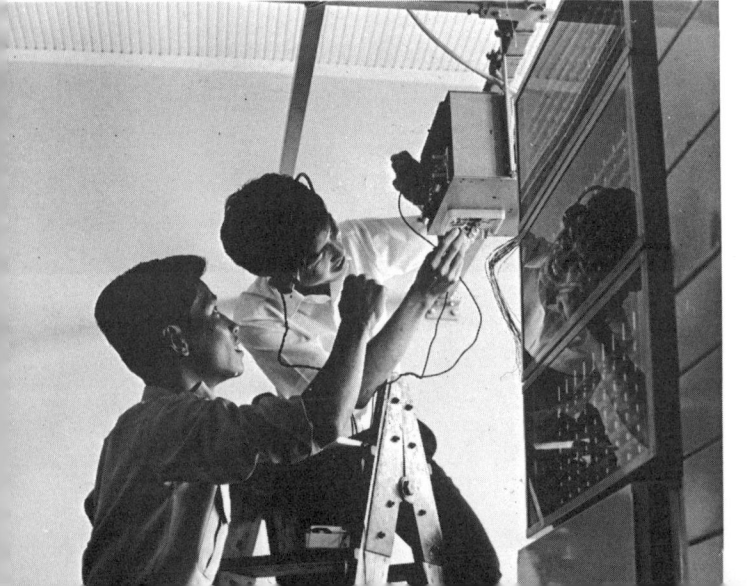

PAKISTAN - A FUTURE IN THE MAKING.
Soil analysis experts of FAO in the Sind Barrage area advise on proper draining, underground water supplies. Pits serve as "On-the-Spot Demonstration Laboratory" for Pakistani Agricultural Engineers.

depressed rather than uplifted. This is the consequence of 'colonialism' on its bad side. When and where white settlers have made their homes in predominantly 'coloured' countries, they have lived in separation and at a higher level than the native peoples, without seeking significantly to raise the standards of the latter. This has been somewhat offset by the arrival of Christian missionaries, but even this has by no means always counteracted the damage done by bad 'colonialism'.

Since the Second World War, however, the conscience of the civilized world has been stirred as never before, and sincere attempts are being made not only to provide physical aid and personal help to the under-privileged, but also to train and encourage leadership which is well-informed and able to discern the right kind of lines on which progress should be made.

There is still a long way to go, but a start has been made. The factors involved will be further considered in sections IV and V of this atlas.

The predominant influence of the spread of Christianity on the growth of 'western' civilization, which we enjoy, demands that we should make a special study of its impact

HAITI TACKLES A PROBLEM. The Government is concentrating its efforts on agriculture. Its Agriculture School at Damien was expanded to teach better cultivation methods; feeding experiments were undertaken to improve poultry breeding (shown here), and training in the utilization of resources was intensified.

and origins. The next two sections of this atlas are devoted to this study.

The fact that we date our calendar from the birth of Christ is evidence that at one time it was considered important enough to scrap all the old points of reference in favour of this outstanding event. The coming of Christ meant the birth of a new world. As J. Middleton Murry once put it, 'Christianity made Europe'.

Before dealing with the geographical background to the historical events of the Old and New Testaments, from which we gain our knowledge of the origins of Christianity, it is important to see how this series of events burst upon the world and made such a tremendous impact on the pattern of 'western' civilization.

Section II will, therefore, illustrate the stages in this development, giving some explanation of the geographical, political and social factors which determined the direction of the expansion of Christianity.

THE OLD AND THE NEW
The donkeys carry away the excavated earth; but the 'Sanderson Cyclone down the hole air hammer' does the job quicker. Modern methods are bringing new life and hope to the arid land of India.

21

DECOLONIZATION.
A UN Visiting Mission meeting the people of the Trust Territory of New Guinea. Although more than 35 territories have achieved statehood since the founding of the United Nations, millions of people still do not govern themselves. The General Assembly has unanimously declared its determination to bring a speedy and unconditional end to all forms of colonialism

THE IMPACT OF CHRISTIANITY
ON WESTERN CIVILIZATION

ONE OF the germinal decisions of history was that made by Saint Paul at Troas, on his second missionary journey. He had a dream in which he saw a 'man of Macedonia' who pleaded with him 'Come over into Macedonia, and help us' (Acts *16*. 9). Moved by this dream, Paul crossed into Europe, to take with him the message of the Christian Gospel.

From that decision it followed that the main expansion of Christianity was westward into Europe, rather than eastward into the continent of Asia, or southward into Africa. In fact, the dream was no doubt inspired by the way Paul's mind had been working. It was the common-sense way to go. All the factors were in favour of westward expansion, as we have already noticed. This was the territory of the great Roman Empire. News travelled fast along the Roman roads, and the trade-routes were busy with traffic. People mixed easily and were ready to exchange ideas and discuss their problems. There was in use a common

language, which made it easy for people to be understood over the whole area covered by the Roman rule.

The religious atmosphere was unsettled and disturbed. The so-called Mystery religions mingled with countless philo-sophical schools, to say nothing of the admixture of Judaism among the Jews who had settled in various parts of the

HEBREW SCROLL. The Books of the Old Testament were recorded by Hebrew scribes from the 3rd century B.C. Copies were made with minute care on lengths of skin which were rolled and kept in the synagogues. These were the Scriptures known and often quoted by our Lord.

Mediterranean area after the Dispersion from Palestine. The preaching of the Gospel of God's love in Christ had an immediately liberating influence, and, although it was opposed and persecuted by those with vested interests in the old order, it eventually won through as a force to be reckoned with. After it had been accepted by the Emperor Constantine and adopted as the religion of the Roman Empire, it made great strides in the development of European unity under the Holy Roman Empire which was founded in the year A.D. 800. Much of European history since then has been closely associated with the divisions which developed within the Christian Church.

Although the main expansion of Christianity was in Europe, there were early missionary thrusts in other directions, including Asia and Africa.

When European trade developed overseas, Christian missionaries 'followed the flag', and Christianity became established in various parts of the world because of the penetration and conquest by 'Christian' nations. Towards the end of the eighteenth century, however, there arose a deep religious concern to spread the Gospel in all the world, in direct obedience to our Lord's command to his disciples (Matt. *28*. 19, 20). This led to the modern missionary movement, and the foundation of missionary societies by all the main Christian denominations. Since 1792, when the Baptist Missionary Society was founded and William Carey was sent to India, the influence of Christianity has spread to nearly all parts of the globe, and during the twentieth century it has been increasing in numbers at a greater rate than ever before in its history. It claims by far the largest number of adherents of any living religion in the world today, equal to about 30% of the world's population.

SYRIAC NEW TESTAMENT 2nd CENTURY.
As the early Church extended its bounds, translation from the Greek became a necessity, and Syriac was one of the earliest versions. In the north of Syria was the great city of Antioch, where the disciples were first called Christians. Syriac continued to be spoken throughout the Middle Ages, and remains as a liturgical language of the Eastern Church.

The missionary character of the Christian religion was first recognised at Pentecost (Acts *2*). The coming of Christ and the assurance of God's love was so important that it needed to be made known everywhere. It was seen to change the idea of the brotherhood of man from a pious hope to a practical programme. It took some time for the first disciples, who were Jews, to realize what was implied in this recognition of the need to spread the good news of the Gospel. It was Paul who gave the first impetus to the expansion of the Church, and it was he who carried the Gospel to Asia Minor and then beyond, into Europe, as we have already noticed.

The difference between the first and second maps in this section is almost entirely due to the activities of Paul as described in the Book of the Acts of the Apostles. In the teeth of opposition from various vested interests, including the Jews of the Dispersion (those scattered from Palestine who had settled in various towns in Asia Minor and Europe), the Christian Church grew very quickly and became established in most of the important towns in the Roman Empire. Opposition continued and developed more than once into official persecution under such emperors as Nero, Decius and Diocletian. Nevertheless the Christian Church continued to grow and became established in the continents of both Asia and Africa, as well as in Europe. There is little detailed evidence of how the Church spread immediately after the period covered by the Acts of the Apostles, but there are various legends and traditions which have survived to account for the appearance of the Christian witness in remote areas. In India, for instance, there is a Church in existence today which claims to have been founded by the Apostle Thomas, and it is even suggested that Thomas travelled as far as China in his missionary journeys.

CODEX SINAITICUS 4th CENTURY.
The Earliest Christian writings we possess are pages of the great Codices, beautifully written on papyrus and vellum during the first four hundred years of the Christian era. Discovered in a monastery on Mount Sinai in the 19th century, this famous manuscript is now treasured in the British Museum.

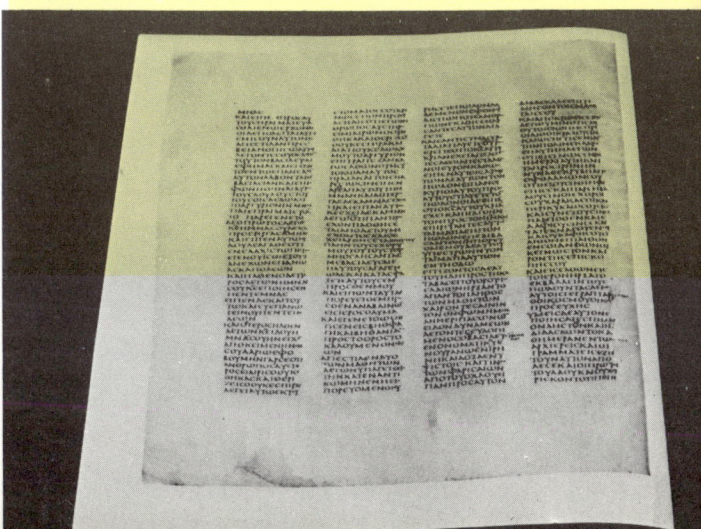

Reliable evidence emerges towards the end of the second century showing that the Christian Church was established beyond Edessa to the East and in parts of North Africa, as well as in Spain and Gaul (France). From that time on the steady and rapid growth of the Church is easily traceable, and it went on in the teeth of violent persecution, until the beginning of the fourth century, when the emperor Constantine accepted the Christian faith and proclaimed it as the official religion of the Roman Empire (Edict of Milan A.D. 313).

The continuing history of the Church is one of set-backs and advances, each set-back being less than the one before and each advance reaching forward to a far greater extent than hitherto. Although it was closely associated with the Roman 'establishment' the Church survived the decline and fall of the Roman empire. It was adversely affected by the wave of advancing Mohammedanism and lost its hold on the places of its origin and early expansion, in Palestine, Asia Minor and North Africa. At the same time it spread throughout most of Europe and became the dominant influence in the political and cultural development of that continent. There is also evidence of the penetration of Christianity across central and eastern Asia in numerous pockets of Christian communities most of which enjoyed a limited period of existence.

As might have been expected, a period of spiritual decline followed the 'palmy days' when the Church enjoyed considerable political power, and it tended to lose the spiritual stimulus which was characteristic of its early days. Lethargy and corruption began to appear and these factors disturbed the consciences of the faithful. This sense of concern led eventually to the Reformation which, although it split the Church,

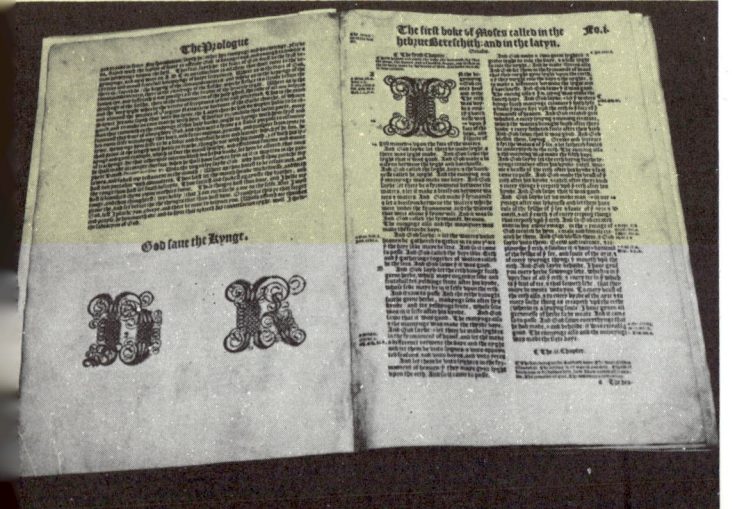

GREAT BIBLE 1539.
This Version by Coverdale was based on Tyndale's translation and the Latin Vulgate. The massive volume, fifteen inches high was the first "Byble in Englyshe" to be officially set up in the churches, where there the people flocked to hear it read.

nevertheless brought new life to it also. Two further influences accompanied and promoted this movement in the Church.

The first of these was the Renaissance. The word means 'rebirth', and refers to a widespread renewal of interest in the arts and literature, and particularly in the study of Christian writings, including primarily, of course, the Bible. The Renaissance has often been associated with the fall of Constantinople (1453) and the subsequent dispersal of learned scholars to the west throughout Europe. This is now thought by students of the period to give too dramatic an explanation of a movement which was much more complicated and less spectacular than this would suggest. Nevertheless, it is certainly true that the doubts and hesitations of many pious churchmen were sustained and encouraged by a new wave of intellectual discussion of opinions and doctrines which had for too long been allowed to pass unquestioned.

Secondly, there was a new and considerable spirit of adventure which led to the discovery of new lands, such as the American continent, Australia and the Pacific Islands, and which promoted the growth of trade, the claims of conquest, and the settlement of Europeans in colonies —western 'enclaves' which exploited the local resources, of men and materials, for the benefit of 'western' civilization. In some cases, colonies were founded by men and women who left their native countries to escape persecution at home, such as the Pilgrim Fathers. Wherever these adventurers, traders or refugees went they took with them their religious faith, and so the Christian Church became established in many new areas. Sometimes by conviction, but sometimes by compulsion, the native populations adopted Christian principles and practices.

Towards the end of the eighteenth cen-

THE AUTHORIZED VERSION 1611.
At the Hampton Court conference of 1604 King James I supported the proposal for a new translation of the Bible. A committee of scholars based their revision on the Great, the Bishops' and the Geneva Bibles, the Rheims New Testament and other sources. The words of Coverdale and Tyndale, the work of Erasmus and Jerome contribute to this great version, part of the English heritage today

tury there arose a genuine spiritual concern for the world-wide spread of the Christian Gospel based on the nature of the New Testament itself. Jesus had commanded his disciples to

> 'go . . . and make all nations my disciples; baptize men everywhere in the name of the Father and the Son and the Holy Spirit, and teach them to observe all that I have commanded you. And be assured, I am with you always, to the end of time.' (Matthew *28*. 19, 20).

The implications of this command were seen to lay an inescapable responsibility on the Christian community to make the Gospel known throughout the world.

In England this concern is associated particularly with the name of William Carey, who was so possessed with the need to awaken the Church to its missionary responsibilities that his enthusiasm broke down the opposition of his fellow ministers and led to the formation of the Baptist Missionary Society in 1792. A year later Carey went as the first missionary of the Society to India, where he overcame many difficulties and gained a foothold for the Gospel which was followed by a glorious company who have gone on to build schools, hospitals, colleges and medical centres as well as to encourage the growth of the worshipping Church in India to its present-day proportions.

The example set by the Baptists was quickly followed by other denominations, and over the next few decades were founded many missionary societies, such as the London Missionary Society (now the Congregational Council for World Mission), the Society for the Propagation of the Gospel (now the U.S.P.G.), The

CORONATION BIBLE 1953.
This beautiful edition of the Authorized Version was specially printed and bound for use in the Coronation Service of Queen Elizabeth II.

British and Foreign Bible Society (which provides translations of the Bible into the languages needed for the spread of the Gospel into different parts of the world), and many others.

The growth of the Christian Church in the nineteenth and early twentieth centuries has been truly phenomenal. In the early years of the twentieth century the success of the Christian witness was apparently so assured that a movement was founded among students (the Student Volunteer Movement) whose seriously avowed aim was to spread the Christian Gospel throughout the whole world 'in our lifetime'! We have no such ambitious illusions in our time, but it is worth recalling that at the time when the World Council of Churches was constituted in 1948 Dr. John Mackay, chairman of the International Missionary Council, could claim that

> 'today in every land save three, Tibet, Afghanistan and Saudi Arabia, there are organized Christian Churches. For the first time in Christian history the Church has become "ecumenical" in the literal meaning of the word. Its boundaries are co-extensive with the habitable globe.'

Since the British and Foreign Bible Society was founded in 1804 the Bible has been translated, in part or in whole, into 1,337 languages (1968 figure) embracing all corners of the globe, and, incidentally, including 23 different dialects of the English language as spoken in various parts of the British Isles.

The present situation is paradoxical. In some parts of the 'western' world the Church seems to be losing ground quickly, and yet in the same places the demand for

The Book of Esther which is read during the Jewish festival of Purim.

Ancient Pillars at Capernaum, Israel.

literature about religious questions is increasing and the many modern translations of the Bible sell in vast numbers. This suggests that, while institutional religion is 'under a cloud', perhaps because its ways are regarded as irrelevant and old-fashioned, the interest in religious problems is very much alive. This is particularly so when these problems are related to the subjects of war, race relations, world hunger, the population explosion, and such matters. These are all 'religious' problems in the true sense of that word, which we have accepted in this atlas. They concern human responsibility.

We seem to be moving away from the older attitudes and moving into a situation where the problems of living together in a world which is getting smaller and smaller demand practical action as well as affecting the principles by which such action can be effectively directed in the right ways.

It is this concern which forms the starting-point from which to consider Sections IV and V of this atlas. Section IV indicates the channels through which the common concern of the nations is expressed through the agencies of the United Nations Organization, and Section V describes the momentum which has gathered and is gathering round the Ecumenical Movement towards unity of action and thought among the Christian Churches in the world. But, meanwhile in Section III we take a closer look at the background and first impact of Christianity on the world as seen in the Old and New Testaments.

THE BACKGROUND OF CHRISTIANITY

The historical importance of the rise of Christianity is not in dispute. It is enshrined in the dating of the calendar from the birth of Christ. Of course, other calendars, such as the Jewish and Moslem, are still observed by those concerned, but it is the Christian calendar which is in most general use throughout the world.

The historical importance of Christianity is matched by its geographical importance. We have already noticed that the spread of Christianity was greatly aided by the amenities afforded by the existence of the Roman Empire with its unifying influences in the use of a common language, the organization of a central government and the provision of good communications by the building of trunk roads throughout the Empire. But this is only a part of the story.

In other ways the geographical position of the 'cradle' of the Christian religion was particularly suitable for the birth of a movement which claims universal relevance. It occupied the strategic centre of the developing world. The inhabitants of this little strip of land at the eastern end of the

The Wailing Wall in Jerusalem. Jews here lament the loss of their Temple and national home.

Jordan River, where John the Baptist baptized Jesus.

MOUNT ZION. The Church of the Dormition on Mount Zion, Jerusalem, was built at the beginning of this century on the site of an earlier building where it was claimed that Mary, the mother of Jesus, passed her life after the crucifixion and eventually 'slept away'.

Mediterranean, or 'Great', Sea, about the size of Wales, and called by various names from time to time, maintained their own peculiar existence, in spite of the pressure of the great empires by which they were surrounded, and who, as they marched to war with one another, treated the land of Palestine (to use the later, but more convenient name for the area) as a doormat on which they respectively wiped their feet as they passed; or, to change the metaphor, as a pawn, lightly to be moved or sacrificed at the behest of the kings, knights and bishops in pursuit of their strategies. The people of Israel were humiliated, their land occupied, their leaders and others deported, but they never lost their identity.

Apart from the fact that Palestine was at the geographical centre of the movements of great empires, it was also at the junction of the three continents of Europe, Asia and Africa. Elements from all three directions influenced the culture and traditions of the people over the years, and this fact ensured that when the Christian religion emerged, with its universal claims, it was by its intrinsic nature 'exportable' over the whole known world in all directions.

The Old Testament is the surviving literature of the Hebrew people, who were

Church of The Transfiguration on Mount Tabor, Israel.

brought up to believe that they were God's chosen nation, founded on the faith of the patriarchs Abraham, Isaac and Jacob. God was their leader and king—never to be seen, but made known in the hearts of the faithful and heard in the wise words of the prophets. Through the agony of their chequered history runs the cry of faith in God, in the early times crudely interpreted, and later expressed in more elevated and ethical terms, but always there explicitly or implicitly, whether in the historical record of the scribe, the judgment of the prophet or the song of the psalmist. No crisis or disaster left them without some spokesman for such faith, and even in the humiliation of exile there were those who found a heart to sing, though it be a dirge; but never without the assurance of faith that God had not forsaken them.

The maps in the Old Testament part of this Section are designed to give some impression of the vast movements which characterized the rise and fall of empires, and the relation of these movements to the land of Palestine and its people. It is not fanciful to liken this little country to a rocky island set in the middle of a raging sea. Battered and beaten by the swirling waves as they strike the rock, it remains the only stable element in the scene. So, too, the faith of this strange, unique people, the

Amphitheatre at Beth Sha'an.

Excavations at Ashkelon, Israel, ancient Philistine City, also associated with the Greeks, the Romans and the Crusaders.

The tomb of Rabbi Moshe Ben Maimon (Maimondes) with Tiberias in the background, Israel.

33

Greek Orthodox Monastery and church at Bethany

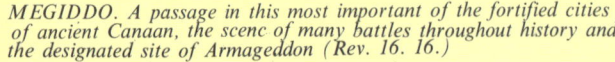

MEGIDDO. A passage in this most important of the fortified cities of ancient Canaan, the scene of many battles throughout history and the designated site of Armageddon (Rev. 16. 16.)

Children of Israel, stands firm amid the chequered fortunes of her mighty neighbours. The history books record how the great warriors rolled back frontiers and redrew maps, as the empires of Egypt, Assyria, Babylonia, Media, Syria, Greece and Rome, successively rose and fell; and yet they seemed to change nothing fundamentally. The lust for power, the selfish greed, the cruelty, the injustice still survived each movement of the tide, one way or the other. But the faith of this insignificant little people of Israel was quietly and steadily changing the values of history. Through the agony of humiliation and frustration there was born a sense of righteousness, forgiveness and love at the heart of things, which demanded acceptance in the face of all that seemed to deny it. It was out of this unconquerable conviction that there emerged the confident expectation that God would vindicate his people and redeem them from their parlous state. This expectation was called the 'Messianic hope' and it dominated the thoughts of some of the later Prophets. It summed up the long *preparatio evangelica* which embraced the whole history of the Hebrew people, and made it natural for the faithful few to see in Jesus Christ the fulfilment of their hopes.

The maps in the New Testament part of this Section illustrate the seriousness with which this fantastic claim of the importance of Jesus Christ for the understanding of the whole of history and of man's nature and destiny needs to be taken. The geography pin-points the history, and vice-versa. The history of the early Church points back to a point of origin in time. Secular historical records make little mention of Jesus of Nazareth, but enough to establish that he existed. For instance, references are to be found in Josephus, Tacitus and Suetonius. The only detailed account of his life and teaching and of the foundation of the Christian movement is to be found in the New Testament, written by those who were followers of Jesus, with the declared intention of persuading others of the truth of the Christian Gospel and its claims. It is possible, however, to give a degree of objectivity to the course of events by reference to the places mentioned in the New Testament.

The maps show the context in which Jesus was born, in terms of the political power of the Roman empire in its wide sweep round the Great Sea (the Mediterranean), and the more intimate context of the small Roman province which constituted Palestine. It was here that Jesus lived, gathered his disciples around him, taught the people about God's love, healed the sick, and enraged the authorities. He was arrested, condemned to death by Pilate at the insistence of the leaders of his

Remains of the Synagogue said to have been built by the Centurion whose servant Jesus healed at Capernaum, on the Sea of Galilee, Israel.

An aerial view of Tel-Aviv.

An aerial view of Ein Kerem, Birthplace of John the Baptist, in the Judaean hills, near Jerusalem, Israel.

Via Dolorosa, Jerusalem.

Nazareth, Israel.

own people, and crucified. His disciples claimed that he rose from the dead and appeared to them. It was this experience that turned a dispirited group of men into fervent advocates, ready to suffer and die for their faith.

It is helpful to be able to pin these events down to places on a map. When we move out from the Gospels to the territory of the Acts and the Epistles we can see how the flame spread and reached out into the wider world. Each place which is marked on these maps recalls a story which is part of a most important period of history.

Robert Browning has a poem which is evocative of great events in English history and their significance simply by the recital of the names of places on a map:

> Nobly, nobly, Cape Saint Vincent to
>   the North-West died away;
> Sunset ran, one glorious blood-red,
>   reeking into Cadiz Bay;
> Bluish mid the burning water, full in
>   face Trafalgar lay;
> In the dimmest North-East distance,
>   dawned Gibraltar grand and gray;
> 'Here and here did England help me:
>   how can I help England?'—say,
> Whoso turns as I, this evening, turn to
>   God to praise and pray,
> While Jove's planet rises yonder,
>   silent over Africa.

A similar sense of the dramatic clings to the place-names reproduced in these maps. 'Here and here'—Bethlehem, Nazareth, Jerusalem, Corinth, Ephesus, Rome &c &c.—did tremendous changes take place, which have had their impact on succeeding generations down to our own times. History is illuminated by geography. Before it is possible to evaluate the truth and worth of Christianity you must know how, where and when the things happened on which alone the evidence for judgment can be gathered and assessed. For this purpose the whole of this section of the atlas is indispensable.

MASADA. Scaling the massive bluff of Masada, where the dramatic and heroic last stand of the Jews against the Romans ended in 'communal suicide' in 73 A. D.

UNITED NATIONS HEADQUARTERS. The majority of the 126 Members of the United Nations are represented throughout the year at it s headquarters. This unique opportunity to meet quickly and informally, away from the glare of publicity, often makes it possible for nations to discuss their differences at an early stage.

SECTION FOUR

THE UNITED NATIONS AND ITS AGENCIES

The overriding concern of this Atlas is to emphasise the essential unity of the world and of the human race. We regard this as a basic fact, but it is one that can easily be overlooked and disregarded. The development of swift communications and the progress of scientific civilisation has underlined this basic fact and made more serious its disregard. The food we eat, the clothes we wear, the news we read, the radio and television programmes we watch and listen to, make us daily conscious that we are linked to the ends of the earth and are compelled to take notice of one another, whether we like it or not.

There is, however, another side to the coin. The very factors which serve to promote unity, can also be seen to intensify disunity, where it exists, and render it more devastating in its effects.

Speed of communication, scientific discovery and inventiveness, and all the other elements that go to make up modern civilisation, render it inevitable that the

View of the armillary sphere, in the Ariana Park, in Geneva, with in the background a corner of the Library wing of the Palais des Nations. The sphere, which was installed in 1939, was a gift of the Woodrow Wilson Foundation to the League of Nations.

A bronze statue by a young Dutch artist, Arthur Spronken, was presented to the World Meteorological Organization (WMO), at a ceremony held at the WMO Headquarters in Geneva. The statue symbolizes the "Taurus of the Sun", and stands near the pool on the north-east of the headquarters.

impact of war will be total and devastating wherever it strikes.

The inability of men and nations to accept the full implications of living together in harmony is reflected in the fact that the sweep of history throughout the ages is punctuated by wars, and as man's control of natural forces has increased, his conduct of war has become more destructive of life and property. For the first time in man's history the twentieth century has known the experience of war on a world-wide scale, and this experience has happened twice. The second world-war (1939–1945) was more sophisticated and more deadly than the first (1914–1918), and was brought to an end with two demonstrations of the destructive power of the atom bomb. A third world-war would start with weapons many times more deadly than any yet used in anger and would bring with it the real possibility of the virtual annihilation, or total pollution of the human race.

Alongside the pessimism so easily engendered by the continuous history of man at war with his fellow men, and by the consequent fact that the economy of most, if not all, nations in the 'civilised' world is based on preparation for possible war, there is the happier evidence of persistent attempts to find a way to guarantee peace. Throughout recorded history such attempts have periodically been made, and many have achieved varying degrees of limited success for limited periods of time. However, no formula has yet been devised to provide universally acceptable conditions for the peaceful settlement of disputes among nations.

The twentieth century has witnessed two outstanding attempts to organise the nations of the world, both for peaceful co-operation and for the prevention of war. After the first world-war the Treaty of Versailles (1919) embodied within its terms the Charter of the League of Nations, designed to promote both of these aims. In the field of co-operation for peaceful purposes, such as the promotion of research and the raising of living standards and working conditions, the League of Nations was eminently successful. It was also instrumental in resolving many disputes which might otherwise have led to the use of force. It was not able, however, to prevent the succession of events leading to the second world-war, and failure in this aim automatically brought to a halt all the good work which was going on in the other spheres of its interest. Failure to prevent a major war is the place of final judgment in the field of international co-operation. Whatever good is being done in other fields immediately comes to a halt when the participating nations are at war with one another.

The second world-war signalised the collapse of the League of Nations, but some of the lessons learned by its successes and its failures led to the inclusion of more realistic principles and practices in the establishment of the second great twentieth-century experiment in international co-operation, the United Nations Organisation, which came into being very soon after the end of the war. Indeed, its planning was actually taking place a year before the war came to an end. The basic principles on which the U.N. was based were laid down at a conference held at Dumbarton Oaks, U.S.A., in August 1944, attended by representatives of the four nations, U.S.A., U.S.S.R., U.K. and China.

The originating Charter was signed on June 26, 1945, and the United Nations Organisation was officially inaugurated on October 24, 1945 when the Charter was ratified by U.S.A., U.S.S.R., U.K., China and France, together with a majority of other signatory nations. From this time the 24th October has been celebrated annually as United Nations Day throughout the world. The five nations named comprise the permanent members of the Security Council, of which more will be said later.

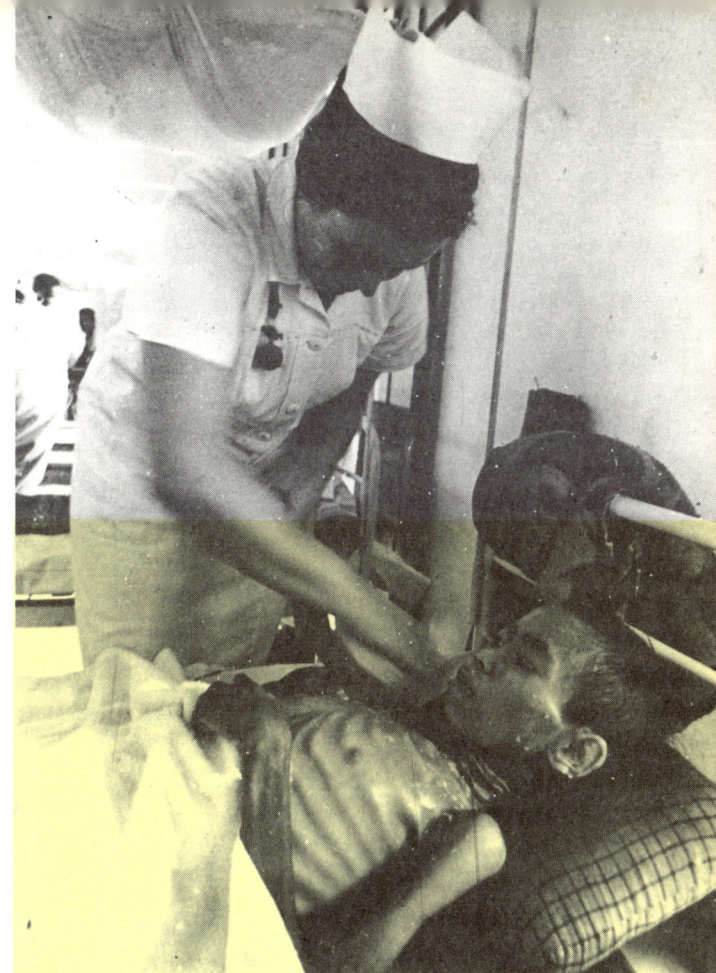

Muriel Jackson, in Vietnam, treats a 10 year old child brought from a refugee village suffering from severe malnutrition.

This section of the Atlas is devoted to an examination of the nature and continuing work of the United Nations Organisation.

THE STRUCTURE OF THE UNITED NATIONS

The membership of the United Nations consists of the Member States who have accepted the obligations and principles of the United Nations Charter and agree with the declared purposes of the U.N.:

TO MAINTAIN international peace and security;

TO DEVELOP friendly relations among nations;

TO BE A CENTRE for harmonising the actions of nations in attaining these common ends.

TO CO-OPERATE internationally in solving international economic, social, cultural and humanitarian problems and in promoting respect for human rights and fundamental freedoms;

UNESCO'S NEW PERMANENT HEADQUARTERS IN PARIS. The modern home of the United Nations Educational, Scientific and Cultural Organization (UNESCO) was opened officially on the 3rd November 1958. Designed by a panel of international architects and decorated with gifts from Member Governments, UNESCO's new permanent headquarters covers a seven and a half acre site fronting the Place de Fontenoy. This photograph of a part of the new site shows a statue in travertine marble by the English sculptor, Henry Moore. This statue, which weighs ten tons, is located in the garden near the "Piazza" entrance of the Secretariat building.

At the time of writing there are 126 members. Membership is open to all peace-loving nations able and willing to carry out the obligations of the Charter. Members may be suspended or expelled by the General Assembly on the recommendation of the Security Council if they persistently violate the principles of the Charter.

The official languages of the U.N. are Chinese, English, French, Russian and Spanish. Its working languages are English, French and Spanish.

All member states belong to the **General Assembly**, which meets once a year in regular session from the third Tuesday in September each year. It can be called together for special sessions at the request of the Security Council, or at the request of any nation with the support of a majority of members. Each state can send up to five representatives to the Assembly, but each state has only one vote.

The General Assembly works through seven Main Committees, which deal with Political, Economic, Social, Administrative, Legal and Trusteeship questions as they are referred to them by the General Assembly.

One of the chief ways in which the U.N. differs from the old League of Nations is that it has a representative body which is in 'continual session' and can take action on behalf of the whole of the membership. This is the **Security Council**. It consists of fifteen members (enlarged from eleven in 1965), five being permanent members (U.S.A., U.S.S.R., U.K., China and France, as indicated earlier) and ten being elected by the General Assembly to serve for two-year periods. These members are not eligible for re-election immediately after their term has expired. The Security Council can call upon member states to take action (such as economic sanctions) or to provide men and materials for military action, where that is undertaken by U.N. forces. On matters requiring action the Security Council must secure a vote of not less than nine of its members, including all five of the permanent members. However, any member concerned in a dispute under discussion must not use his vote on any resolution calling for action.

The **Economic and Social Council** consists of twenty-seven members, nine being elected each year by the General Assembly for a three-year period, after which they are eligible for re-election. This organ of the U.N. is responsible for the economic and social activities of the U.N. It can initiate studies, negotiate agreements, promote appropriate causes and perform services for member states and for the specialised agencies of the U.N. It also sets up commissions and committees to further its interests in such fields as human rights, social development, the status of women, the traffic in drugs, the problems of population etc. It supports four regional commissions which deal with problems of economic development in (i) Europe, (ii) Asia and the Far East, (iii) Latin America, (iv) Africa, as well as special committees appointed as necessary, to deal with housing, building and planning, science and technology, and other such fields of interest.

The **Trusteeship Council** is appointed to supervise the administration of 'trust territories', those territories which were formerly under the 'mandate' of the League of Nations and have not yet won their independence. These are administered respectively by Australia, New Zealand, the United Kingdom and the United States of America.

The Trusteeship Council consists of these administering members, the other permanent members of the Security Council and enough other members to make an equality of numbers between administering and non-administering countries. These latter members are elected by the General Assembly for three-year periods, and are then eligible for re-election.

A view of the Headquarters of the International Labour Organization. (ILO)   ILO was established on April 11, 1919, when its constitution was adopted as Part XIII of the Treaty of Versailles. In 1946, it became the first specialized agency associated with the United Nations.

The **International Court of Justice** has its origins away back in the early part of the twentieth-century and is situated at The Hague, in Holland. Its Statute is an integral part of the U.N. Charter and so includes all members of the United Nations. It is the principal judicial body of the U.N. and deals with any matters referred to it by any state or states, who may agree to accept its jurisdiction in advance by declaration or by signing a treaty or convention to this effect. The Court consists of fifteen judges elected by the General Assembly and the Security Council voting independently. They are chosen on the basis of their qualifications and not for their nationality. However, care is taken to see that the principal legal systems of the world are represented, and no two judges can be nationals of the same state. Each judge serves for a term of nine years and may be re-elected at the end of that time. The judges are not allowed to engage in any other occupation during their term of office.

The last of the main organs in the structure of the United Nations Organisation is the **Secretariat.** This consists of the Secretary General, appointed by the General Assembly on the recommendation of the Security Council, and 'such staff as the Organisation may require'.

The Secretary General, as chief administrative officer of the U.N., is a very important person. Three persons have so far held this position. Trygve Lie, of Norway, was the first, elected on February 1, 1946, for five years. In November 1950 he was confirmed in office for three more years, but resigned in November 1952. In April 1953 Dag Hammarskjold, of Sweden, succeeded to the office, being appointed for five years, and reappointed for five years in September 1957. He died in a plane crash in Africa on September 17, 1961. In November 1961 U Thant, of Burma, was appointed to complete the unexpired period of Hammarskjold's term, and then confirmed in his

TECHNICAL ASSISTANCE TO SOUTH-EAST ASIA (FAO),RICE.

HOPE FOR ASIA'S MILLIONS.

One of the special activities of the International Rice Commission of the Food and Agriculture Organisation of the U.N. (FAO) is the Rice Hybridization Project at Cuttack, in Orissa, India, where nine nations participate in the FAO scheme for improving yields of rice. Beneath microscope, growth is examined in experimental paddy. In artificial cross-breeding, station has pollinated 60,000 rice plants, has collected 13,000 hybridized seeds.

office in November 1962 (his five-year term ending in 1966, as from November 1961). In November 1966 he was appointed for a further five-year term.

The Secretary General is assisted by a large staff, covering the various departments of the United Nations responsibilities. The personnel are of the highest efficiency and integrity, and are recruited on the basis of world-wide representation. As members of the U.N. staff they assume a supra-national loyalty, and elevate the interests of world service above those of their own national patriotism.

Such are the main organs of the United Nations Organisation. Under their authority and sometimes at their initiative the programme of positive achievements accomplished is impressive. These achievements can be classified under the following general headings:

(1) The preservation or restoration of peace

Action has been taken, sometimes by the appointment of a commission to determine facts, sometimes by helping to effect an agreement between parties in conflict and sometimes by military or economic action, in the following areas: *Kashmir, Cyprus, the Dominican Republic, the Congo, West New Guinea, the Middle East, Korea, South Africa, Rhodesia, Israel and the United Arab Republic.*

The U.N. has not always solved problems, but its presence has provided a moderating, and sometimes a decisive, influence.

(2) Economic and Social Problems

The United Nations Conference on Trade and Development (UNCTAD) was set up at the end of 1964 to promote international trade and accelerate economic growth, and it provides a forum for international discussion of problems

FOOD. Harvesting wheat in Morocco. After a long period when food production scarcely kept up with population growth, the output of the world's farmers and fishermen has begun to rise. This is due in large part to greater emphasis by governments on agriculture and the long-term efforts by the world community to combat famine.

SHARING SKILLS. Brickmakers set out their products to dry near Baghdad, Iraq. The expansion and development of small-scale businesses is an important part of the economic plans of some countries. Through the UN Development Programme they are able to obtain the advice and experience of other countries with similar problems.

and the formulation of conventions and agreements to further these aims.

In November 1965 the General Assembly set up the United Nations Development Programme (UNDP) which is designed to initiate projects and to give practical help, sometimes through the various agencies and sometimes directly. It is financed by voluntary governmental contributions.

The United Nations Institute for Training and Research (UNITAR) trains personnel for national and U.N. administrative service.

The United Nations Industrial Development Organisation (UNIDO) is designed to help developing countries with the problems of industrialisation.

The World Food Programme is sponsored jointly by the U.N. and the Food and Agricultural Organisation (FAO) and helps to meet the emergency needs for food created by earthquakes, floods and other disasters, as well as in other appropriate circumstances.

(3) **Areas of special need**

These comprise such varied activities as the United Nations Children's Fund (UNICEF), the United Nations High Commissioner for Refugees (UN HCR) and the United Nations Relief and Works Agency (UNRWA), whose functions are obvious from their titles.

(4) **Human rights**

The Universal Declaration of Human Rights was adopted by the General Assembly on 10 December 1948. It consists of thirty articles, covering civil, political, social and cultural rights which are accepted as a 'yard-stick' by which the standards of nations can be judged and to which all nations have agreed consciously to aspire.

(5) National Independence

The United Nations has encouraged and welcomed the emergence to nationhood of former colonial territories, and continues to supervise the administration of the territories under trusteeship, as referred to earlier. The declared aim is to prepare such territories for independence as soon as appropriately possible.

(6) International Law

The International Court of Justice has dealt with some twenty-four out of thirty-six cases submitted to it. The remainder were adjudged outside its competence. It has settled or pronounced on matters of national boundaries, interpretation of treaties, and fishing rights, among others.

The International Law Commission was set up in 1947 and is concerned to promote the ordered development of international law.

On the periphery of the U.N.O. but closely associated with it, are certain so-called 'Inter-governmental' agencies which provide a pattern of international co-operation of incalculable value. Some of these agencies have survived from their original association with the League of Nations, but others have sprung up since the end of the Second World War. Together they represent the collaboration of the world's experts on science, health, economics, and a host of other essential spheres of service to an extent wider and more thoroughgoing than at any time in the previous history of the world. In assessing the value of this multiplicity of co-operative enterprises it must always be borne in mind that their survival and development is balanced on the razor-edge of continuing world peace.

The agencies coming into this category are separate and autonomous, but they are closely associated with the U.N. through

NATURAL RESOURCES. A crew at work on an oil-drilling rig in Bolivia. Many developing countries need assistance in exploring the wealth-producing possibilities of their resources.
The UN Development Programme helps them not only with surveys but with training engineers and technicians to continue and expand the investigations.

ATOMIC ENERGY. Radio-isotopes production and research at the Bhaha Atomic Research Centre in Trombay, India, is an important example of the progress being made by some countries in developing and increasing the peaceful uses of atomic energy.

the Economic and Social Council. The U.N. Charter refers to these as 'specialised agencies' and recognises thirteen of them, which are required to report annually to the Economic and Social Council.

A fourteenth agency was established in 1957 'under the aegis of the U.N.'. This is the *International Atomic Energy Agency* (IAEA), which reports annually to the General Assembly and, as appropriate, to the Security Council and the Economic and Social Council. The purpose of the IAEA is concerned solely to promote the peaceful development of nuclear power and is required to ensure that any assistance it may provide is not used to further any military purpose.

The other thirteen agencies are as follows:

The *International Labour Organisation* (ILO), which was established in 1919 and had its constitution incorporated in the Treaty of Versailles. In 1946 it was the first 'specialised agency' associated with the United Nations. It is concerned to improve labour conditions and living standards and to promote economic and social stability.

The *Food and Agriculture Organisation* (FAO) was established in 1945, its constitution being accepted at Quebec in October of that year. Its obvious purposes are to improve the production and distribution of food and agricultural products, to raise levels of nutrition and the conditions of country dwellers and workers. It launched the Freedom from Hunger campaign in 1960 and co-operates with the U.N. in the World Food Programme.

The *United Nations Educational, Scientific and Cultural Organisation* (UNESCO) established in 1946, has a wide interest in all matters connected with the application of education, science and culture to the furtherance of justice, human rights and freedom for peoples of all races, creeds, languages and nationalities.

The *World Health Organisation* (WHO) established in 1946, is dedicated to the 'attainment by all peoples of the highest possible level of health'. To this end it operates on three fronts: to provide world services, to give aid to individual countries when required and to encourage and carry out medical research. Its achievements in the furtherance of these purposes have been in many cases dramatic and in others, though less spectacular, effective in pushing back the frontiers of disease.

The *International Bank for Reconstruction and Development* (WORLD BANK) was established in 1945 to facilitate the reconstruction and development of member states by encouraging both private and governmental investment and by granting loans to assist member states in various appropriate circumstances. It also provides technical assistance when required.

The *International Development Association* (IDA) is administered by the World Bank. It came into existence in 1960 to provide help in raising the standards of living in the less developed areas of the world by providing finance at favourable terms for this purpose.

The *International Finance Corporation* (IFC), set up in 1956, became a 'specialised agency' of the U.N. in 1957. It is separate from the World Bank, but closely associated with it, and is specially concerned with the encouragement of private enterprise projects in the less developed areas.

The *International Monetary Fund* (FUND), set up in 1945, is concerned to promote exchange stability and to assist in reducing the problems of international currency transactions by eliminating restrictions which hamper world trade.

The *International Civil Aviation Organisation* (ICAO), was established in 1947 to draw up international standards and regulations for civil aviation, to encourage the acceptance of common procedures for traffic control, safety measures, meteorological services and other facilities which may further the development of international civil aviation across the world.

The *Universal Postal Union* (UPO) was set up as far back as 1875 to form a single postal territory of countries for the reciprocal exchange of correspondence and to improve the organisation of postal services between the nations of the world.

The *International Telecommunication Union* (ITU) goes back even further, to 1865, and has continued for more than a hundred years to promote international co-operation in telegraph, telephone and radio services and to encourage their extension and development.

The *World Meteorological Organisation* (WMO) was brought into being by the convention adopted by the twelfth Conference of Directors of the International Meteorological Organisation, held in Washington in 1947. The convention came into force in 1950. The purpose of the WMO is to provide a world-wide service of meteorological information in standardised and commonly accepted form for the use of aviation, shipping, agriculture etc.

The *Inter-Government Maritime Consultative Organisation* (IMCO), established by a convention which came into effect in 1958, is concerned to establish standards of maritime safety and efficient navigation and to remove restrictions and discriminatory action by governments with regard to international shipping.

In addition to these thirteen 'specialised agencies' attempts were made to find agreement on a charter for an international trade organisation to encourage the expansion of world trade and the rise in standards of living. Such a charter was drawn up in 1948, known as the Havana Charter; but when it was clear that this would not command the consent of some important trading nations, it was set aside. Nevertheless, there has emerged an international concern for this field of co-operation, and a treaty was entered into and became effective in 1948. This is known as the *General Agreement on Tariffs and Trade* (GATT), and under its auspices much valuable co-operation has been effected. In 1964, for instance, the International Trade Centre was established within GATT to provide information on export markets and to help developing countries to work out the best techniques of export promotion and the training of personnel.

Such is the pattern of international co-operation that has emerged with the development of the United Nations and its associated agencies. As we have already noted, the extent of co-operation over so many fields is greater than ever before. With the interdependence of the nations of the world becoming more and more pronounced every day, the existence of the machinery provided through the United Nations may well ensure the maximum benefit for all peoples of the new possibilities now made available by science and man's inventiveness.

There still remains, however, the shadow of a mushroom-cloud over the future of humanity to remind us that all the good work represented by the U.N. is in jeopardy unless we can learn to live together as members of one family, seeking the good of all.

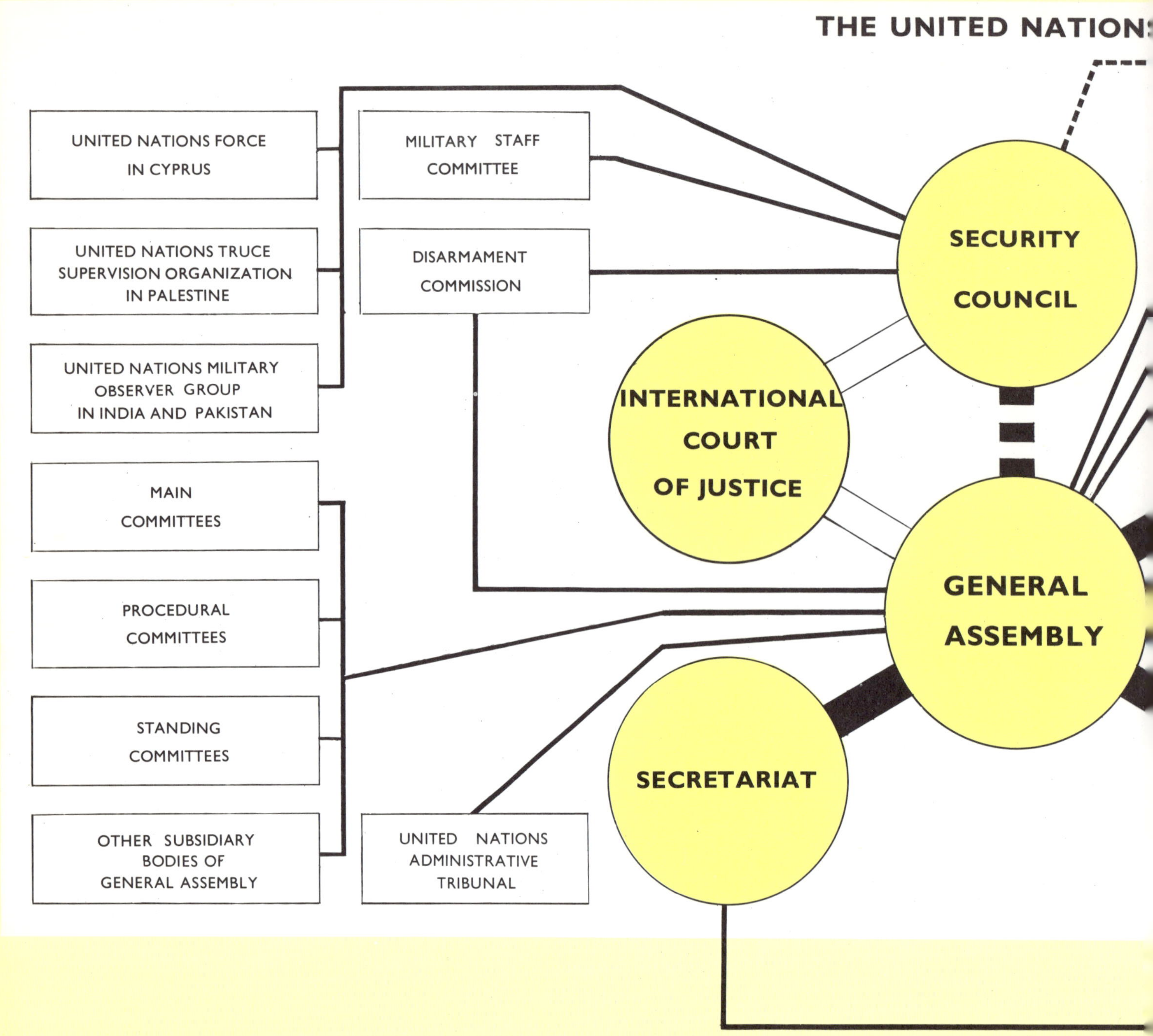

THE UNITED NATION:

UNITED NATIONS FORCE
IN CYPRUS

UNITED NATIONS TRUCE
SUPERVISION ORGANIZATION
IN PALESTINE

UNITED NATIONS MILITARY
OBSERVER GROUP
IN INDIA AND PAKISTAN

MAIN
COMMITTEES

PROCEDURAL
COMMITTEES

STANDING
COMMITTEES

OTHER SUBSIDIARY
BODIES OF
GENERAL ASSEMBLY

MILITARY STAFF
COMMITTEE

DISARMAMENT
COMMISSION

UNITED NATIONS
ADMINISTRATIVE
TRIBUNAL

SECURITY
COUNCIL

INTERNATIONAL
COURT
OF JUSTICE

GENERAL
ASSEMBLY

SECRETARIAT

THE SPECIALIZEI

INTERNATIONAL LABOUR
ORGANIZATION (ILO)

UNITED NATIONS
FOOD AND AGRICULTURE
ORGANIZATION (FAO)

UNITED NATIONS EDUCATIONAL
SCIENTIFIC AND CULTURAL
ORGANIZATION (UNESCO)

WORLD HEALTH
ORGANIZATION (WHO)

INTERNATIONAL
CIVIL AVIATION
ORGANIZATION (ICAO)

INTERNATIONAL
TELECOMMUNICATION
UNION (ITU)

UNIVERSAL POSTAL UNION
(UPU)

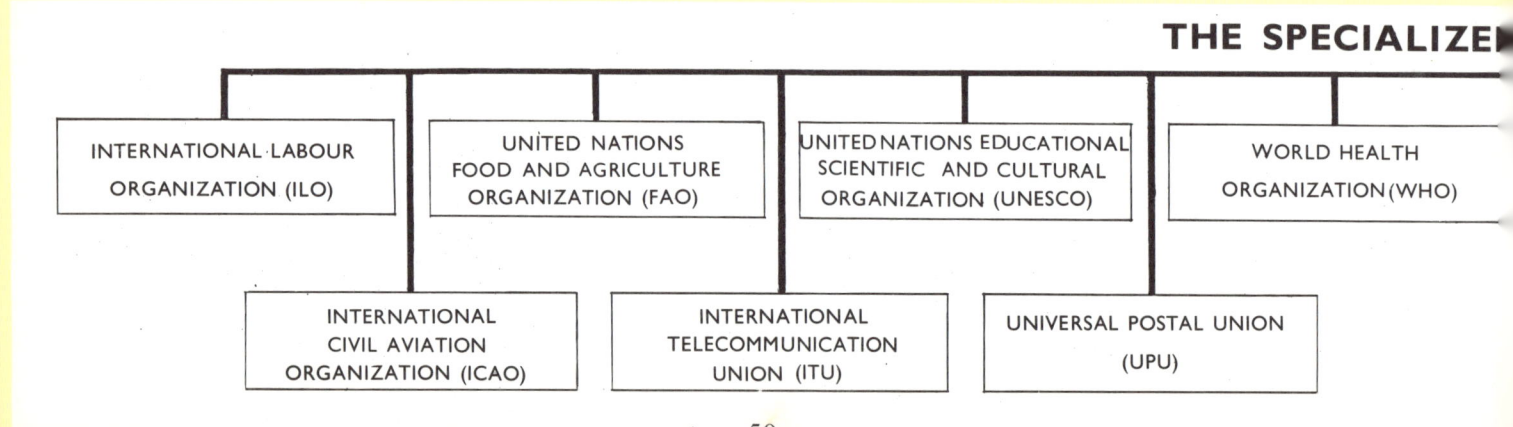

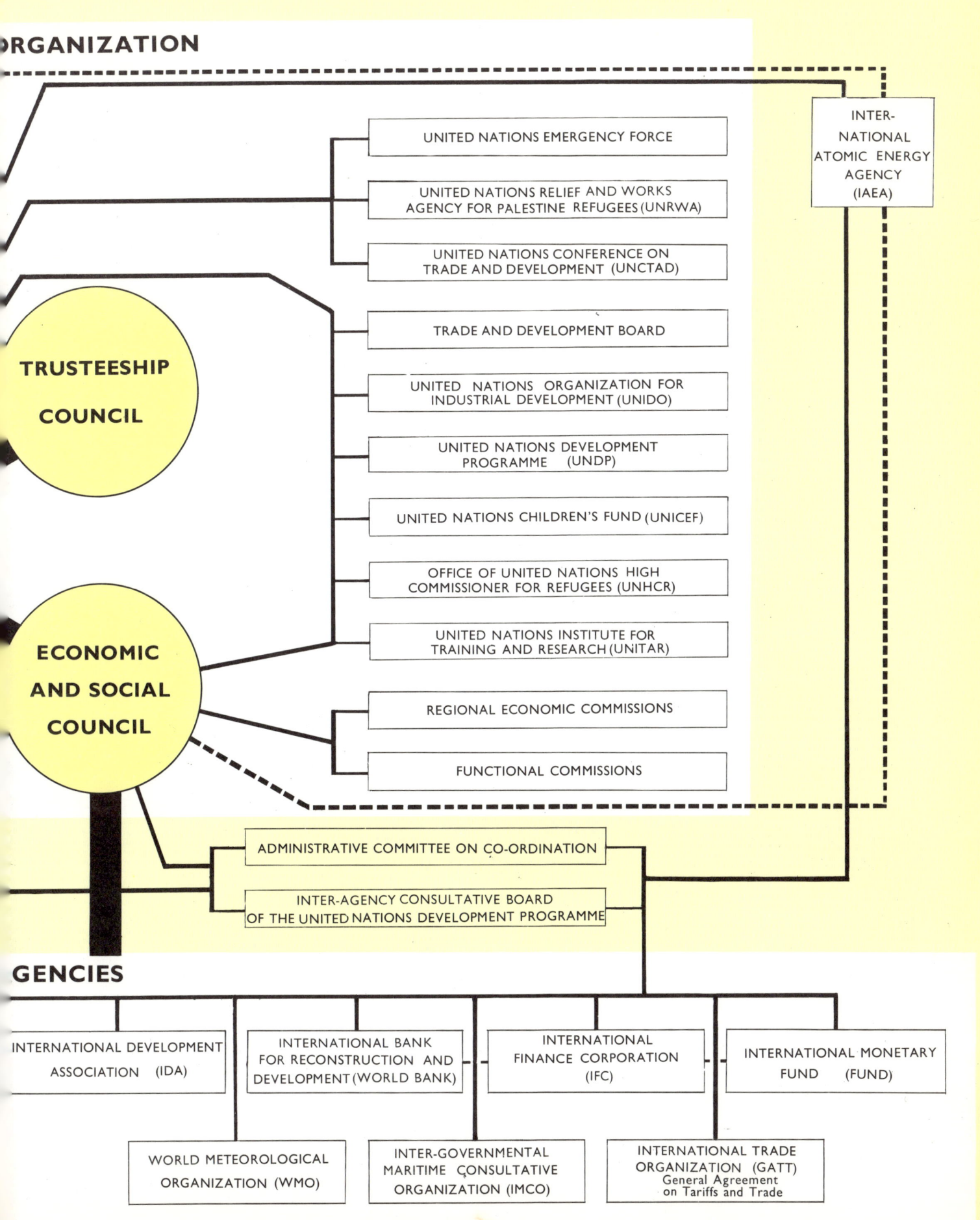

ZATION AND RELATED AGENCIES

ORGANIZATION

TRUSTEESHIP COUNCIL

ECONOMIC AND SOCIAL COUNCIL

UNITED NATIONS EMERGENCY FORCE

UNITED NATIONS RELIEF AND WORKS AGENCY FOR PALESTINE REFUGEES (UNRWA)

UNITED NATIONS CONFERENCE ON TRADE AND DEVELOPMENT (UNCTAD)

TRADE AND DEVELOPMENT BOARD

UNITED NATIONS ORGANIZATION FOR INDUSTRIAL DEVELOPMENT (UNIDO)

UNITED NATIONS DEVELOPMENT PROGRAMME (UNDP)

UNITED NATIONS CHILDREN'S FUND (UNICEF)

OFFICE OF UNITED NATIONS HIGH COMMISSIONER FOR REFUGEES (UNHCR)

UNITED NATIONS INSTITUTE FOR TRAINING AND RESEARCH (UNITAR)

REGIONAL ECONOMIC COMMISSIONS

FUNCTIONAL COMMISSIONS

INTER-NATIONAL ATOMIC ENERGY AGENCY (IAEA)

ADMINISTRATIVE COMMITTEE ON CO-ORDINATION

INTER-AGENCY CONSULTATIVE BOARD OF THE UNITED NATIONS DEVELOPMENT PROGRAMME

GENCIES

INTERNATIONAL DEVELOPMENT ASSOCIATION (IDA)

INTERNATIONAL BANK FOR RECONSTRUCTION AND DEVELOPMENT (WORLD BANK)

INTERNATIONAL FINANCE CORPORATION (IFC)

INTERNATIONAL MONETARY FUND (FUND)

WORLD METEOROLOGICAL ORGANIZATION (WMO)

INTER-GOVERNMENTAL MARITIME CONSULTATIVE ORGANIZATION (IMCO)

INTERNATIONAL TRADE ORGANIZATION (GATT) General Agreement on Tariffs and Trade

51

PEACEKEEPING.

The vital task of keeping the peace is entrusted to the Security Council. The only organ in continuous session, it is able to meet whenever there is an outbreak or threat of hostilities which might spread or erupt into international conflict

UNIVERSAL

DECLARATION

OF

HUMAN RIGHTS

ON DECEMBER 10, 1948, The General
Assembly of the United Nations adopted
and proclaimed the Universal Declaration
of Human Rights, the full text of which
appears in the following pages. Following
this historic act the Assembly called upon
all Member countries to publicize the text
of the Declaration and 'to cause it to be
disseminated, displayed, read and ex-
pounded principally in schools and other
educational institutions, without distinction based on the political status of countries or territories.'

UNIVERSAL DECLARATION OF HUMAN RIGHTS

PREAMBLE

Whereas recognition of the inherent dignity and of the equal and inalienable rights of all members of the human family is the foundation of freedom, justice and peace in the world,

Whereas disregard and contempt for human rights have resulted in barbarous acts which have outraged the conscience of mankind, and the advent of a world in which human beings shall enjoy freedom of speech and belief and freedom from fear and want has been proclaimed as the highest aspiration of the common people,

Whereas it is essential, if man is not to be compelled to have recourse, as a last resort, to rebellion against tyranny and oppression, that human rights should be protected by the rule of law,

Whereas it is essential to promote the development of friendly relations between nations,

Whereas the peoples of the United Nations have in the Charter reaffirmed their faith in fundamental human rights, in the dignity and worth of the human person and in the equal rights of men and women and have determined to promote social progress and better standards of life in larger freedom,

Whereas Member States have pledged themselves to achieve, in co-operation with the United Nations, the promotion of universal respect for and observance of human rights and fundamental freedoms,

Whereas a common understanding of these rights and freedoms is of the greatest importance for the full realization of this pledge,

Now, Therefore,

THE GENERAL ASSEMBLY

proclaims

THIS UNIVERSAL DECLARATION OF HUMAN RIGHTS as a common standard of achievement for all peoples and all nations, to the end that every individual and every organ of society, keeping this Declaration constantly in mind, shall strive by teaching and education to promote respect for these rights and freedoms and by progressive measures, national and international, to secure their universal and effective recognition and observance, both among the peoples of Member States themselves and among the peoples of territories under their jurisdiction.

Article 1. *All human beings are born free and equal in dignity and rights. They are endowed with reason and conscience and should act towards one another in a spirit of brotherhood.*

Article 2. *Everyone is entitled to all the rights and freedoms set forth in this Declaration, without distinction of any kind, such as race, colour, sex, language, religion, political or other opinion, national or social origin, property, birth or other status.*

Furthermore, no distinction shall be made on the basis of the political, jurisdictional or international status of the country or territory to which a person belongs, whether it be independent, trust, non-self-governing or under any other limitation of sovereignty.

Article 3. *Everyone has the right to life, liberty and security of person.*

Article 4. *No one shall be held in slavery or servitude; slavery and the slave trade shall be prohibited in all their forms.*

Article 5. *No one shall be subjected to torture or to cruel, inhuman or degrading treatment or punishment.*

Article 6. *Everyone has the right to recognition everywhere as a person before the law.*

Article 7. *All are equal before the law and are entitled without any discrimination to equal protection of the law. All are entitled to equal protection against any discrimination in violation of this Declaration and against any incitement to such discrimination.*

Article 8. *Everyone has the right to an effective remedy by the competent national tribunals for acts violating the fundamental rights granted him by the constitution or by law.*

Article 9. *No one shall be subjected to arbitrary arrest, detention or exile.*

Article 10. *Everyone is entitled in full equality to a fair and public hearing by an independent and impartial tribunal, in the determination of his rights and obligations and of any criminal charge against him.*

Article 11. (1) *Everyone charged with a penal offence has the right to be presumed innocent until proved guilty according to law in a public trial at which he has had all the guarantees necessary for his defence.*

(2) *No one shall be held guilty of any penal offence on account of any act or omission which did not constitute a penal offence, under national or international law, at the time when it was committed. Nor shall a heavier penalty be imposed than the one that was applicable at the time the penal offence was committed.*

Article 12. *No one shall be subjected to arbitrary interference with his privacy, family, home or correspondence, nor to attacks upon his honour and reputation. Everyone has the right to the protection of the law against such interference or attacks.*

Article 13. (1) *Everyone has the right to freedom of movement and residence within the borders of each state.*

(2) *Everyone has the right to leave any country, including his own, and to return to his country.*

Article 14. (1) *Everyone has the right to seek and to enjoy in other countries asylum from persecution.*

(2) *This right may not be invoked in the case of prosecutions genuinely arising from non-political crimes or from acts contrary to the purposes and principles of the United Nations.*

Article 15. (1) *Everyone has the right to a nationality.*

(2) *No one shall be arbitrarily deprived of his nationality nor denied the right to change his nationality.*

Article 16. (1) *Men and women of full age, without any limitation due to race, nationality or religion, have the right to marry and to found a family. They are entitled to equal rights as to marriage, during marriage and at its dissolution.*

(2) *Marriage shall be entered into only with the free and full consent of the intending spouses.*

(3) *The family is the natural and fundamental group unit of society and is entitled to protection by society and the State.*

Article 17. (1) *Everyone has the right to own property alone as well as in association with others.*

(2) *No one shall be arbitrarily deprived of his property.*

Article 18. *Everyone has the right to freedom of thought, conscience and religion; this right includes freedom to change his religion or belief, and freedom, either alone or in community with others and in public or private, to manifest his religion or belief in teaching, practice, worship and observance.*

Article 19. *Everyone has the right to freedom of opinion and expression; this right includes freedom to hold opinions without interference and to seek, receive and impart information and ideas through any media and regardless of frontiers.*

Article 20. (1) *Everyone has the right to freedom of peaceful assembly and association.*

(2) *No one may be compelled to belong to an association.*

Article 21. (1) *Everyone has the right to take part in the government of his country, directly or through freely chosen representatives.*

(2) *Everyone has the right of equal access to*

public services in his country.

(3) The will of the people shall be the basis of the authority of government; this will shall be expressed in periodic and genuine elections which shall be by universal and equal suffrage and shall be held by secret vote or by equivalent free voting procedures.

Article 22. *Everyone, as a member of society, has the right to social security and is entitled to realization, through national effort and international co-operation and in accordance with the organization and resources of each State, of the economic, social and cultural rights indispensable for his dignity and the free development of his personality.*

Article 23. *(1) Everyone has the right to work, to free choice of employment, to just and favourable conditions of work and to protection against unemployment.*

(2) Everyone, without any discrimination, has the right to equal pay for equal work.

(3) Everyone who works has the right to just and favourable remuneration ensuring for himself and his family an existence worthy of human dignity, and supplemented, if necessary, by other means of social protection.

(4) Everyone has the right to form and to join trade unions for the protection of his interests.

Article 24. *Everyone has the right to rest and leisure, including reasonable limitation of working hours and periodic holidays with pay.*

Article 25. *(1) Everyone has the right to a standard of living adequate for the health and well-being of himself and of his family, including food, clothing, housing and medical care and necessary social services, and the right to security in the event of unemployment, sickness, disability, widowhood, old age or other lack of livelihood in circumstances beyond his control.*

(2) Motherhood and childhood are entitled to special care and assistance. All children, whether born in or out of wedlock, shall enjoy the same social protection.

Article 26. *(1) Everyone has the right to education. Education shall be free, at least in*

the elementary and fundamental stages. Elementary education shall be compulsory. Technical and professional education shall be made generally available and higher education shall be equally accessible to all on the basis of merit.

(2) Education shall be directed to the full development of the human personality and to the strengthening of respect for human rights and fundamental freedoms. It shall promote understanding, tolerance and friendship among all nations, racial or religious groups, and shall further the activities of the United Nations for the maintenance of peace.

(3) Parents have a prior right to choose the kind of education that shall be given to their children.

Article 27. *(1) Everyone has the right freely to participate in the cultural life of the community, to enjoy the arts and to share in scientific advancement and its benefits.*

(2) Everyone has the right to the protection of the moral and material interests resulting from any scientific, literary or artistic production of which he is the author.

Article 28. *Everyone is entitled to a social and international order in which the rights and freedoms set forth in this Declaration can be fully realized.*

Article 29. *(1) Everyone has duties to the community in which alone the free and full development of his personality is possible.*

(2) In the exercise of his rights and freedoms, everyone shall be subject only to such limitations as are determined by law solely for the purpose of securing due recognition and respect for the rights and freedoms of others and of meeting the just requirements of morality, public order and the general welfare in a democratic society.

(3) These rights and freedoms may in no case be exercised contrary to the purposes and principles of the United Nations.

Article 30. *Nothing in this Declaration may be interpreted as implying for any State, group or person any right to engage in any activity or to perform any act aimed at the destruction of any of the rights and freedoms set forth herein.*

SECTION FIVE

THE WORLD COUNCIL OF CHURCHES

It has been made clear that this Atlas of Man and Religion is compiled according to deliberate principles of selectivity. It seeks to illustrate the theme of its title by consciously concentrating on the heritage of western civilisation and its dependence on the traditions of the Christian religion. We believe this approach to be justified on the grounds already given in Section 1.

There is, however, a further justification which is illustrated in this final section, which is concerned with the World Council of Churches. The Christian religion incorporates in its very nature a missionary and evangelistic element which can be paralleled in no other religion, and it has permeated the variety of world cultures to an extent beyond that of other religions. This claim is set down objectively as a fact of history and does not preclude the consequent question, which may reasonably be argued in the present state of the world, as to whether the Christian influence has always been for the good of those affected by it. There is no doubt that the honest

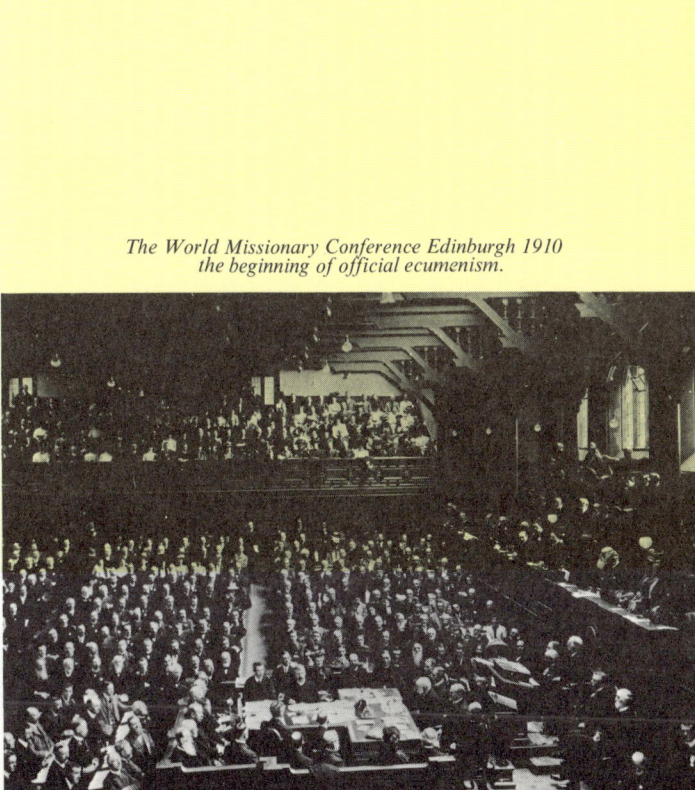

The World Missionary Conference Edinburgh 1910 the beginning of official ecumenism.

The Central Committee of the World Council of Churches held its annual meeting in the University of Kent at Canterbury, August 1969. This picture shows: His Eminence Joseph Diangienda of the Church of Christ on Earth by the Prophet Simon Kimbangu conducts evening worship with Pastor Luntindila, Mr. Mark Schomer and another pastor.

CONTRASTS. At the New Delhi Assembly (1961) new member-churches were admitted to the World Council of Churches. These included the highly liturgical, colourful and dramatic Russian Orthodox and the simple unsophisticated Pentecostal churches.

Christian historian must concede that much of the good flowing from the true preaching and living of the gospel has been vitiated by the bitter divisions which have marred the story of the Christian Church, setting Christian against Christian in a most unholy conflict.

We are not concerned here to dwell on the 'unhappy divisions' which have served to obscure the good news of the gospel. We have the much happier task of recording the story which signalises the past 180 years, and has now come to dominate the Christian ecclesiastical landscape—the story of the persistent attempts to heal the divisions and break down the barriers which have separated those claiming to be brothers in Christ.

The impetus towards reunion began to gather momentum towards the end of the eighteenth century, when a new sense of missionary urgency brought fresh life to many churches, both in Britain and other parts of the western world. In Britain, under the leadership of such men as William Carey and John Williams, the consciences of Christian men and women were stirred to obey more literally than hitherto the command of the risen Lord to his disciples to 'go into all the world and make disciples of all nations'. Many missionary societies were founded at the turn of the 18th and 19th centuries. They were mostly founded within the several denominations of the Christian community, but some did set out to recruit missionaries from all denominations without discrimination.

The surge of missionary enterprise throughout the nineteenth century met with very great success and proved the channel through which education, medical care and other accompanying benefits were first introduced to many parts of the world hitherto illiterate and disease-ridden. As time went on, it became more and more apparent that to those hearing and responding to the gospel for the first time the channels into which the Church was divided were bewildering and a very real hindrance to the true understanding of Christianity and its practical demands. Indeed, many of those responsible for the practical service of the Christian gospel in the mission field found themselves drawn together across denominational frontiers in order to do their work effectively.

In the light of this spontaneous pressure attempts were made to find ways of full and unfettered co-operation among the different denominations. Eventually a World Missionary Conference was convened in Edinburgh in the year 1910. This proved to be an outstanding landmark in the development of what is called the modern 'ecumenical' movement. The word 'ecumenical' comes from the Greek word *Oikoumene* which means 'world-wide'. It is the word used of the Councils of the Church in the fourth and fifth centuries, when the Church was indeed united in structure and purpose, and thought of itself as responsible for preserving the integrity of the Christian gospel for the sake of the whole world.

The Edinburgh Conference was like a pebble dropped in a still pool. It sent out ripples which extended further than anyone could have foreseen. In the light of the present advanced situation it is difficult for us to realise how great were the achievements of that historic meeting. The many missionary societies there represented entered into agreements and understandings which were designed to use their resources more efficiently and to preclude wasteful overlapping by working out agreed areas of operation.

The most significant result of the Edinburgh Conference was the serious determination shown by the appointment of a Continuation Committee under the chairmanship of the young American, John R. Mott, with the Scotsman J. H. Oldham as secretary. These two men were

A FRIENDLY CALL. The official Roman Catholic attitude of non-recognition of the World Council of Churches was replaced by friendly conversations after 'Vatican 2'. In 1965 Cardinal Bea leaves his hat in the cloakroom on the occasion of this momentous visit to discuss future relations.

Pope Paul signs the visitors' book in the office of Dr. Eugene Carson Blake, World Council of Churches' general secretary.

Common Prayer at the Ecumenical Centre during the visit of Pope Paul on June 10th 1969. right to left: Jan Cardinal Willebrands, president of the Vatican Secretariat for Promoting Christian Unity; Pope Paul; Dr. Eugene Carson Blake, general secretary of the World Council of Churches; Mr. M. M. Thomas, chairman of the Central Committee of the WCC; Miss Pauline M. Webb and Metropolitan Meliton of Chalcedon, vice-chairman of the Central Committee.

to play an outstanding part in the progress of the ecumenical movement. Soon after the Edinburgh Conference, and as a direct result of its Continuation Committee's work, there was established the International Missionary Council, responsible for providing a firm basis for missionary co-operation over the whole range of world concern as represented by the co-operating societies. (At this time there was no possibility of co-operation between the Protestant and Roman Catholic Churches.)

Alongside the firm establishment of the International Missionary Council two other essential fields of interest were entered more tentatively, but with hope that some progress towards agreement might be made. These were the fields represented by the *Faith and Order* movement, and the *Life and Work* movement. These were concerned to bring Christians together to discuss their ecclesiastical and theological differences on the one hand, and to seek ways of co-operation in the field of social action on the other. As one would expect, the Life and Work movement, being more practical and less affected by theological differences, made more obvious advance in common areas of interest than the Faith and Order movement, which was concerned to tackle the hard core of ecclesiastical and theological disagreement.

However, both these streams continued active discussion over the next thirty years. The Faith and Order movement held an important conference at Lausanne in 1927, and the Life and Work movement in Stockholm in 1925. Again the Stockholm conference seemed to be more successful than that at Lausanne. Both streams persisted in their co-operative endeavours and agreed to convene further conferences to take place close together in time and place. The Faith and Order conference took place in Edinburgh, the Life and Work conference in Oxford; both in the summer of 1937.

These conferences reaped the reward of persistence and led directly to the great leap of faith, by which the World Council of Churches became a real possibility. Indeed, in 1938 the churches co-operating in the fields of Faith and Order and Life and Work made a solemn and binding 'declaration of intent' after meeting together at Utrecht, in Holland. This declaration brought into being the World Council of Churches 'in process of formation'. This phrase indicated that the W.C.C. enjoyed a kind of 'suspended animation', which proved to be of considerable spiritual value during the years of the Second World War. Across the frontiers of war Christians were praying together for peace and for one another. In particular, the members of the anti-Hitler Confessional Church in Germany were much enheartened by the knowledge that they were not without spiritual support. In the inaugural address at his installation as Archbishop of Canterbury in 1944, while the war was still raging, Dr. William Temple spoke of the ecumenical movement as 'the great new fact of our era'. This was a high claim, indeed, but not without justification.

When the war ended representatives of the Churches quickly came together again, and by 1948 they were prepared to complete the operation begun in 1938. At Amsterdam in a service of solemn commitment representatives of 147 Churches throughout the world joined in the act by which the World Council of Churches at last came into existence. This was a triumph of faith and hope which would have been considered quite impossible of achievement at the beginning of the twentieth century.

There was still a long way to go, however. The 147 member-Churches of the W.C.C. represented the main Protestant communions in the world, but there were notable exceptions even among the Protestants. More significant was the manifest gulf which still separated the Protestant from

Church reconstruction in Nuremberg, Germany. Funds have come from several churches abroad to help the Protestant churches of Germany rebuild.

Christian-Marxist dialogue sponsored by WCC's department on Church and Society held in Geneva April 1968. Mr Neffa in heated discussion with Rev. Paul Blanquart, French Dominican. Dr. Sergio Arce of Cuba, and Gonzalez Ruiz.

Lady Jackson (Barbara Ward), author of several books on economics, made an impassioned plea for Christians to spearhead "A propaganda campaign to spread the ideas of development and justice among the general citizen body". Flanking her are conference co-chairman, B. T. B. Chidzero (left) and Prof Jon Tirbergen.

the Roman Catholic Christians. Little progress had been recorded in bridging this gulf. Moreover, the Russian Orthodox Church, which had shown some interest in the ecumenical movement, refused to accept an invitation to send 'observers' to the Amsterdam Assembly of the W.C.C. in 1948. Other Churches in the 'Orthodox' camp were also disinterested. However, the willingness of the W.C.C. to extend practical help to the Orthodox in the task of rehabilitating and rebuilding the stricken areas of Eastern Europe warmed their hearts (and widened their theology?). Conversations were entered into in 1958 and were brought to a happy conclusion at the New Delhi Assembly of the W.C.C. in 1961, when the Russian Orthodox Church was received into membership, accompanied by the Orthodox Churches of Romania and Bulgaria. Soon after this, the Lutheran Church of Estonia and Latvia, and the Russian Baptist Church, successfully applied for membership. This association with the Churches within the Russian orbit was a notable 'breakthrough'.

In 1948, then, a great step forward towards Christian unity had been taken; and this provided a base from which to go further. In 1952 a conference was held at Lund, in Sweden, at which the concerns of the old Life and Work movement were examined in the light of the new climate created by the formation of the W.C.C. From that conference came the germinal phrase which has captured the imagination and stirred the consciences of those engaged in local parish situations. This formulated the strong recommendation that, in Christian life and work 'nothing should be done separately which could be done together'. This provides a continuing criterion by which so much denominational activity at the local level is judged and often condemned.

The Second Assembly of the W.C.C. was held at Evanston, Illinois, U.S.A., in 1954, and it was clearly demonstrated that the first six years of the World Council had strengthened the fellowship and the determination of the members.

The Third Assembly was held in 1961 at New Delhi. We have already made reference to the admission of several member Churches from Russia and elsewhere behind the Iron Curtain. But the New Delhi Assembly was notable for other important signs of advance. Together with the Orthodox Churches there were admitted to membership also some Pentecostal Churches from South America. Hitherto these 'extreme evangelical' Churches had held aloof from any co-operation with other Churches, as had the Orthodox. Now representatives from these two opposite wings of Christian churchmanship were joined together in common acceptance of the aims and basis of the W.C.C. The basis of membership (slightly changed from the original basis of 1948) states:

The World Council of Churches is a fellowship of churches which confess the Lord Jesus Christ as God and Saviour according to the scriptures and therefore seek to fulfil together their common calling to the glory of the one God, Father, Son, and Holy Spirit.

Furthermore, for the first time, the Roman Catholic Church sent official 'observers' to the New Delhi Assembly. But perhaps the most important feature of this very notable Assembly was the unification in one body of the International Missionary Council and the W.C.C. Up to this time the I.M.C., which we have already seen to be the 'senior' ecumenical organisation, had maintained its separate existence. Since its formation in 1921 its work had expanded and intensified. In a series of conferences at Jerusalem (1928) Madras (1938) Whitby (1947) Willingen (1952) and Ghana (1958)

it had registered the change of leadership in the evangelistic task from the older to the younger Churches. Now it was recognised, on both sides, that the I.M.C. and the W.C.C. needed to give outward form to the growing consciousness that Church and Mission belonged together. This was accomplished by the unanimous and common agreement of the members of the two bodies, and they became one in the World Council of Churches, now enlarged in its scope by the inclusion of a *Division of World Mission and Evangelism* (DWME).

The Fourth Assembly coincided with the twentieth anniversary of the formation of the World Council. It was held in 1968 at Uppsala, Sweden, a city closely associated with Bishop Nathan Söderblom, one of the pioneers of the modern ecumenical movement, who was particularly concerned with the practical problems dealt with by the Life and Work movement. At the Uppsala Assembly Roman Catholic 'observers' were again present, but their presence was more than a formality. They took part in sectional discussions and contributed greatly to the deeper understanding of their point of view. This new level of co-operation was a direct result of the new spirit of Christian fellowship encouraged on the Roman Catholic

RHODESIA. The Mindolo Ecumenical Centre near Kitwe, Northern Rhodesia, is located in the Copperbelt, second largest copper producing area in the world. Here an inter-racial, international, and interdenomi-national staff is conducting a programme which has a threefold emphasis. It is attemting to meet needs for leadership, research and consultation, particularly among laity.

side by the Second Vatican Council, called by Pope John XXIII in 1962, and continued by his successor Pope Paul VI. This spirit had been demonstrated by the readiness of the Roman Catholic Church to join in talks with the Secretary of the World Council of Churches, then Dr. W. A. Visser 't Hooft. Cardinal Bea entered whole-heartedly into such conversations, and in 1969 Pope Paul VI himself made an official visit to the Ecumenical Centre in Geneva to convey his greetings and good wishes to the World Council of Churches. Such 'fraternising' shows how completely the atmosphere has changed within a very short time, and it augurs well for ultimate unity among the Christian Churches.

Meanwhile, the work of the World Council has been carried out in all three fields of interest represented by the movements initiated after the Edinburgh conference of 1910—the fields of the Life and Work movement, the Faith and Order movement, and the International Missionary Council.

Coming into existence, as it did, immediately after the Second World War, the W.C.C. was faced with an obvious field of practical co-operation among all Christians. The rehabilitation of a war-torn world called for the recruitment and organisation of all the goodwill which alone could tackle the tasks of feeding the hungry, clothing the naked, rehousing the homeless and comforting the refugee. In many parts of Europe the local churches were seeking to rebuild not only the shattered buildings but also the community life of the people. In this enterprise the World Council of Churches took a lead by setting up its division of Inter-Church Aid. As time passed the responsibilities assumed by this division grew; and it became involved in all the problems of helping people to help themselves, as well as providing emergency aid to those in need of any sort. The name given to the organisation which now set itself to gather funds and establish expert teams to administer them was enlarged to the *Division of Inter-Church Aid, Refugee and World Service* (DICARWS).

The DWME, which we have already referred to, has also found its field of service enlarged to provide means of training people to write and produce books of their own in places where literacy is only beginning to appear. Over against the older conception of Mission as being to send missionaries out to preach, teach and live the gospel, there is a growing need to join in the tasks now laid upon the conscience of the 'younger churches', helping them with expert advice and willing service.

The awareness of a world struggle for peace and justice has led to the establishment of a *Commission of the Churches on International Affairs*, which has tried to find a common Christian mind on the complex problems thrown up by the technical and social revolutions in all parts of the world.

The change in moral standards and ethical attitudes has brought bewilderment to many people, and a forum for the ordered discussion of the issues involved is provided by the *Division of Ecumenical Action*, through its departments on *Laity, Youth*, and *Co-operation of Men and Women*. This division takes seriously the problems involved in trying to retain the values of Christian community and worship without being afraid to develop new ideas as to how this can best be done.

The *Commission of Faith and Order* keeps alive the conversation between Churches of different traditions and convictions, encouraging movements towards the union of Churches where they are taking place. It also provides channels for conversations with the Roman Catholic Church, not only on theological matters, but also on practical matters, such as mixed marriages and religious liberty.

It will be seen from this necessarily brief summary of the activities of the World Council of Churches that during the twenty-two years of its existence it has made possible the development of real co-operation in action and in lively discussion between those who are yet deeply divided in their theological and ecclesiastical convictions. This has led to a deeper understanding of each others' points of view and, in not a few instances, has helped those who were divided to overcome their divisions.

A stage has now been reached when discussion is possible, not only between churchmen who previously would not recognise one another as Christians, but also between Christians and Communists. Here there is no expectation on either side that any full reconciliation could be reached between two such different ideologies, but it is recognised that there are areas of common concern which it might be profitable to explore. How far this may lead is yet to be seen; but a start has been made.

Throughout the world, wherever there are member-Churches of the W.C.C. National Christian Councils have been set up to promote channels of communication and common activity among the Churches, both nationally and internationally.

Western civilisation has dominated the world for many centuries now. It has been responsible for the rise of modern science and technology, and has enriched life with the many elements of culture which have grown with it. It has also brought the world the experience of untold misery and disaster. In this Atlas we have tried to discern the elements which make up this world in which we live, and through eyes trained to look out from within the experience of the western world and the Christian tradition to draw a true picture of what is going on. The emergence at such a time as this of the United Nations and the World Council of Churches justifies a measure of hope, and invites all men to search their hearts to find the truth by which men can live together in peace and true brotherhood.

It is the claim of the Christian gospel that the clue to realising this aspiration can be found in the evidence of God's love made known in Jesus Christ. Before this claim is brushed aside it is worth pondering together with all other relevant evidence. The writer hopes that what is here may help the reader to understand some of the factors involved in his search.

AMSTERDAM 1948. The World Council of Churches is born. The inaugural Service.

THE WORLD COUNCIL OF CHURCHES ASSEMBLY

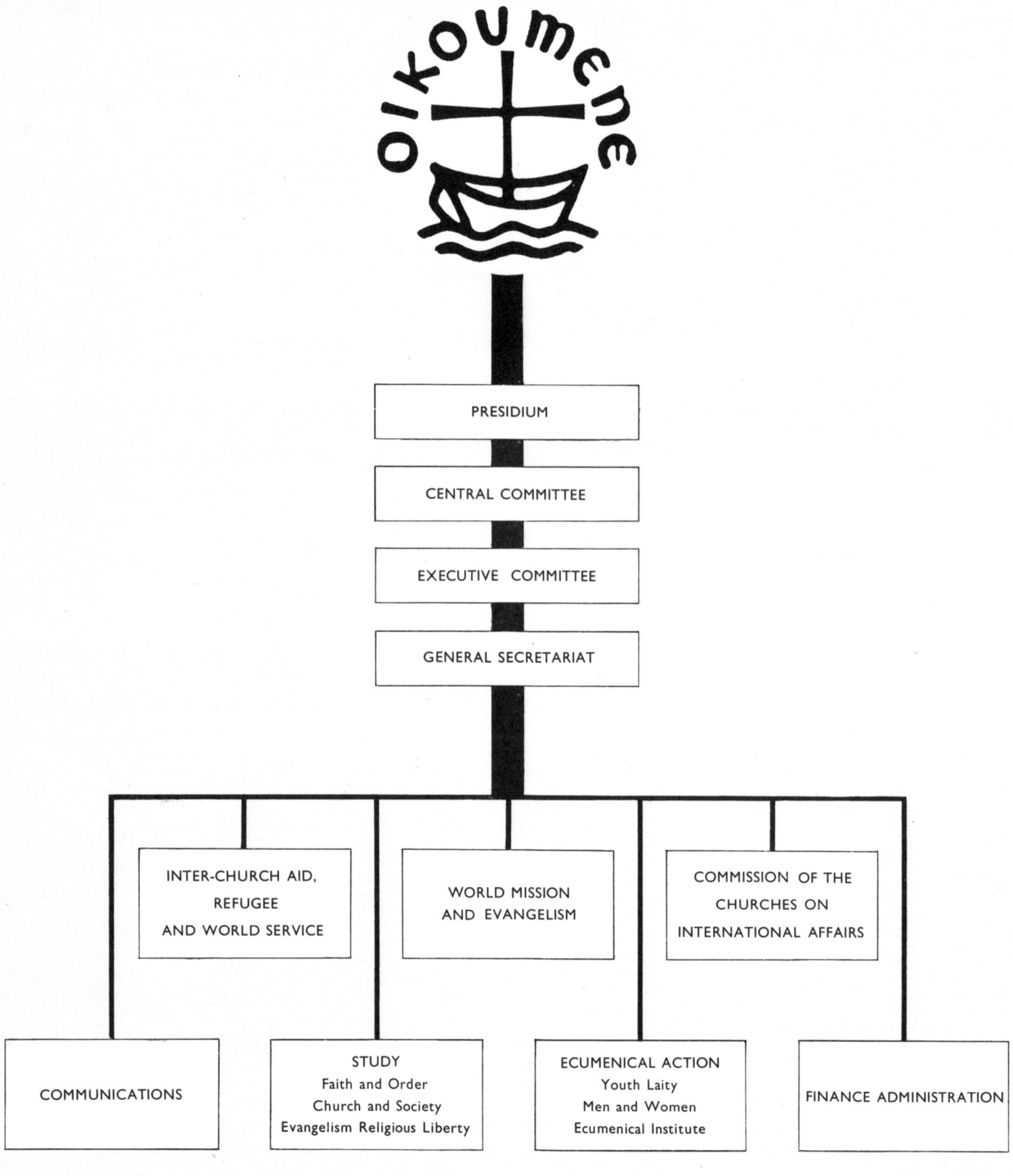

WORLD COUNCIL OF CHURCHES

List of Member Churches

ARGENTINA
   IGLESIA EVANGELICA DEL RIO DE LA
   PLATA (Evangelical Church of the River Plata)
AUSTRALASIA
   METHODIST CHURCH OF AUSTRALASIA
AUSTRALIA
   CHURCHES OF CHRIST IN AUSTRALIA
   THE CHURCH OF ENGLAND IN AUSTRALIA
   CONGREGATIONAL UNION OF AUSTRALIA
   PRESBYTERIAN CHURCH OF AUSTRALIA
AUSTRIA
   ALT-KATHOLISCHE KIRCHE ÖSTERREICHS
      (Old Catholic Church of Austria)
   EVANGELISCHE KIRCHE A.u.H.B. IN
   ÖSTERREICH (Evangelical Church of
      the Augsburg and Helvetic Confession)
BELGIUM
   EGLISE CHRETIENNE MISSIONNAIRE BELGE
      (Belgian Christian Missionary Church)
   EGLISE EVANGELIQUE PROTESTANTE DE
   BELGIQUE (Evangelical Protestant Church of
      Belgium)
BRAZIL
   IGREJA EPISCOPAL DO BRASIL
      (Episcopal Church of Brazil)
   IGREJA EVANGELICA DE CONFISSAO
   LUTHERANA NO BRASIL (Evangelical Church
      of Lutheran Confession in Brazil)
   IGREJA METODISTA DO BRASIL
      (Methodist Church of Brazil)
BULGARIA
   BULGARIAN ORTHODOX CHURCH
      (Eglise orthodoxe de Bulgarie)
BURMA
   THE BURMA BAPTIST CONVENTION

CAMEROON
   EGLISE EVANGELIQUE DU CAMEROUN
      (Evangelical Church of Cameroon)
   EGLISE PRESBYTERIENNE CAMEROUNAISE
      (Presbyterian Church of Cameroon)
   PRESBYTERIAN CHURCH IN WEST
   CAMEROON
   UNION DES EGLISES BAPTISTES DU
   CAMEROUN (Union of Baptist Churches
      of Cameroon)
CANADA
   THE ANGLICAN CHURCH OF CANADA
   CANADIAN YEARLY MEETING OF THE
   RELIGIOUS SOCIETY OF FRIENDS
   CHURCHES OF CHRIST (DISCIPLES)
   THE EVANGELICAL LUTHERAN CHURCH
   OF CANADA
   THE PRESBYTERIAN CHURCH IN CANADA
   THE UNITED CHURCH OF CANADA
CENTRAL AFRICA
   CHURCH OF THE PROVINCE OF CENTRAL
   AFRICA
CEYLON
   METHODIST CHURCH, CEYLON
CHILE
   IGLESIA EVANGELICA LUTERANA EN CHILE
      (Evangelical-Lutheran Church in Chile)
   IGLESIA PENTECOSTAL DE CHILE
      (Pentecostal Church of Chile)
CHINA
   CHINA BAPTIST COUNCIL
   CHUNG-HUA CHI-TU CHIAO-HUI
      (Church of Christ in China)

CHUNG HUA SHENG KUNG HUI
(Anglican Church in China)
HUA PEI KUNG LI HUI
(North China Congregational Church)
CONGO (Brazzaville)
EGLISE EVANGELIQUE DU CONGO
(Evangelical Church of the Congo)
CONGO (Kinshasa)
EGLISE DU CHRIST AU CONGO
(Disciples du Christ)
EGLISE EVANGELIQUE DE MANIANGA-
MATADI (Manianga-Matadi Evangelical Church)
CYPRUS
CHURCH OF CYPRUS
CZECHOSLOVAKIA
CESKOBRATRSKA CIRKVE EVANGELICKA
(Evangelical Church of Czech Brethren)
CESKOSLOVENSKA CIRKEV
(Czechoslovak Church)
EVANGELICKA CIRKEV A.V. NA SLOVENSKU
(Evangelical Church in Czechoslovakia,
Augsburg Confession)
ORTHODOX CHURCH OF CZECHOSLOVAKIA
REF. KREST CIRKVI NA SLOVENSKU
(Reformed Christian Church in Slovakia)
SLEZSKA CIRKEV EVANGELICKA A. V.
(Evangeligal Church of the Augsburg
Confession in Silesia)
DENMARK
THE BAPTIST UNION OF DENMARK
DEN EVANGELISKLUTHERSKE
FOLKEKIRKE I DANMARK (Church
of Denmark)
EAST AFRICA
CHURCH OF THE PROVINCE OF EAST
AFRICA
THE PRESBYTERIAN CHURCH OF EAST
AFRICA
EGYPT
COPTIC EVANGELICAL CHURCH -
THE SYNOD OF THE NILE
COPTIC ORTHODOX CHURCH

GREEK ORTHODOX PATRIARCHATE OF
ALEXANDRIA
ETHIOPIA
ETHIOPIAN ORTHODOX CHURCH
FINLAND
SUOMEN EVANKELIS - LUTERILAINEN
KIRKKO (Evangelical Lutheran Church of Finland)
FRANCE
EGLISE DE LA CONFESSION D'AUGSBOURG
D'ALSACE ET DE LORRAINE (Evangelical
Church of the Augsburg Confession in
Alsace and Lorraine)
EGLISE EVANGELIQUE LUTHERIENNE DE FRANCE)
EGLISE REFORMEE D'ALSACE ET DE LORRAINE
(Reformed Church of Alsace and Lorraine)
EGLISE REFORMEE DE FRANCE
(Reformed Church of France)
GABON
EGLISE EVANGELIQUE DU GABON
GERMANY
ALT-KATHOLISCHE KIRCHE IN DEUTSCHLAND
(Old Catholic Church in Germany)
EVANGELISCHE BRÜDER-ÜNITAT
(Moravian Church)
EVANGELISCHE KIRCHE IN DEUTSCHLAND
(Evangelical Church in Germany)
EVANGELISCHE KIRCHE IN BERLIN-
BRANDENBURG
EVANGELISCHE LANDESKIRCHE GREIFSWALD
EVANGELISCHE KIRCHE DES KIRCHENGEBIETES
GÖRLITZ
EVANGELISCHE KIRCHE DER KIRCHENPROVINZ
SACHSEN
EVANGELISCHE KIRCHE VON WESTFALEN
EVANGELISCHE KIRCHE IM RHEINLAND
★ EVANGELISCH-LUTHERISCHE LANDESKIRCHE
SACHSENS
★ EVANGELISCH-LUTHERISCHE LANDESKIRCHE
HANNOVERS
★ EVANGELISCH-LUTHERISCHE KIRCHE IN BAYERN
EVANGELISCH-LUTHERISCHE KIRCHE IN
THURINGEN

* EVANGELISCH-LUTHERISCHE LANDESKIRCHE
  SCHLESWIG-HOLSTEINS
* EVANGELISCH-LUTHERISCHE LANDESKIRCHE
  IM HAMBURGISCHEN STAATE
* EVANGELISCH-LUTHERISCHE LANDESKIRCHE
  MECKLENBURGS
* BRAUNSCHWEIGISCHE EVANGELISCH-
  LUTHERISCHE LANDESKIRCHE
* EVANGELISCH-LUTHERISCHE KIRCHE
  IN LÜBECK
* EVANGELISCH-LUTHERISCHE LANDESKIRCHE
  VON SCHAUMBURG-LIPPE
EVANGELISCHE LANDESKIRCHE IN
  WÜRTTEMBURG
EVANGELISCH-LUTERISCHE KIRCHE IN
  OLDENBURG
EVANGELISCH-LUTHERISCHE LANDESKIRCHE
  EUTIN
EVANGELISCHE KIRCHE IN HESSEN UND
  NASSAU
EVANGELISCHE LANDESKIRCHE
  VON KURHESSEN-WALDECK
EVANGELISCHE LANDESKIRCHE IN BADEN
VEREINIGTE PROTESTANTISCH-
  EVANGELISCH-CHRISTLICHE KIRCHE
  DER PFALZ
EVANGELISCHE LANDESKIRCHE ANHALTS
BREMISCHE EVANGELISCHE KIRCHE
EVANGELISCH-REFORMIERTE KIRCHE IN
  NORDWESTDEUTSCHLAND
LIPPISCHE LANDESKIRCHE

* This Church is directly a member of the World Council of Churches in accordance with the resolution of the General Synod of the United Evangelical Lutheran Church of Germany, dated 27 January 1949, which recommended that the member churches of the United Evangelical Lutheran Church should make the following declaration to the Council of the Evangelical Church in Germany concerning their relation to the World Council of Churches: "The Evangelical Church in Germany has made it clear through its constitution that it is a federation (Bund) of confessionally determined churches. Moreover, the conditions of membership of the World Council of Churches have been determined at the Assembly at Amsterdam. Therefore, this Evangelical Lutheran Church declares concerning its membership in the World Council of Churches:

  i) It is represented in the World Council as a church of the Evangelical Lutheran confession.
  ii) Representatives which it sends to the World Council are to be identified as Evangelical Lutherans.
  iii) Within the limits of the competence of the Evangelical Church in Germany it is represented in the World Council through the intermediary of the Council of the Evangelical Church in Germany."

VEREINIGUNG DER DEUTSCHEN
  MENNONITENGEMEINDEN (Mennonite Church)

GHANA
EVANGELICAL PRESBYTERIAN CHURCH
THE METHODIST CHURCH, GHANA
PRESBYTERIAN CHURCH OF GHANA

GREECE
EKKLESIA TES ELLADOS
  (Church of Greece)
GREEK EVANGELICAL CHURCH

HONG KONG
THE CHURCH OF CHRIST IN CHINA,
  THE HONG KONG COUNCIL

HUNGARY
MAGYARORSZAGI BAPTISTA EGYHAZ
  (Baptist Church of Hungary)
MAGYARORSZAGI EVANGELIKUS EGYHAZ
  (Lutheran Church of Hungary)
MAGYARORSZAGI REFORMATUS EGYHAZ
  (Reformed Church of Hungary)

ICELAND
EVANGELICAL LUTHERAN CHURCH

INDIA
CHURCH OF INDIA, PAKISTAN, BURMA
  AND CEYLON

CHURCH OF SOUTH INDIA

FEDERATION OF EVANGELICAL LUTHERAN
CHURCHES IN INDIA

MAR THOMA SYRIAN CHURCH OF
MALABAR

THE ORTHODOX SYRIAN CHURCH OF
THE EAST

THE SAMAVESAM OF TELUGU BAPTIST
CHURCHES

THE UNITED CHURCH OF NORTHERN INDIA

INDONESIA

GEREDJA GEREDJA KRISTEN DJAWA DI
DJAWA TENGAH
(Christian Churches of Mid-Java)

GEREDJA KALIMANTAN EVANGELIS
(Evangelical Church in Kalimantan)

GEREDJA KRISTEN DJAWA WETAN
(Christian Church of East Java)

GEREDJA KRISTEN INDJILI DI IRIAN BARAT
(Evangelical Christian Church in West Irian)

GEREDJA KRISTEN INDONESIA
(Indonesian Christian Church)

GEREDJA KRISTEN PASUNDAN
(Sundanese Protestant Church of West Java)

GEREDJA KRISTEN SULAWESI TENGAH
(Christian Church in Mid-Sulawesi)

GEREDJA MASEHI INDJILI MINAHASA
(Christian Evangelical Church in Minahasa)

GEREDJA MASEHI INDJILI DI TIMOR
(Protestant Evangelical Church in Timor)

GEREDJA PROTESTAN DI INDONESIA
(Protestant Church in Indonesia)

GEREDJA PROTESTAN MALUKU
(Protestant Church of the Moluccas)

GEREDJA TORADJA (Toradja Church)

HURIA KRISTEN BATAK PROTESTAN
(Protestant Christian Batak Church)

KARO (Karo Batak Protestant Church)

IRAN

SYNOD OF THE EVANGELICAL CHURCH
OF IRAN

ITALY

CHIESA EVANGELICA METODISTA D'ITALIA
(Evangelical Methodist Church of Italy)

CHIESA EVANGELICA VALDESE
(Waldensian Church)

JAMAICA

THE UNITED CHURCH OF JAMAICA
AND GRAND CAYMAN

THE MORAVIAN CHURCH IN JAMAICA.

JAPAN

NIPPON KIRISUTO KYODAN
(The United Church of Christ in Japan)

NIPPON SEI KO KAI
(Anglican-Episcopal Church in Japan)

JERUSALEM

GREEK ORTHODOX PATRIARCHATE OF
JERUSALEM

KENYA (see also under East Africa)

THE METHODIST CHURCH IN KENYA

KOREA

THE KOREAN METHODIST CHURCH

THE PRESBYTERIAN CHURCH IN THE
REPUBLIC OF KOREA

THE PRESBYTERIAN CHURCH IN KOREA

LEBANON

ARMENIAN APOSTOLIC CHURCH

UNION OF THE ARMENIAN EVANGELICAL
CHURCHES IN THE NEAR EAST

LESOTHO

EVANGELICAL CHURCH

LIBERIA

PRESBYTERIAN CHURCH

MADAGASCAR

EGLISE DU CHRIST A MADAGASCAR
(Church of Christ in Madagascar)

EGLISE DES AMIS A MADAGASCAR
(Malagasy Friends Church)

EGLISE EVANGELIQUE DE MADAGASCAR
(Evangelical Church of Madagascar)

EGLISE LUTHERIENNE MALGACHE
(Malagasy Lutheran Church)

MEXICO
IGLESIA METODISTA DE MEXICO
(Methodist Church of Mexico)
NETHERLANDS
ALGEMENE DOOPSGEZINDE SOCIETEIT
(General Mennonite Society)
EVANGELISCH-LUTHERSE KERK
(Evangelical Lutheran Church)
NEDERLANDSE HERVORMDE KERK
(Netherlands Reformed Church)
OUD-KATHOLIEKE KERK VAN NEDERLAND
(Old Catholic Church of the Netherlands)
REMONSTRANTSE BROEDERSCHAP
(Remonstrant Brotherhood)
NEW CALEDONIA
EGLISE EVANGELIQUE EN NOUVELLE
CALEDONIE ET AUX ILES LOYAUTE
(Evangelical Church in New Caledonia and
the Loyalty Isles)
NEW HEBRIDES
PRESBYTERIAN CHURCH
NEW ZEALAND
ASSOCIATED CHURCHES OF CHRIST
IN NEW ZEALAND
THE BAPTIST UNION OF NEW ZEALAND
CHURCH OF THE PROVINCE OF NEW
ZEALAND
THE CONGREGATION UNION
THE METHODIST CHURCH OF NEW
ZEALAND
THE PRESBYTERIAN CHURCH OF NEW
ZEALAND
NIGERIA (see also West Africa)
METHODIST CHURCH
THE PRESBYTERIAN CHURCH OF NIGERIA
NORWAY
NORSKE KIRKE (Church of Norway)
PAKISTAN
UNITED PRESBYTERIAN CHURCH
PHILIPPINES
IGLESIA FILIPINA INDEPENDIENTE
(Philippine Independent Church)

UNITED CHURCH OF CHRIST IN THE
PHILIPPINES
POLAND
EGLISE AUTOCEPH. ORTHODOXE EN POLOGNE
(Orthodox Church of Poland)
KOSCIOL EWANGELICKO-AUGSBURSKI W POLSCE
(Evangelical Church of the Augsburg
Confession in Poland)
POLISH MANAVITE CHURCH
KOSCIOL POLSKOKATOLICKI W P R L
(Polish-Catholic Church in Poland)
RUMANIA
EVANGELICAL SYNODAL PRESBYTERIAL CHURCH
OF THE AUGSBURG CONFESSION IN THE
SOCIALIST REPUBLIC OF RUMANIA
BISERICA EVANGELICA DUPA CONFESIUNEA
DELA AUGSBURG (Evangelical Church of
the Augsburg Confession)
BISERICA ORTODOXA ROMANE
(Rumanian Orthodox Church)
BISERICA REFORMATA DIN ROMANIA
(Reformed Church of Rumania)
SAMOA
THE CONGREGATIONAL CHRISTIAN
CHURCH IN SAMOA
SIERRA LEONE
THE METHODIST CHURCH
SOUTH AFRICA
THE BANTU PRESBYTERIAN CHURCH
CHURCH OF THE PROVINCE OF SOUTH AFRICA
EVANGELICAL LUTHERAN CHURCH IN
SOUTHERN AFRICA (SOUTH-EASTERN
REGION) & (TRANSVAAL REGION)
THE METHODIST CHURCH OF SOUTH AFRICA
MORAVIAN CHURCH IN SOUTH AFRICA
MORAVIAN CHURCH EASTERN PROVINCE
THE PRESBYTERIAN CHURCH OF
SOUTHERN AFRICA
THE UNITED CONGREGATIONAL CHURCH
OF SOUTHERN AFRICA
SPAIN
IGLESIA EVANGELICA ESPANOLA

SWEDEN
    SVENSKA KYRKAN (Church of Sweden)
    SVENSKA MISSIONSFÖRBUNDET
        (The Mission Covenant Church of Sweden)
SWITZERLAND
    CHRISTKATHOLISCHE KIRCHE DER SCHWEIZ
        (Old Catholic Church of Switzerland)
    SCHWEIZERISCHER EVANGELISCHER
    KIRCHENBUND FEDERATION DES EGLISES
    PROTESTANTES DE LA SUISSE
        (Swiss Protestant Church Federation)
SYRIA
    THE NATIONAL EVANGELICAL SYNOD
        OF SYRIA AND LEBANON
    PATRIARCAT GREC-ORTHODOXE
        D'ANTIOCHE ET DE TOUT L'ORIENT
        (Greek Orthodox Patriarchate of Antioch
        and All the East)
    SYRIAN ORTHODOX PATRIARCHATE OF
        ANTIOCH AND ALL THE EAST
TAHITI
    EGLISE EVANGELIQUE DE POLYNESIE
        FRANCAISE
        (Evangelical Church of French Polynesia)
TAIWAN
    TAI-OAN KI-TOK TIU-LO KAU-HOE
        (The Presbyterian Church of Formosa)
TANZANIA
    EVANGELICAL LUTHERAN CHURCH
        IN TANZANIA
THAILAND
    THE CHURCH OF CHRIST IN THAILAND
TOGO
    EGLISE EVANGELIQUE DU TOGO
        (Evangelical Church of Togo)
TRINIDAD
    THE PRESBYTERIAN CHURCH IN
        TRINIDAD & GRENADA
TURKEY
    ECUMENICAL PATRIARCHATE OF
        CONSTANTINOPLE

UGANDA
    THE CHURCH OF UGANDA, RWANDA
        AND BURUNDI
UNITED KINGDOM AND EIRE
    THE BAPTIST UNION OF GREAT BRITAIN
        AND IRELAND
    CHURCHES OF CHRIST IN GREAT BRITAIN
        AND IRELAND
    CHURCH OF ENGLAND
    CHURCH OF IRELAND
    THE CHURCH OF SCOTLAND
    CHURCH IN WALES
    THE CONGREGATIONAL CHURCH IN
        ENGLAND AND WALES
    THE CONGREGATIONAL UNION OF SCOTLAND
    EPISCOPAL CHURCH IN SCOTLAND
    THE METHODIST CHURCH
    THE METHODIST CHURCH IN IRELAND
    THE MORAVIAN CHURCH IN GREAT
        BRITAIN AND IRELAND
    PRESBYTERIAN CHURCH OF ENGLAND
    THE PRESBYTERIAN CHURCH IN IRELAND
    THE PRESBYTERIAN CHURCH OF WALES
    THE SALVATION ARMY
    UNION OF WELSH INDEPENDENTS
    UNITED FREE CHURCH OF SCOTLAND
UNITED STATES OF AMERICA
    AFRICAN METHODIST EPISCOPAL CHURCH
    AFRICAN METHODIST EPISCOPAL ZION CHURCH
    AMERICAN BAPTIST CONVENTION
    THE AMERICAN LUTHERAN CHURCH
    CHRISTIAN METHODIST EPISCOPAL CHURCH
    CHURCH OF THE BRETHREN
    CHURCH OF THE EAST (ASSYRIAN)
    EPISCOPAL CHURCH
    THE HUNGARIAN REFORMED CHURCH
        IN AMERICA
    THE CHRISTIAN CHURCH
        (Disciples of Christ)
    LUTHERAN CHURCH IN AMERICA

THE MORAVIAN CHURCH IN AMERICA
(NORTHERN PROVINCE)
MORAVIAN CHURCH IN AMERICA
(SOUTHERN PROVINCE)
NATIONAL BAPTIST CONVENTION OF
AMERICA
THE NATIONAL BAPTIST CONVENTION,
U.S.A., INC.
POLISH NATIONAL CATHOLIC CHURCH
OF AMERICA
THE PRESBYTERIAN CHURCH IN THE
UNITED STATES
REFORMED CHURCH IN AMERICA
RELIGIOUS SOCIETY OF FRIENDS
FRIENDS GENERAL CONFERENCE
FRIENDS UNITED MEETING
THE ROMANIAN ORTHODOX EPISCOPATE
OF AMERICA
RUSSIAN ORTHODOX GREEK CATHOLIC
CHURCH OF AMERICA
SEVENTH DAY BAPTIST GENERAL
CONFERENCE
SYRIAN ANTIOCHIAN ORTHODOX CHURCH
(Archdiocese of New York and North America)
UNITED CHURCH OF CHRIST
UNITED METHODIST CHURCH
THE UNITED PRESBYTERIAN CHURCH IN
THE UNITED STATES OF AMERICA
UNION OF SOVIET SOCIALIST REPUBLICS
ARMENIAN APOSTOLIC CHURCH
ESTONIAN EVANGELICAL LUTHERAN
CHURCH
EVANGELICAL LUTHERAN CHURCH
OF LATVIA
GEORGIAN ORTHODOX CHURCH
ORTHODOX CHURCH OF RUSSIA
THE UNION OF EVANGELICAL CHRISTIAN
BAPTISTS OF USSR
WEST AFRICA (see also Nigeria)
THE CHURCH OF THE PROVINCE OF
WEST AFRICA
WEST INDIES
CHURCH IN THE PROVINCE OF THE
WEST INDIES

METHODIST CHURCH IN THE CARIBBEAN
AND THE AMERICAS
YUGOSLAVIA
REFORMED CHRISTIAN CHURCH OF
YUGOSLAVIA
SERBIAN ORTHODOX CHURCH
SLOVAK EVANGELICAL CHURCH OF THE
AUGSBURG CONFESSION IN YUGOSLAVIA
ZAMBIA
UNITED CHURCH OF ZAMBIA
OTHER CHURCHES
EESTI EVANGEELIUMI LUTERI USU KIRIK
(Estonian Evangelical Lutheran Church)

ASSOCIATED CHURCHES
CAMEROON
EGLISE PROTESTANTE AFRICAINE
CUBA
IGLESIA METODISTA EN CUBA
(Methodist Church in Cuba)
IGLESIA PRESBITERIANA -REFORMADA EN CUBA
(Presbyterian-Reformed Church in Cuba)
INDIA
BENGAL-ORISSA-BIHAR BAPTIST CONVENTION
JAPAN
THE KOREAN CHRISTIAN CHURCH IN JAPAN
NETHERLANDS ANTILLES
UNION OF PROTESTANT CHURCHES IN
THE NETHERLANDS ANTILLES
PORTUGAL
IGREJA EVANGELICA PRESBITERIANA
DE PORTUGAL
(Evangelical Presbyterian Church of Portugal)
IGREJA LUSITANA CATOLICA APOSTOLICA
EVANGELICA
(Lusitanian Church, Portugal)
SPAIN
IGLESIA ESPANOLA REFORMADA EPISCOPAL
(Spanish Reformed Episcopal Church)
SUDAN
THE PRESBYTERIAN CHURCH IN THE
SUDAN (Upper Nile)

WEST AFRICA
    THE EVANGELICAL PRESBYTERIAN
        CHURCH IN RIO MUNI
LIBERIA
    THE PRESBYTERIAN CHURCH
ARGENTINA
    UNITED EVANGELICAL LUTHERAN
        CHURCH IN ARGENTINA

ACKNOWLEDGEMENT OF PHOTOGRAPHS USED

Page 7   United Nations

Page 8   Israel Government Tourist Office.

Page 9   United Nations

Page 10   United Nations Asian Film project

Page 11   United Nations

Page 12   Top: United Nations Relief & Works Agency

        Bottom: The People (Oxfam)

Page 13   Top: United Nations

        Bottom: Oxfam

Page 14   Top: United Nations

        Bottom: Oxfam

Page 15   United Nations Relief & Works Agency

Page 16   Top: Oxfam

        Bottom: Contra la Faim (Oxfam)

Page 17   Top: United Nations (UNIDO)

        Bottom: Gerard Klijn-Holland (Oxfam)

Page 18   United Nations (UNFAO, UNILO,)

Page 19   Top: United Nations

        Bottom left: U. S. aid (Oxfam)

        Bottom right: United Nations. (UNWHO)

Page 20   United Nations

Page 21   United Nations

        Bottom: Derek Garnier (Oxfam)

Page 22   United Nations

Page 29   Israel Government Tourist Office

Page 30   Israel Government Tourist Office

Page 31   Israel Government (J. Allan Cash)

Page 32   Israel Government Tourist Office

Page 33   Israel Government Tourist Office

Page 34   Israel Government Tourist Office

Page 35   Israel Government Tourist Office

Page 36-37 Israel Government Tourist Office

Page 38   United Nations

Page 39   United Nations

Page 40   United Nations (WMO)

Page 41   Daily Mirror (Oxfam)

Page 42   United Nations (UNESCO)

Page 43   United Nations (ILO)

Page 44   United Nations (UNFAO)

Page 45   United Nations

Page 46   United Nations

Page 47   United Nations

Page 52   United Nations

Page 57   World Council of Churches

Page 58   Top: World Council of Churches

        Bottom: World Council of Churches (John Taylor)

Page 59   World Council of Churches (John Taylor)

Page 60   World Council of Churches (Peter Solbjerghoj)

Page 61   World Council of Churches

Page 62   World Council of Churches (John Taylor)

Page 63   World Council of Churches (John Taylor)

Page 65   World Council of Churches

LIST OF MAPS

ARCTIC

BEAUFORT SEA

Queen Elizabeth Islands

West of Green

BANKS I.

DEVON I.

ELLESMERE ISLAND

VICTORIA ISLAND

BAFFIN BAY

GREENLAND
(Denmark)

GREENLAND SEA

Jan Mayen (Nor.)

BAFFIN ISLAND

NORWEGI SEA

UNITED STATES
(ALASKA)

Arctic Circle

HUDSON BAY

ICELAND

Faeroe Is (Denmark)

Shetland Is (U.K.)
Orkney Is

BERING SEA

Kodiak I.

C A N A D A

ALEUTIAN ISLANDS
(U.S.A.)

Queen Charlotte Islands

NEWFOUNDLAND

UNITED DENM
NOR SEA

Vancouver I.

St Pierre & Miquelon (Fr.)

IRELAND KINGDOM
NETHERLAND

U N I T E D
S T A T E S

BERMUDA
(U.K.)

BELGIUM

FRANC
SWITZERLA

HAWAIIAN IS
(U.S.A.)

Tropic of Cancer

PORTUGAL SPAIN

Azores (Port.)

COR
SARD

Johnston I.
(U.S.A.)

GULF OF MEXICO

M E X I C O

BAHAMA IS. (U.K.)

GIBRALTAR
(U.K.) 15

MEL

Madeira (Port.)

MOROCCO

CUBA

TURKS & CAICOS IS (U.K.)

Canary Islands (Sp.)

ALGERIA

Revilla Gigedo Is
(Mexico)

CAYMAN IS
(U.K.)

HAITI

DOMINICAN REP.

SPANISH SAHARA

MAURITANIA

MALI

Palmyra I.
(U.S.A.)

JAMAICA

PUERTO RICO
(U.S.A.)

ANTIGUA

GUADELOUPE (FR.)

Cape Verde Is (Port.)

BRITISH HONDURAS

11

DOMINICA

MARTINIQUE (FR.)

SENEGAL
PORT.

UPPER VOLTA

Christmas I.
(U.K.)

GUATEMALA HONDURAS

ST VINCENT

ST LUCIA
BARBADOS

GAMBIA
GUINEA

Jarvis I.
(U.S.A.)

EL SALVADOR

NICARAGUA

GRENADA

SIERRA LEONE

IVORY COAST

GHANA
DAHOMEY

Clipperton I.
(Fr.)

COSTA RICA

13

TRINIDAD & TOBAGO

EQUATOR
GUI

LINE

Christmas I.

150°W

Equator

140°W

130°W

120°W

110°W

100°W

PANAMA

VENEZUELA

Galapagos Is
(Ecuador)

NETH. (FR.)
GUIANA

São Tomé & Príncipe Is (Port.)

ISLANDS
(U.K.)

Cocos I.
(Costa Rica)

Malpelo I.
(Col.)

COLOMBIA

40°W

St Peter & St Paul Rocks (Braz.)

10°N

Annobón (Sp.)

Marquesas Is

ECUADOR

Rocas I. Fernando de Noronha I.
(Braz.)

CA
(to Ang

FRENCH TUAMOTU
ARCH.

P E R U

B R A Z I L

Ascension I.
(U.K.)

Society Is

COOK IS (N.Z.) Cook Is

POLYNESIA

BOLIVIA

St Helena
(U.K.)

WA
(Re

Tubuai Is

PITCAIRN
(U.K.)

Tropic of Capricorn

PARAGUAY

Trindade
(Braz.)

Easter I.
(Chile)

Desventurados Is
(Chile)

A R G E N T I N A

C H I L E

Tristan da Cunha Group
(U.K.)

Pitcairn I.

URUGUAY

Juan Fernández Is
(Chile)

Gough
(U.K.)

Chiloé I.

FALKLAND IS
(U.K.)

South Georgia
(U.K.)

Bouvet I.
(Nor.)

Tierra del Fuego

SCOTIA SEA

South Sandwich Is
(U.K.)

South Shetland Is

South Orkney Is

ANTARCTIC PENINSULA

WEDDELL SEA

West of Greenwich QUEEN M.

MARIE BYRD LAND

Antarctic Circle

Peter I Island

AMUNDSEN SEA

ATLANTIC OCEAN

PACIFIC OCEAN

1.	ANDORRA	10.	ST CHRISTOPHER (ST KITTS)
2.	LIECHTENSTEIN		NEVIS AND ANGUILLA IS
3.	LUXEMBOURG	11.	MONTSERRAT (U. K.)
4.	MONACO	12.	SWAN IS (U. S. A.)
5.	SAN MARINO	13.	CORN IS (Nicar., U. S. A.)
6.	VATICAN CITY	14.	CANAL ZONE (Panama, U.S.A.)
7.	VIRGIN IS OF THE U. S. A	15.	SPANISH NORTH AFRICA (CEUTA AND MELILLA;
8.	BRITISH VIRGIN IS		ALHUCEMAS, CHAFARINAS AND PÉÑON DE VÉLE.
9.	NETHERLANDS ANTILLES	16.	WEST BERLIN

MAP 1   World: Political   76

© Pergamon Press Ltd

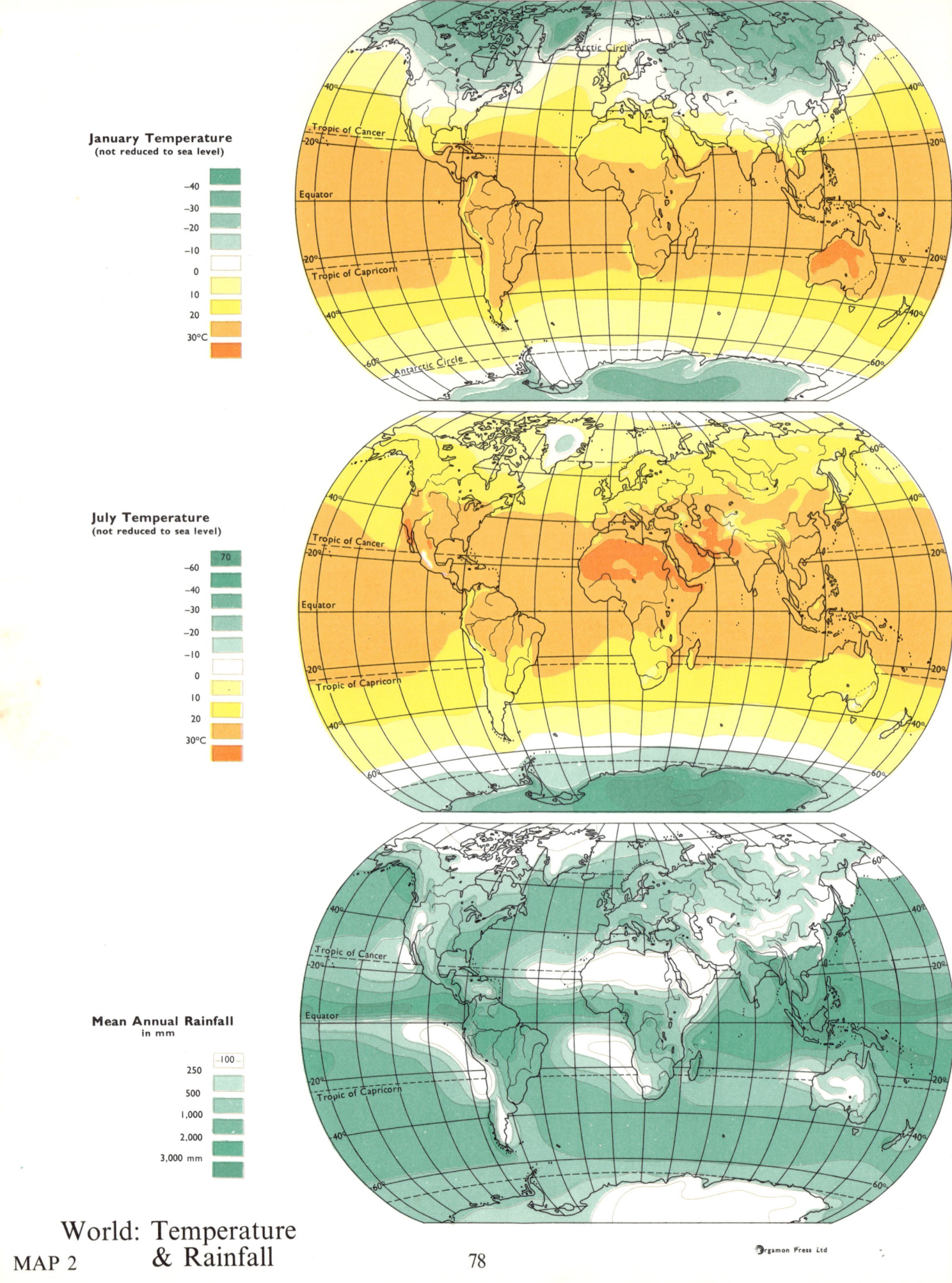

January Temperature
(not reduced to sea level)

-40
-30
-20
-10
0
10
20
30°C

July Temperature
(not reduced to sea level)

70
-60
-40
-30
-20
-10
0
10
20
30°C

Mean Annual Rainfall
in mm

-100-
250
500
1,000
2,000
3,000 mm

World: Temperature
& Rainfall

MAP 2

78

Pergamon Press Ltd

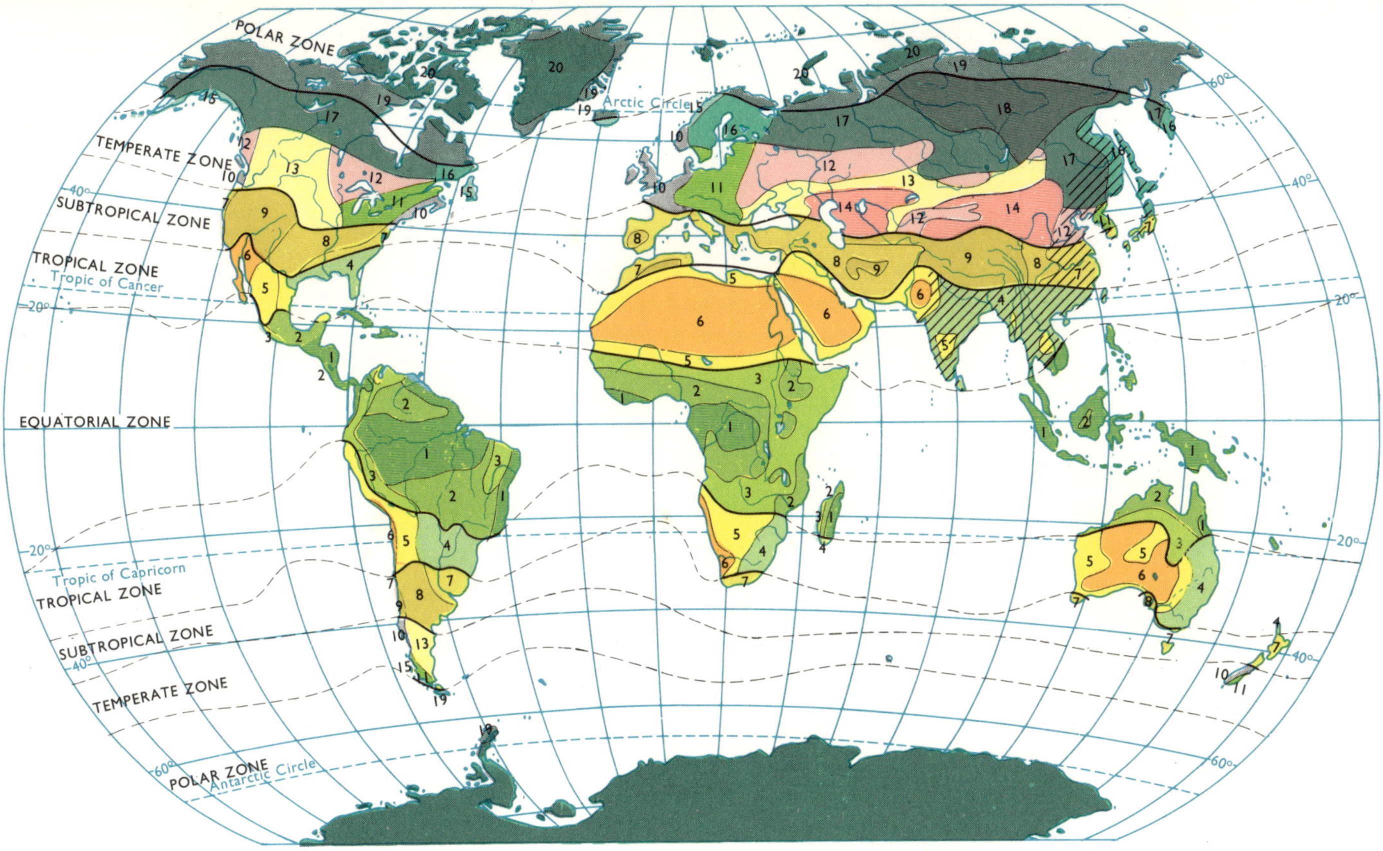

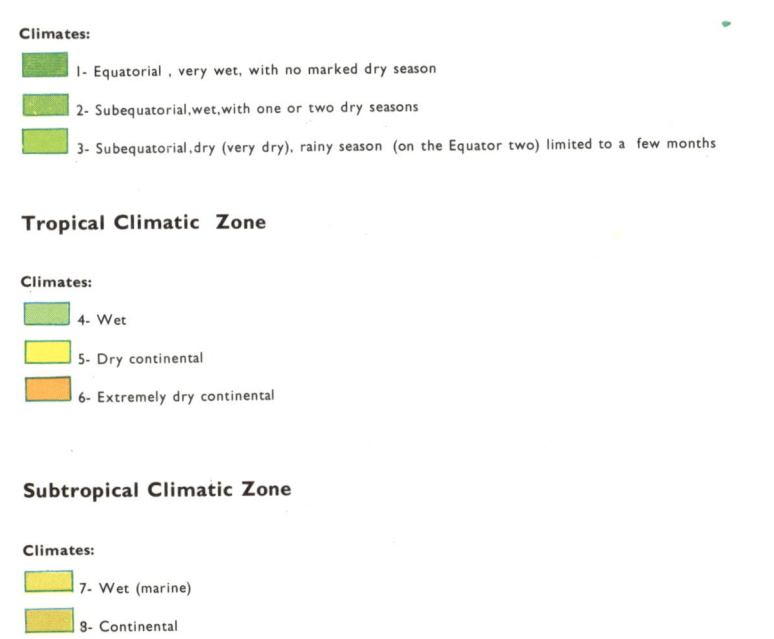
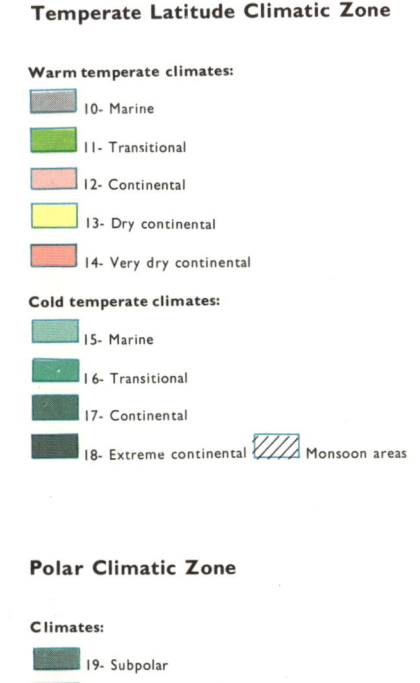

Equatorial Climatic Zone

Climates:

- 1- Equatorial, very wet, with no marked dry season
- 2- Subequatorial, wet, with one or two dry seasons
- 3- Subequatorial, dry (very dry), rainy season (on the Equator two) limited to a few months

Tropical Climatic Zone

Climates:

- 4- Wet
- 5- Dry continental
- 6- Extremely dry continental

Subtropical Climatic Zone

Climates:

- 7- Wet (marine)
- 8- Continental
- 9- Very dry continental

Temperate Latitude Climatic Zone

Warm temperate climates:

- 10- Marine
- 11- Transitional
- 12- Continental
- 13- Dry continental
- 14- Very dry continental

Cold temperate climates:

- 15- Marine
- 16- Transitional
- 17- Continental
- 18- Extreme continental   Monsoon areas

Polar Climatic Zone

Climates:

- 19- Subpolar
- 20- Polar

World: Climatic Zones   MAP 3

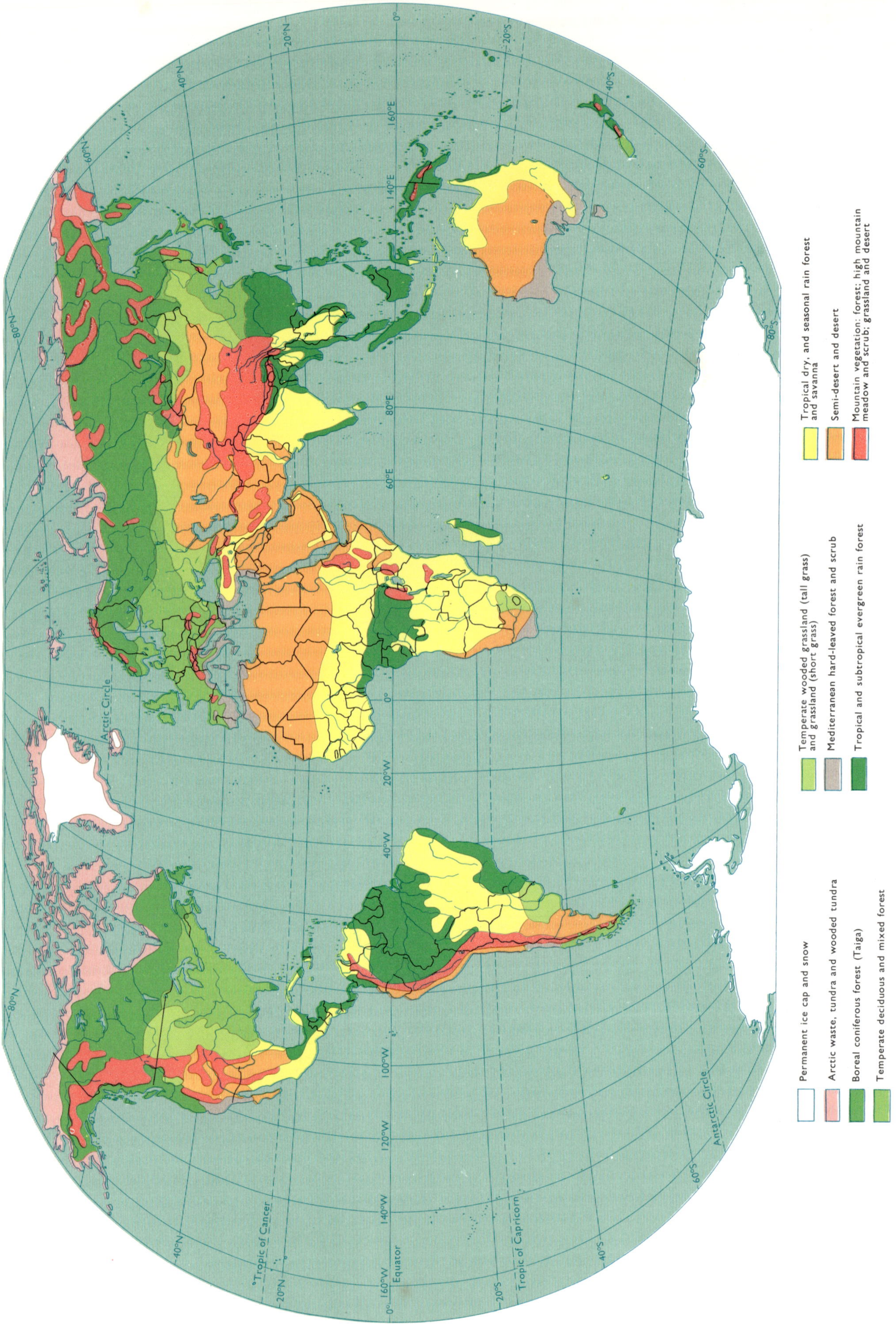

Permanent ice cap and snow

Arctic waste, tundra and wooded tundra

Boreal coniferous forest (Taiga)

Temperate deciduous and mixed forest

Temperate wooded grassland (tall grass) and grassland (short grass)

Mediterranean hard-leaved forest and scrub

Tropical and subtropical evergreen rain forest

Tropical dry, and seasonal rain forest and savanna

Semi-desert and desert

Mountain vegetation: forest; high mountain meadow and scrub; grassland and desert

MAP 4   World: Vegetation   80

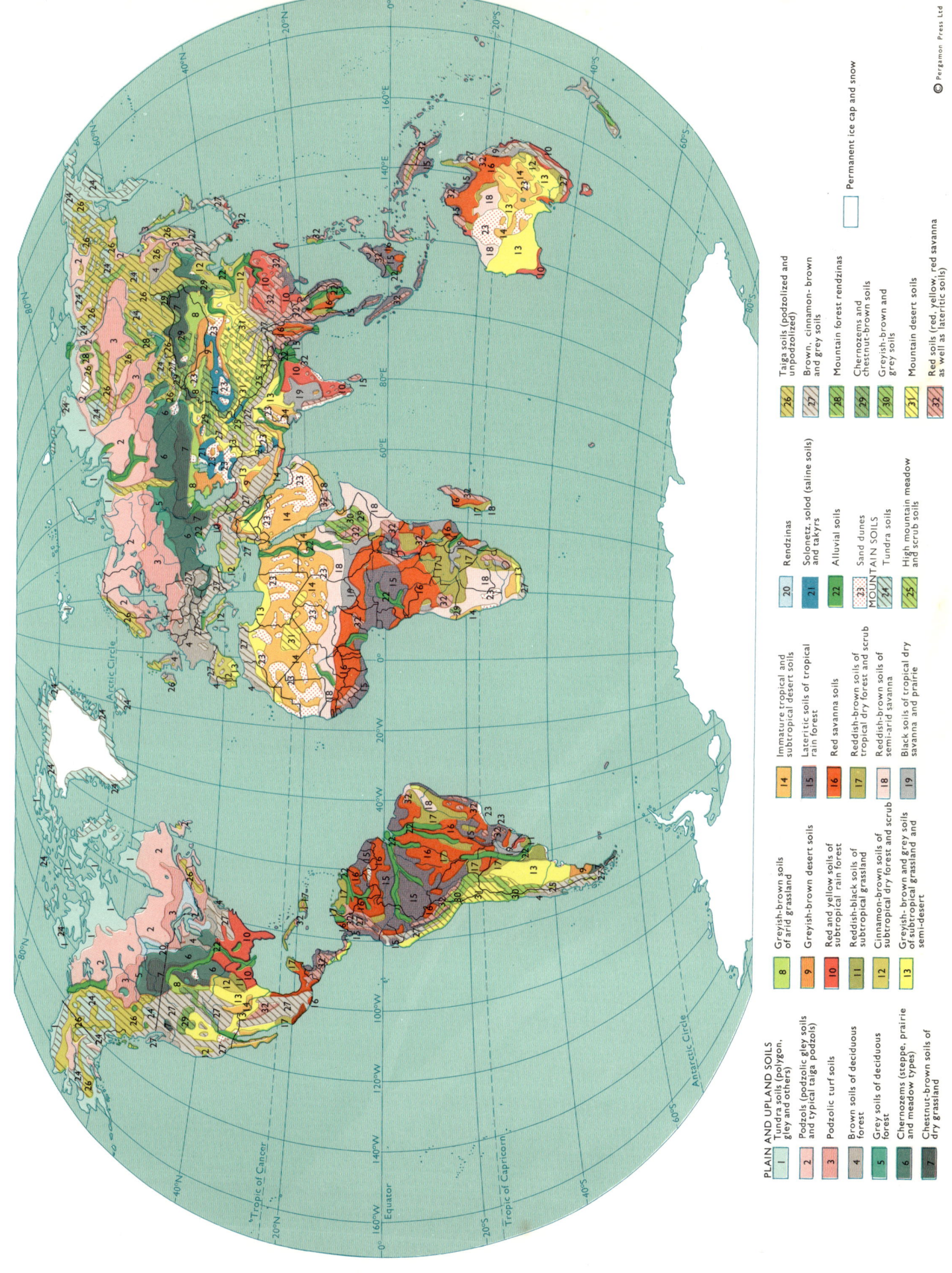

PLAIN AND UPLAND SOILS

1	Tundra soils (polygon, gley and others)
2	Podzols (podzolic gley soils and typical taiga podzols)
3	Podzolic turf soils
4	Brown soils of deciduous forest
5	Grey soils of deciduous forest
6	Chernozems (steppe, prairie and meadow types)
7	Chestnut-brown soils of dry grassland
8	Greyish-brown soils of arid grassland
9	Greyish-brown desert soils
10	Red and yellow soils of subtropical rain forest
11	Reddish-black soils of subtropical grassland
12	Cinnamon-brown soils of subtropical dry forest and scrub
13	Greyish-brown and grey soils of subtropical grassland and semi-desert
14	Immature tropical and subtropical desert soils
15	Lateritic soils of tropical rain forest
16	Red savanna soils
17	Reddish-brown soils of tropical dry forest and scrub
18	Reddish-brown soils of semi-arid savanna
19	Black soils of tropical dry savanna and prairie
20	Rendzinas
21	Solonetz, solod (saline soils) and takyrs
22	Alluvial soils

MOUNTAIN SOILS

23	Sand dunes
24	Tundra soils
25	High mountain meadow and scrub soils
26	Taiga soils (podzolized and unpodzolized)
27	Brown, cinnamon- brown and grey soils
28	Mountain forest rendzinas
29	Chernozems and chestnut-brown soils
30	Greyish-brown and grey soils
31	Mountain desert soils
32	Red soils (red, yellow, red savanna as well as lateritic soils)

Permanent ice cap and snow

MAP 5   World : Soils   81

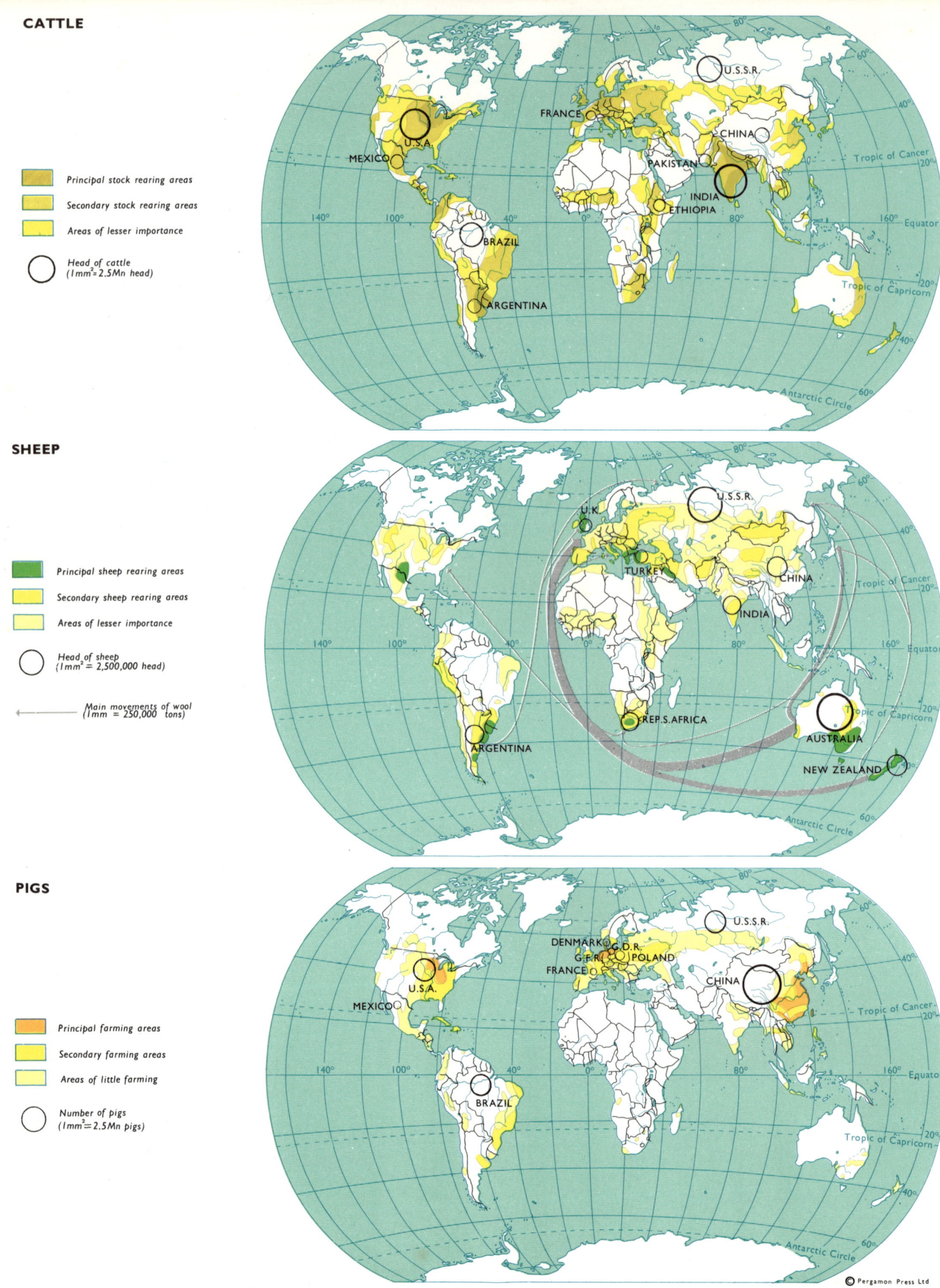

CATTLE

Principal stock rearing areas

Secondary stock rearing areas

Areas of lesser importance

Head of cattle
(1mm² = 2.5Mn head)

U.S.S.R.
FRANCE
CHINA
PAKISTAN
INDIA
ETHIOPIA
U.S.A
MEXICO
BRAZIL
ARGENTINA

Tropic of Cancer
Equator
Tropic of Capricorn
Antarctic Circle

SHEEP

Principal sheep rearing areas

Secondary sheep rearing areas

Areas of lesser importance

Head of sheep
(1mm² = 2,500,000 head)

Main movements of wool
(1mm = 250,000 tons)

U.K.
U.S.S.R.
TURKEY
CHINA
INDIA
ARGENTINA
REP.S.AFRICA
AUSTRALIA
NEW ZEALAND

Tropic of Cancer
Equator
Tropic of Capricorn
Antarctic Circle

PIGS

Principal farming areas

Secondary farming areas

Areas of little farming

Number of pigs
(1mm² = 2.5Mn pigs)

U.S.S.R.
DENMARK
G.D.R.
G.F.R.
POLAND
FRANCE
CHINA
U.S.A.
MEXICO
BRAZIL

Tropic of Cancer
Equator
Tropic of Capricorn
Antarctic Circle

© Pergamon Press Ltd

MAP6   World: Animal Husbandry   82

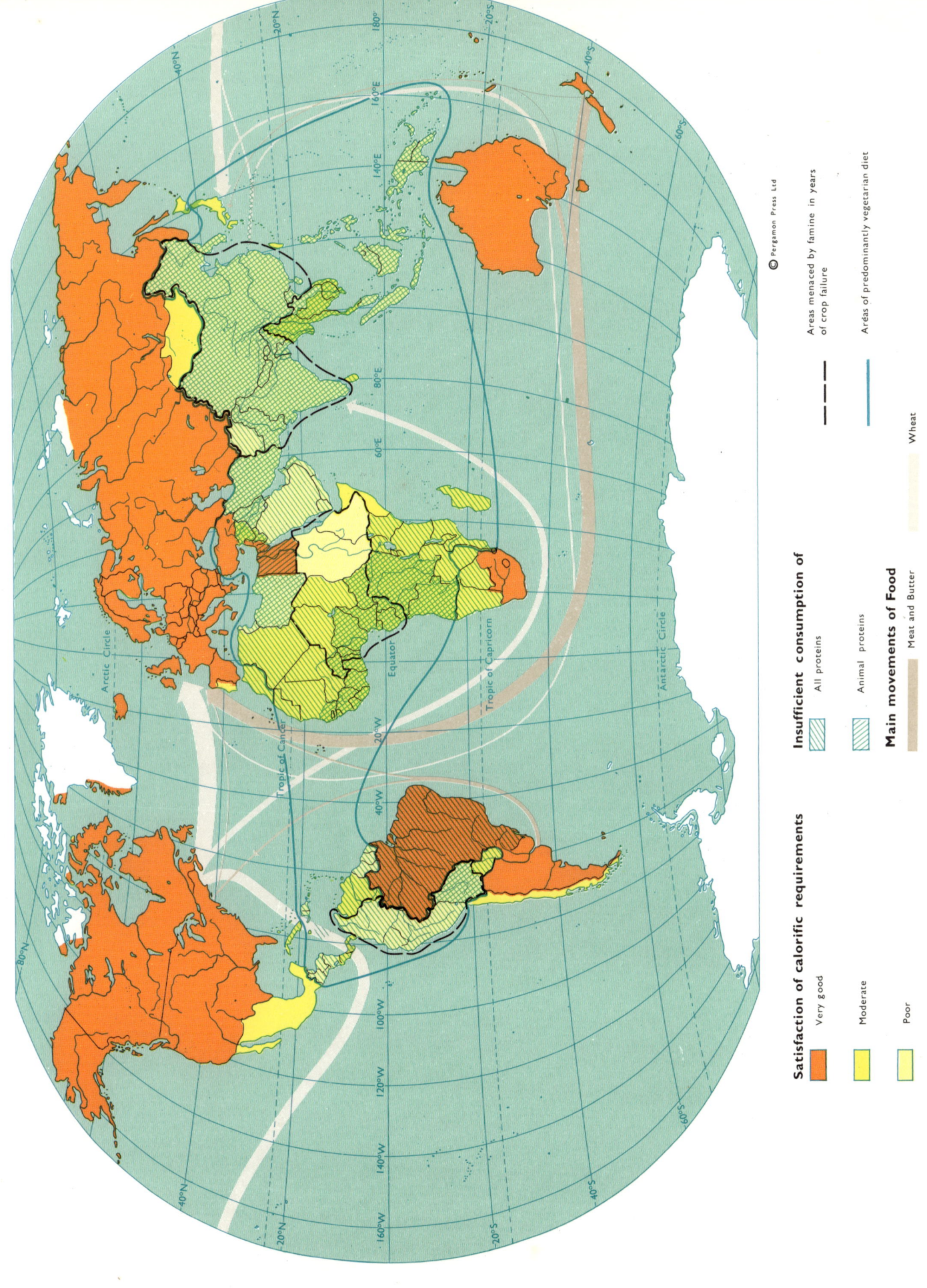

Satisfaction of calorific requirements

Very good

Moderate

Poor

Insufficient consumption of

All proteins

Animal proteins

Main movements of Food

Meat and Butter

Wheat

Areas menaced by famine in years of crop failure

Areas of predominantly vegetarian diet

© Pergamon Press Ltd

MAP 7   World: Food supply   83

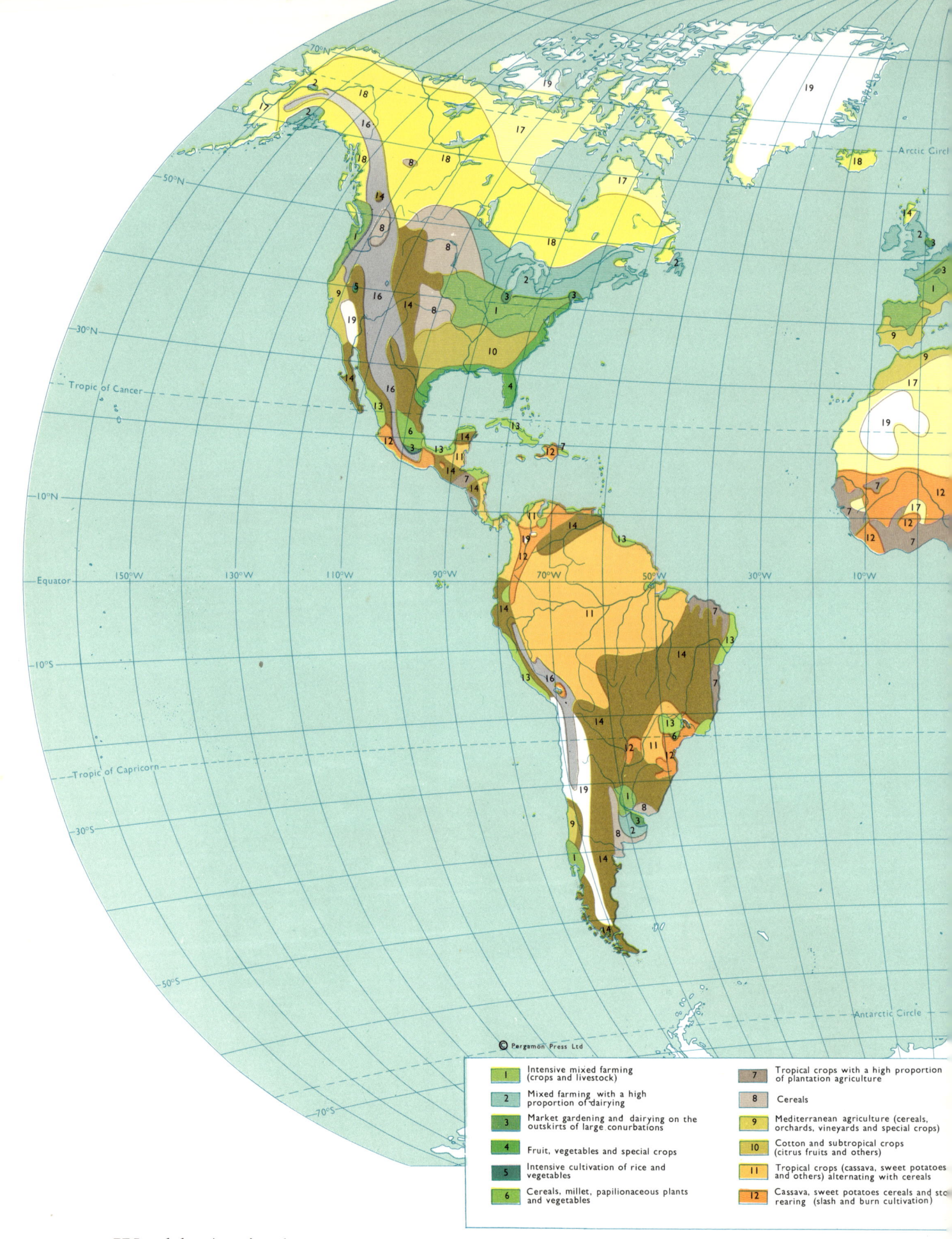

Arctic Circl

Antarctic Circle

© Pergamon Press Ltd

1	Intensive mixed farming (crops and livestock)		7	Tropical crops with a high proportion of plantation agriculture
2	Mixed farming with a high proportion of dairying		8	Cereals
3	Market gardening and dairying on the outskirts of large conurbations		9	Mediterranean agriculture (cereals, orchards, vineyards and special crops)
4	Fruit, vegetables and special crops		10	Cotton and subtropical crops (citrus fruits and others)
5	Intensive cultivation of rice and vegetables		11	Tropical crops (cassava, sweet potatoes and others) alternating with cereals
6	Cereals, millet, papilionaceous plants and vegetables		12	Cassava, sweet potatoes cereals and sto rearing (slash and burn cultivation)

MAP 8   World: Agriculture   84

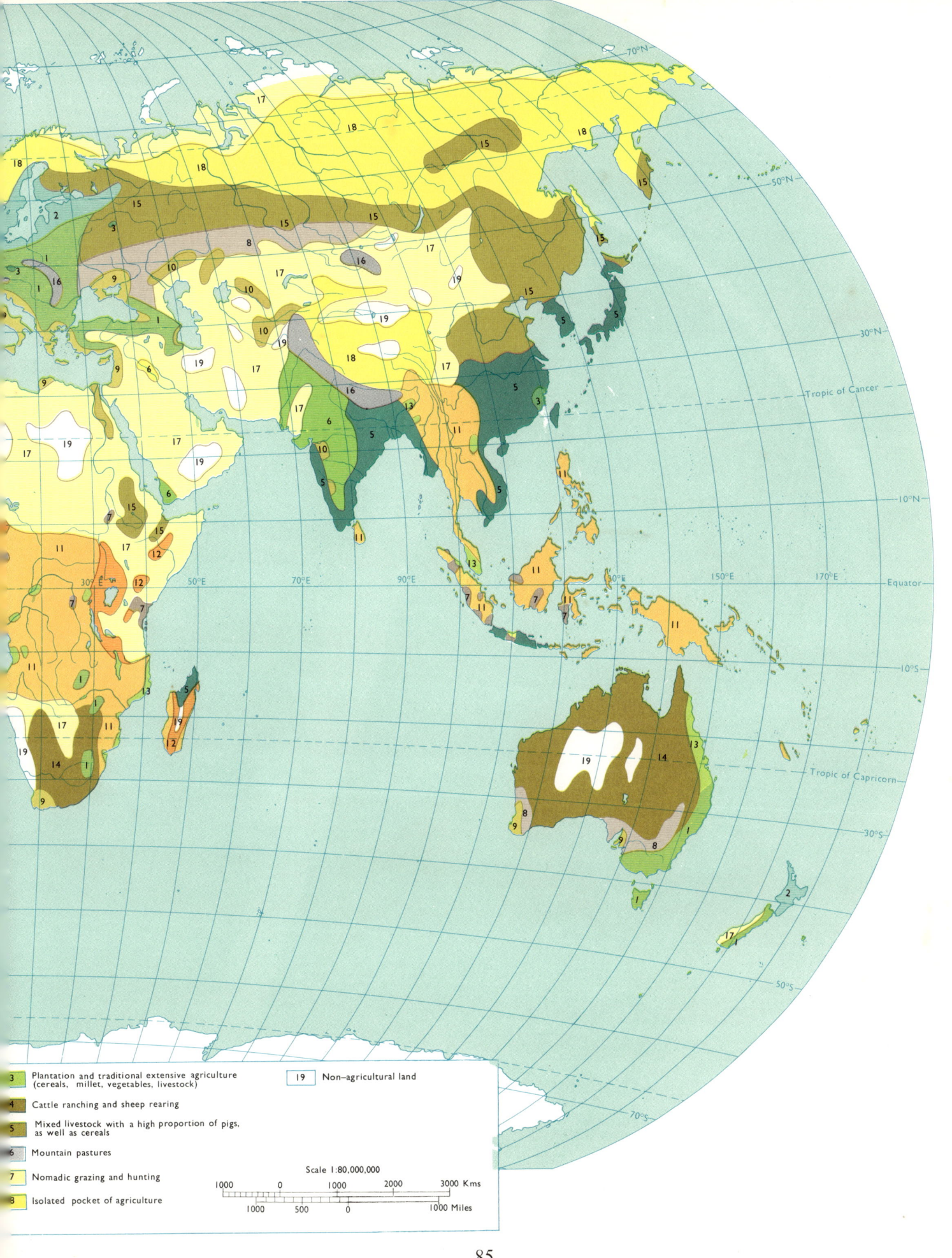

3	Plantation and traditional extensive agriculture (cereals, millet, vegetables, livestock)
4	Cattle ranching and sheep rearing
5	Mixed livestock with a high proportion of pigs, as well as cereals
6	Mountain pastures
7	Nomadic grazing and hunting
8	Isolated pocket of agriculture
19	Non-agricultural land

Scale 1:80,000,000

1000 0 1000 2000 3000 Kms

1000 500 0 1000 Miles

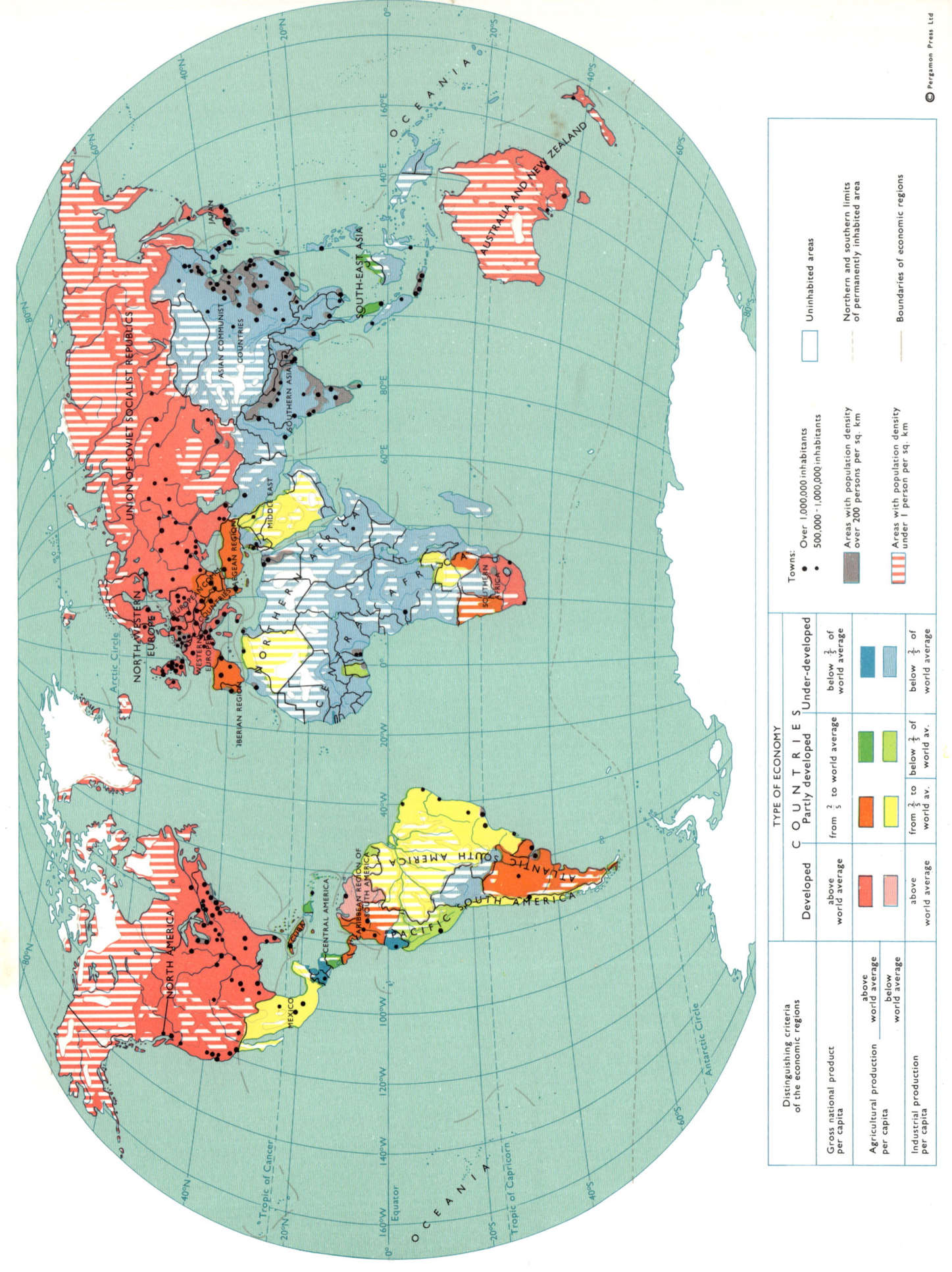

Towns:
● Over 1,000,000 inhabitants
• 500,000 - 1,000,000 inhabitants

▨ Areas with population density over 200 persons per sq. km
▤ Areas with population density under 1 person per sq. km

☐ Uninhabited areas

╌╌╌ Northern and southern limits of permanently inhabited area

──── Boundaries of economic regions

TYPE OF ECONOMY

Distinguishing criteria of the economic regions	Developed	Partly developed		Under-developed	
	above world average	from 2/5 to world average	below 2/5 of world average		
Gross national product per capita				below 2/5 of world average	
Agricultural production per capita	above world average				below 2/5 of world average
	below world average				
Industrial production per capita	above world average	from 2/5 to world av.	below 2/5 of world av.		

MAP 9   World: Economic Regions   86

© Pergamon Press Ltd

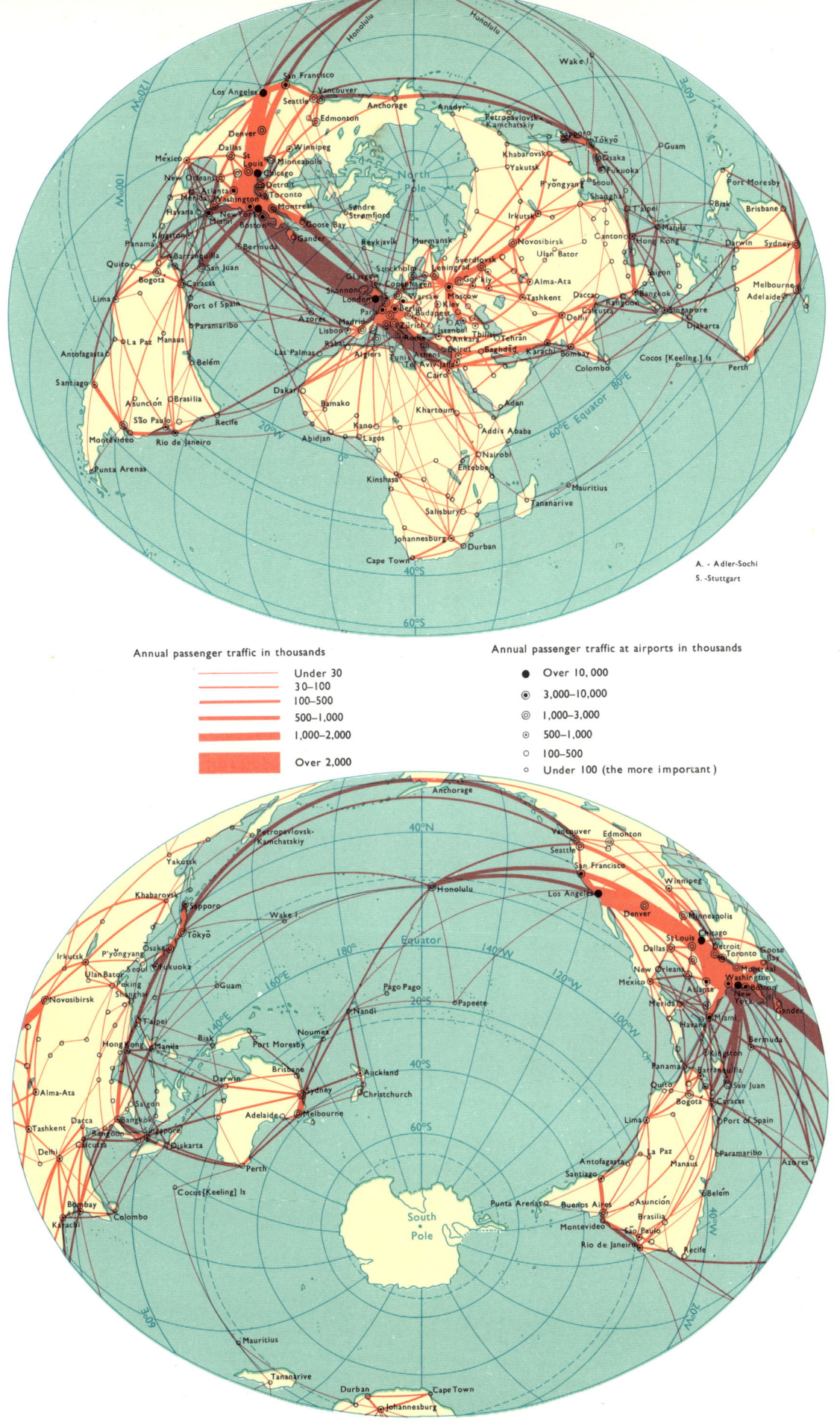

Annual passenger traffic in thousands

	Under 30
	30–100
	100–500
	500–1,000
	1,000–2,000
	Over 2,000

Annual passenger traffic at airports in thousands

● Over 10,000
◉ 3,000–10,000
◎ 1,000–3,000
⊙ 500–1,000
○ 100–500
○ Under 100 (the more important)

A. - Adler-Sochi
S. - Stuttgart

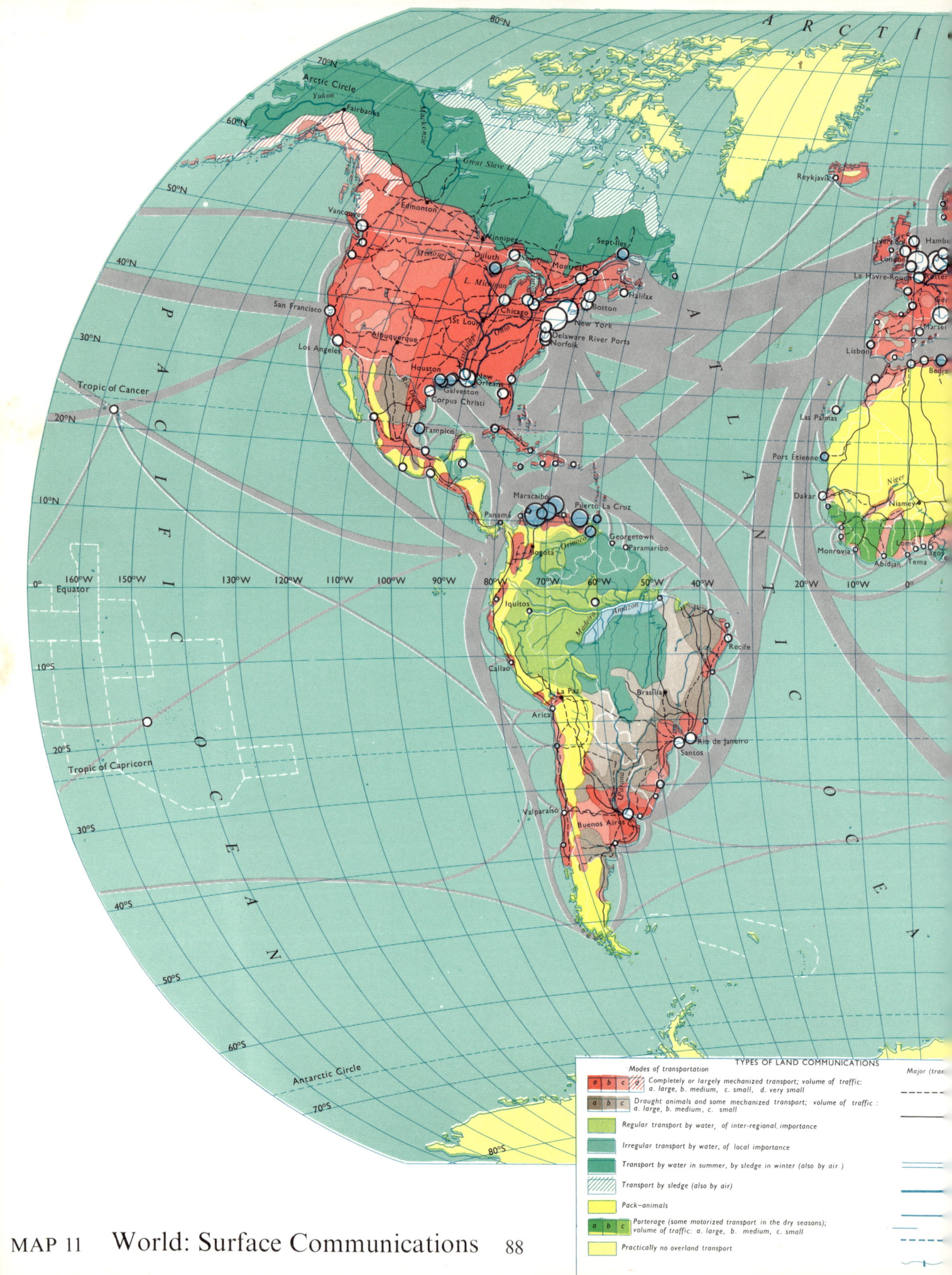

MAP 11 World: Surface Communications 88

TYPES OF LAND COMMUNICATIONS

Modes of transportation

Completely or largely mechanized transport; volume of traffic: a. large, b. medium, c. small, d. very small

Draught animals and some mechanized transport; volume of traffic: a. large, b. medium, c. small

Regular transport by water, of inter-regional importance

Irregular transport by water, of local importance

Transport by water in summer, by sledge in winter (also by air)

Transport by sledge (also by air)

Pack-animals

Porterage (some motorized transport in the dry seasons); volume of traffic: a. large, b. medium, c. small

Practically no overland transport

Major (tra

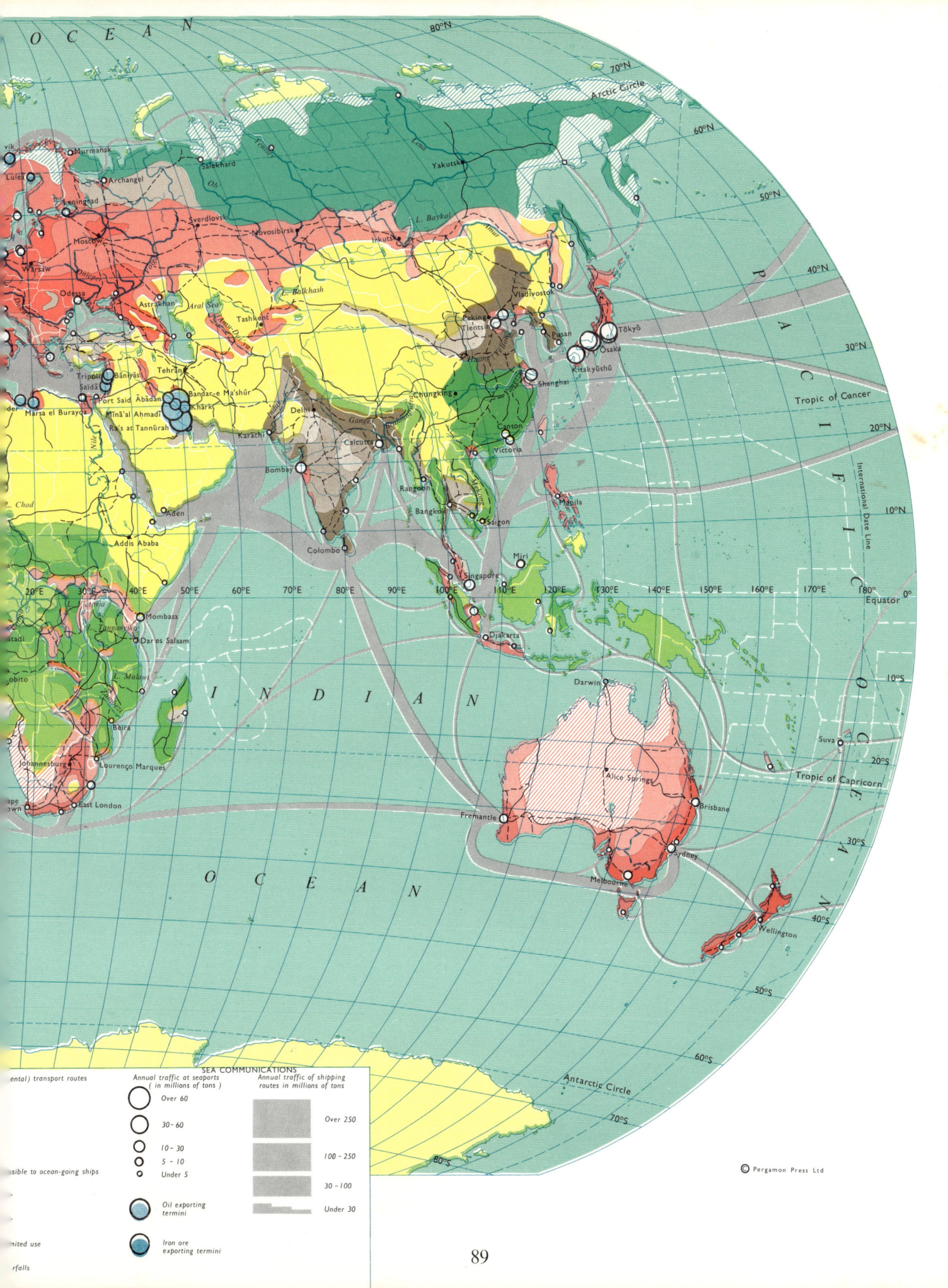

OCEAN

80°N
70°N
Arctic Circle
60°N
50°N

Sørvik
Murmansk
Luleå
Archangel
Salekhard
Ob
Yenisey
Lena
Yakutsk

Leningrad
Moscow
Warsaw
Dnieper
Odessa
Sverdlovsk
Novosibirsk
Irkutsk
L. Baykal
Amur
Vladivostok
40°N

Astrakhan
Aral Sea
Syr Darya
Tashkent
L. Balkhash
Peking
Tientsin
Huang (Yellow)
Pusan
Tōkyō
Osaka
Kitakyūshū
30°N

Tripoli
Saidā
Bāniyās
Port Said
Ābādān
Mīnā'al Ahmadī
Ra's at Tannūrah
Khārk
Tehrān
Bandar-e Ma'shūr
Delhi
Indus
Ganges
Chungking
Brahmaputra
Yangtze
Shanghai
Shanghai
PACIFIC

Marsa el Burayqa
der
Nile
Karāchi
Calcutta
Canton
Victoria
Tropic of Cancer
20°N

Chad
Aden
Bombay
Rangoon
Mekong
Manila
International Date Line
10°N

Addis Ababa
Colombo
Bangkok
Saigon
Miri
OCEAN
Equator 0°

20°E
30°E
40°E
50°E
60°E
70°E
80°E
90°E
100°E
110°E
120°E
Singapore
130°E
140°E
150°E
160°E
170°E
180°

bito
L. Malawi
Mombasa
Dar es Salaam
Djakarta
10°S

INDIAN
Darwin
Suva
20°S

Beira
Alice Springs
Tropic of Capricorn

Johannesburg
Lourenço Marques
Fremantle
Brisbane
30°S

Cape
Town
East London
Sydney
Melbourne
40°S
Wellington

OCEAN
50°S

60°S

Antarctic Circle
70°S

80°S

SEA COMMUNICATIONS

ental) transport routes

Annual traffic at seaports
(in millions of tons)

○ Over 60
○ 30 - 60
○ 10 - 30
○ 5 - 10
○ Under 5

sible to ocean-going ships

○ Oil exporting
termini

nited use

○ Iron ore
exporting termini

rfalls

Annual traffic of shipping
routes in millions of tons

Over 250
100 - 250
30 - 100
Under 30

© Pergamon Press Ltd

89

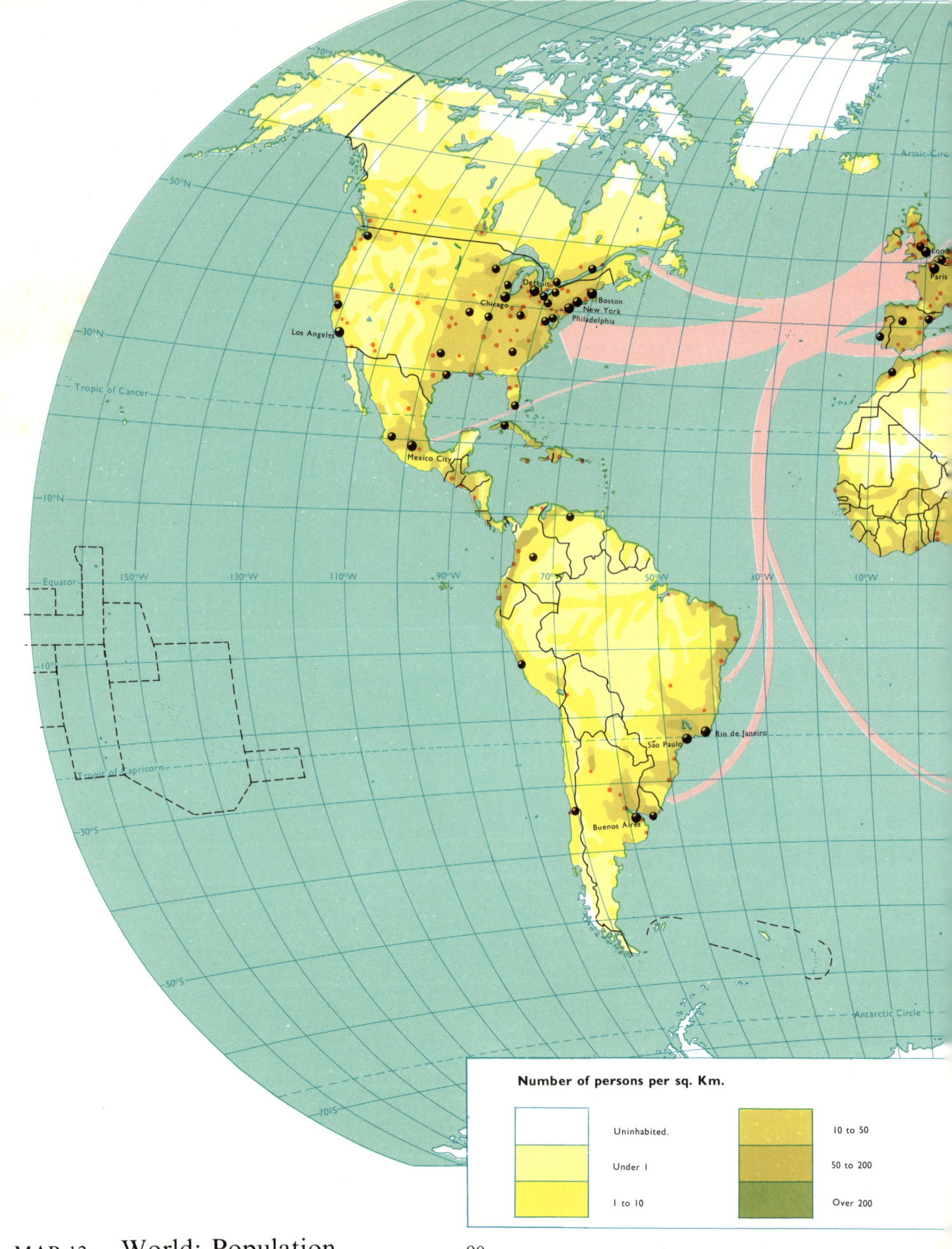

Number of persons per sq. Km.

Uninhabited.

Under 1

1 to 10

10 to 50

50 to 200

Over 200

MAP 12   World: Population   90

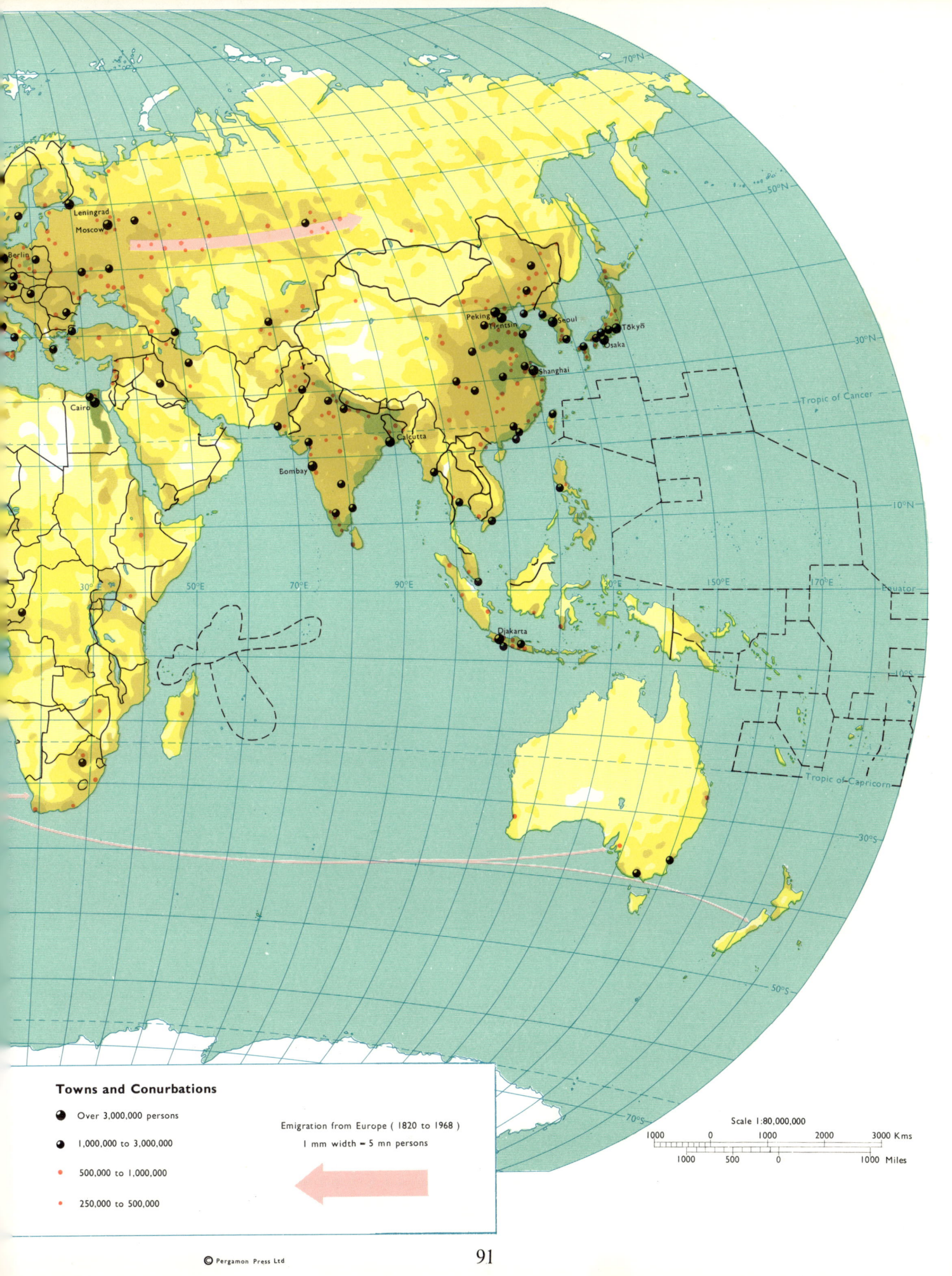

Towns and Conurbations

- ⬤ Over 3,000,000 persons
- ◗ 1,000,000 to 3,000,000
- • 500,000 to 1,000,000
- · 250,000 to 500,000

Emigration from Europe (1820 to 1968)
1 mm width = 5 mn persons

Scale 1:80,000,000

1000   0   1000   2000   3000 Kms

1000   500   0   1000 Miles

© Pergamon Press Ltd

91

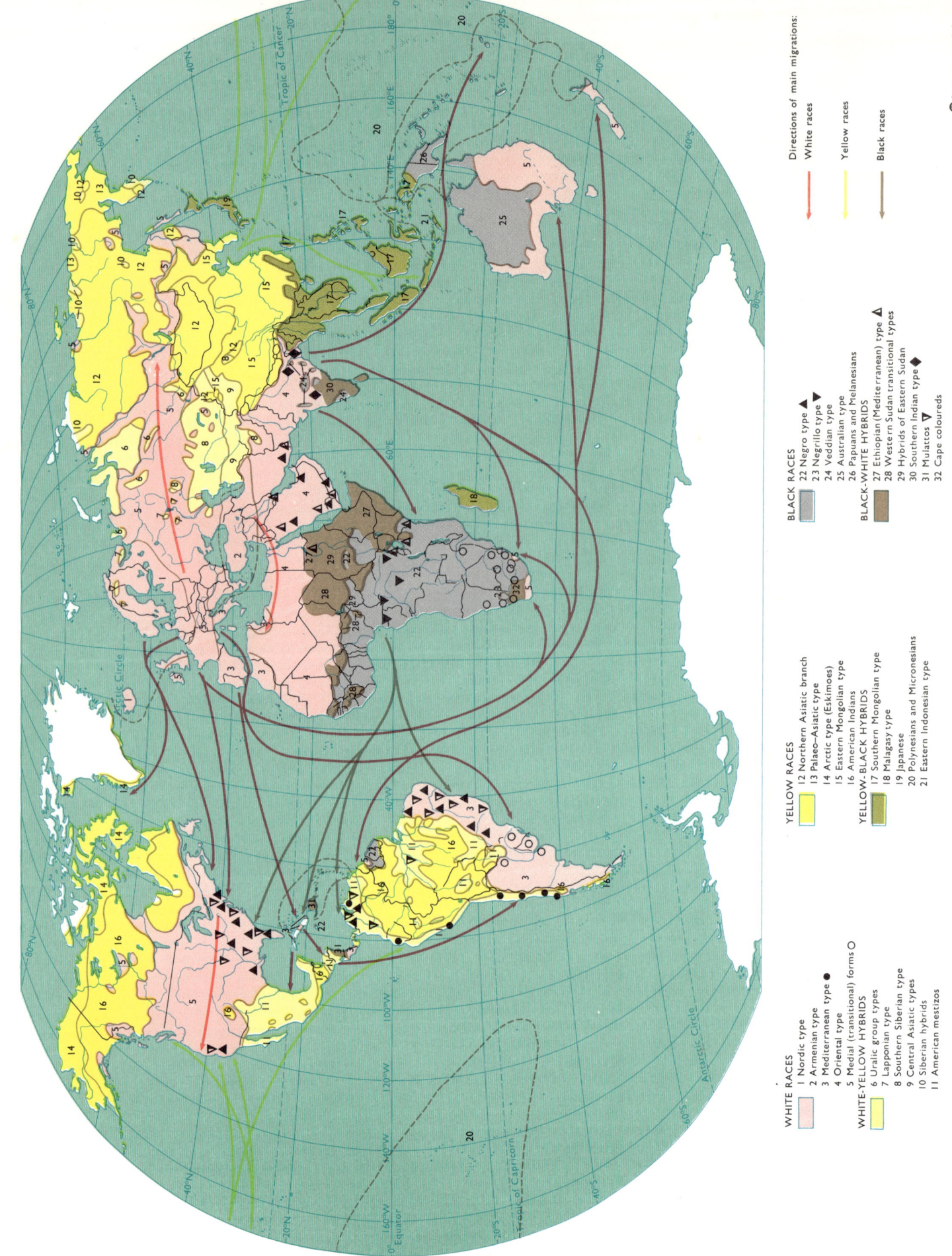

© Pergamon Press Ltd

WHITE RACES
1 Nordic type
2 Armenian type
3 Mediterranean type
4 Oriental type
5 Medial (transitional) forms ○

WHITE-YELLOW HYBRIDS
6 Uralic group types
7 Lapponian type
8 Central Asiatic types
9 Southern Siberian type
10 Siberian hybrids
11 American mestizos

YELLOW RACES
12 Northern Asiatic branch
13 Palaeo-Asiatic type
14 Arctic type (Eskimoes)
15 Eastern Mongolian type
16 American Indians

YELLOW-BLACK HYBRIDS
17 Southern Mongolian type
18 Malagasy type
19 Japanese
20 Polynesians and Micronesians
21 Eastern Indonesian type

BLACK RACES
22 Negro type ▲
23 Negrillo type ▼
24 Veddian type
25 Australian type
26 Papuans and Melanesians

BLACK-WHITE HYBRIDS
27 Ethiopian (Mediterranean) type △
28 Western Sudan transitional types
29 Hybrids of Eastern Sudan
30 Southern Indian type ▽
31 Mulattos
32 Cape coloureds

Directions of main migrations:
White races
Yellow races
Black races

MAP 13   World: Races   92

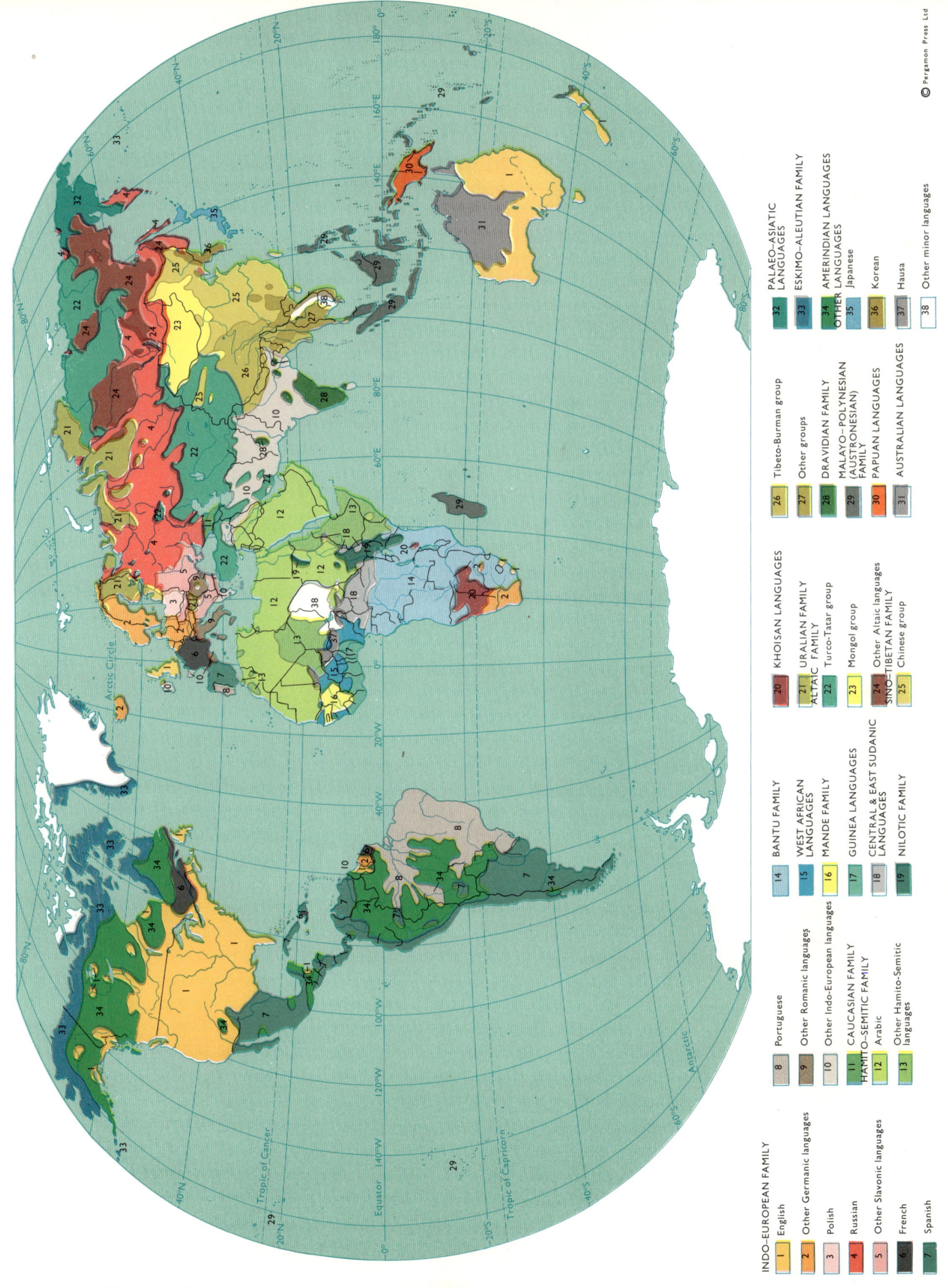

INDO-EUROPEAN FAMILY

1	English
2	Other Germanic languages
3	Polish
4	Russian
5	Other Slavonic languages
6	French
7	Spanish
8	Portuguese
9	Other Romanic languages
10	Other Indo-European languages

CAUCASIAN FAMILY

11	

HAMITO-SEMITIC FAMILY

12	Arabic
13	Other Hamito-Semitic languages

14	BANTU FAMILY
15	WEST AFRICAN LANGUAGES
16	MANDE FAMILY
17	GUINEA LANGUAGES
18	CENTRAL & EAST SUDANIC LANGUAGES
19	NILOTIC FAMILY
20	KHOISAN LANGUAGES

URALIAN FAMILY

21	

ALTAIC FAMILY

22	Turco-Tatar group
23	Mongol group
24	Other Altaic languages

SINO-TIBETAN FAMILY

25	Chinese group
26	Tibeto-Burman group
27	Other groups
28	DRAVIDIAN FAMILY
29	MALAYO-POLYNESIAN (AUSTRONESIAN) FAMILY
30	PAPUAN LANGUAGES
31	AUSTRALIAN LANGUAGES
32	PALAEO-ASIATIC LANGUAGES
33	ESKIMO-ALEUTIAN FAMILY
34	AMERINDIAN LANGUAGES

OTHER LANGUAGES

35	Japanese
36	Korean
37	Hausa
38	Other minor languages

© Pergamon Press Ltd

MAP 14   World: Languages   93

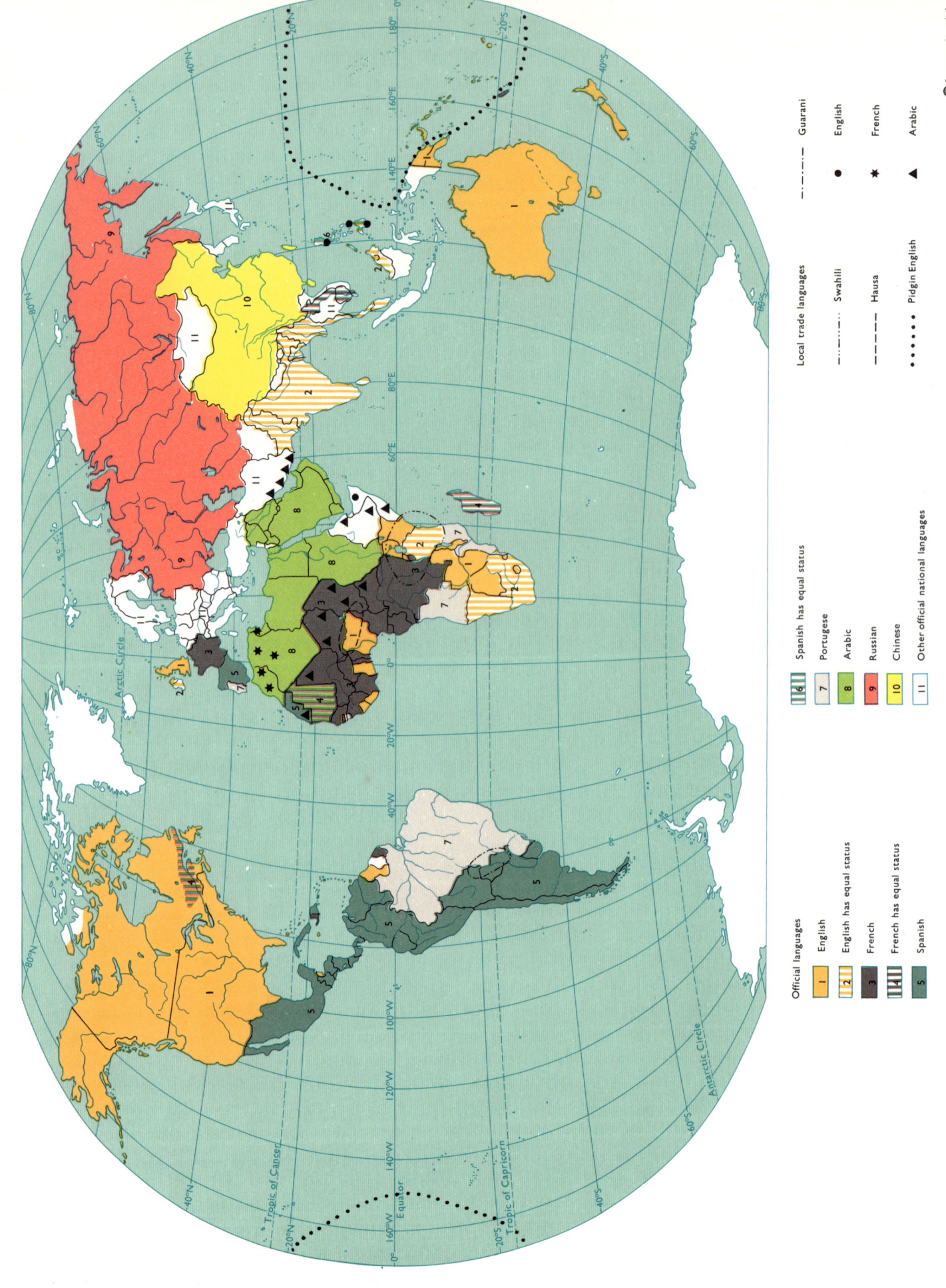

Official languages

1	English
2	English has equal status
3	French
4	French has equal status
5	Spanish

6	Spanish has equal status
7	Portugese
8	Arabic
9	Russian
10	Chinese
11	Other official national languages

Local trade languages

— · — · —	Guarani
— · · — · · —	Swahili
— — —	Hausa
· · · · · ·	Pidgin English

●	English
★	French
▲	Arabic

© Pergamon Press Ltd

MAP 15   World: Trade Languages   94

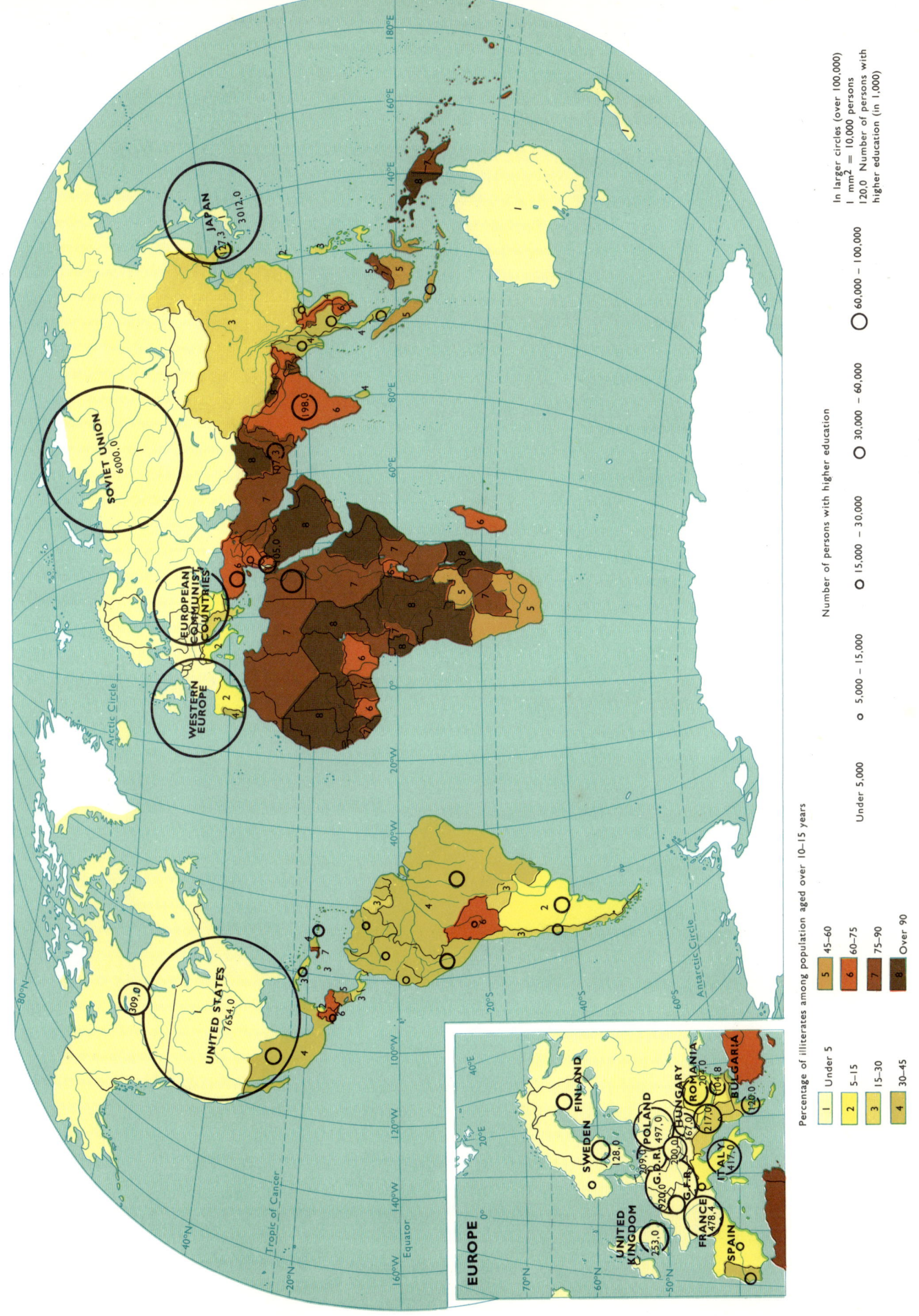

In larger circles (over 100,000)
1 mm² = 10,000 persons
120,0 = Number of persons with
         higher education

Number of persons with higher education

○ 60,000 – 100,000

○ 30,000 – 60,000

○ 15,000 – 30,000

○ 5,000 – 15,000

○ Under 5,000

Percentage of illiterates among population aged over 10–15 years

1 Under 5
2 5–15
3 15–30
4 30–45
5 45–60
6 60–75
7 75–90
8 Over 90

JAPAN
3012,0
27,3

SOVIET UNION
6000,0

EUROPEAN
COMMUNIST
COUNTRIES

WESTERN
EUROPE

UNITED STATES
7654,0
309,0

98,0

EUROPE

SWEDEN
28,0

FINLAND

POLAND
497,0

G.D.R.
209,0

HUNGARY
67,0

ROMANIA
217,0

BULGARIA
120,0

G.F.R.
920,0

ITALY
417,0

UNITED
KINGDOM
253,0

FRANCE
478,4

SPAIN

64,8
204,0

MAP 16   World: Education   95

© Pergamon Press Ltd

Legend:

- 1 doctor –1,000 persons
- 1 doctor –1,000–5,000 persons
- 1 doctor –5,000–20,000 persons
- 1 docto...
- 1 docte...

Quarantinable diseases

Infected areas — April 1969

Cholera

Yellow fever

Smallpox

Typhus fever

20,000–50,000 persons

over 50,000 persons

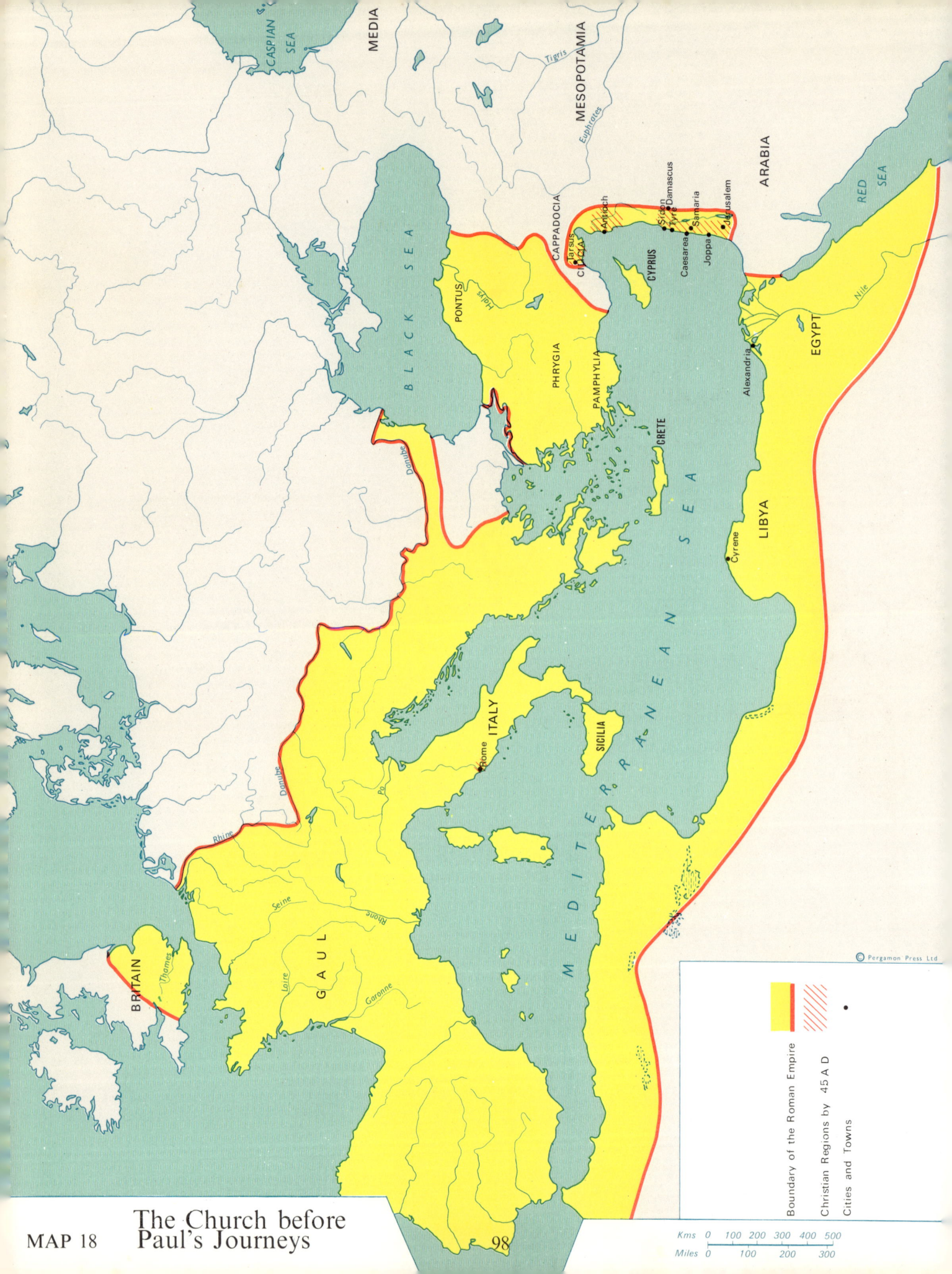

The Church before
Paul's Journeys

MAP 18

98

CASPIAN SEA

MEDIA

MESOPOTAMIA

Tigris

Euphrates

ARABIA

RED SEA

BLACK SEA

Halys

PONTUS

CAPPADOCIA

Antioch

Tarsus

CILICIA

Sidon
Damascus
Tyre

CYPRUS

Caesarea

Samaria

Joppa

Jerusalem

PHRYGIA

PAMPHYLIA

CRETE

Alexandria

EGYPT

Nile

LIBYA

Cyrene

M E D I T E R R A N E A N   S E A

SICILIA

Rome

ITALY

Po

Danube

Rhine

Seine

Rhone

GAUL

Loire

Garonne

BRITAIN

Thames

© Pergamon Press Ltd

Boundary of the Roman Empire

Christian Regions by 45 A D

Cities and Towns

Kms 0 100 200 300 400 500

Miles 0 100 200 300

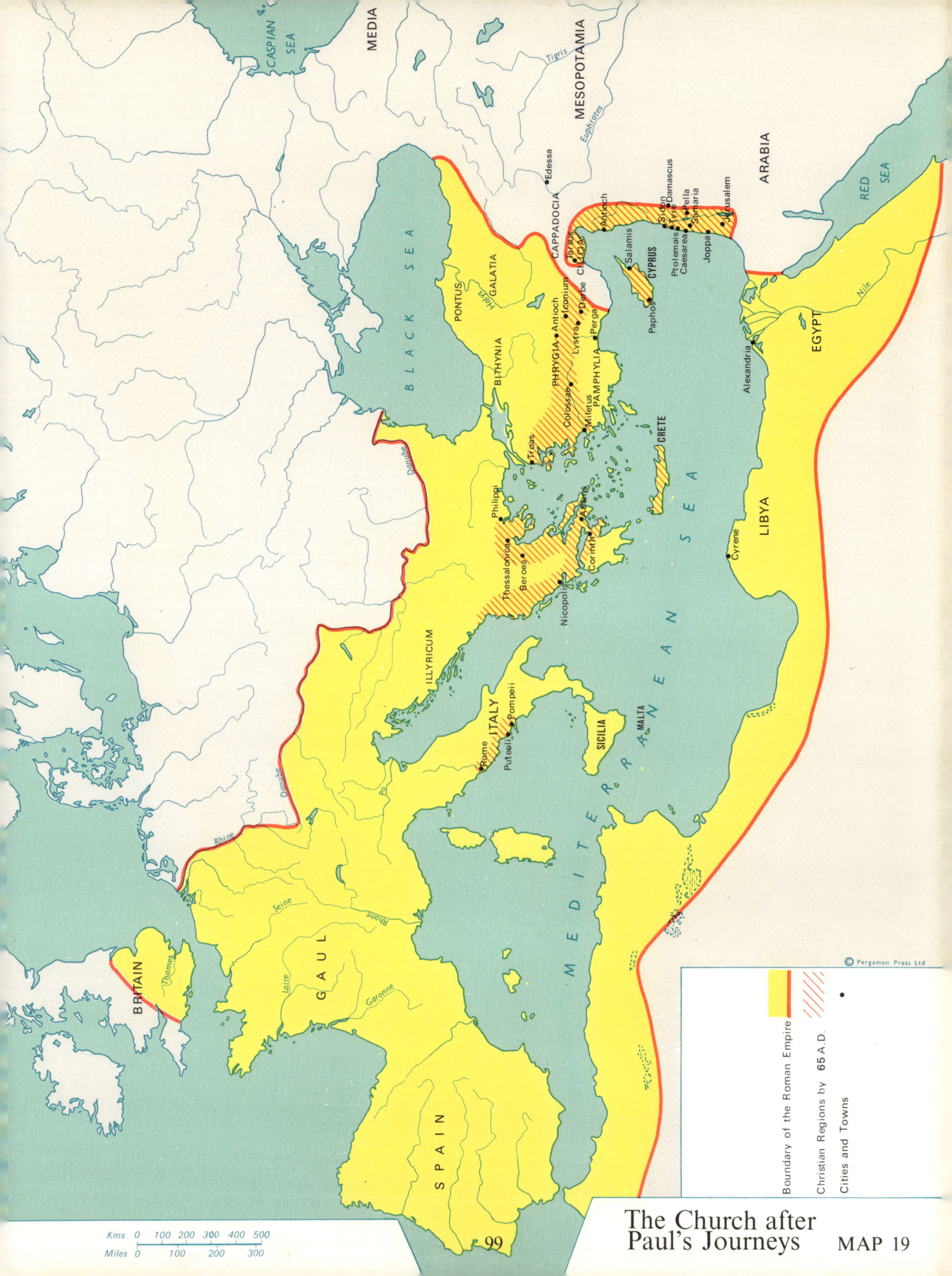

The Church after Paul's Journeys   MAP 19

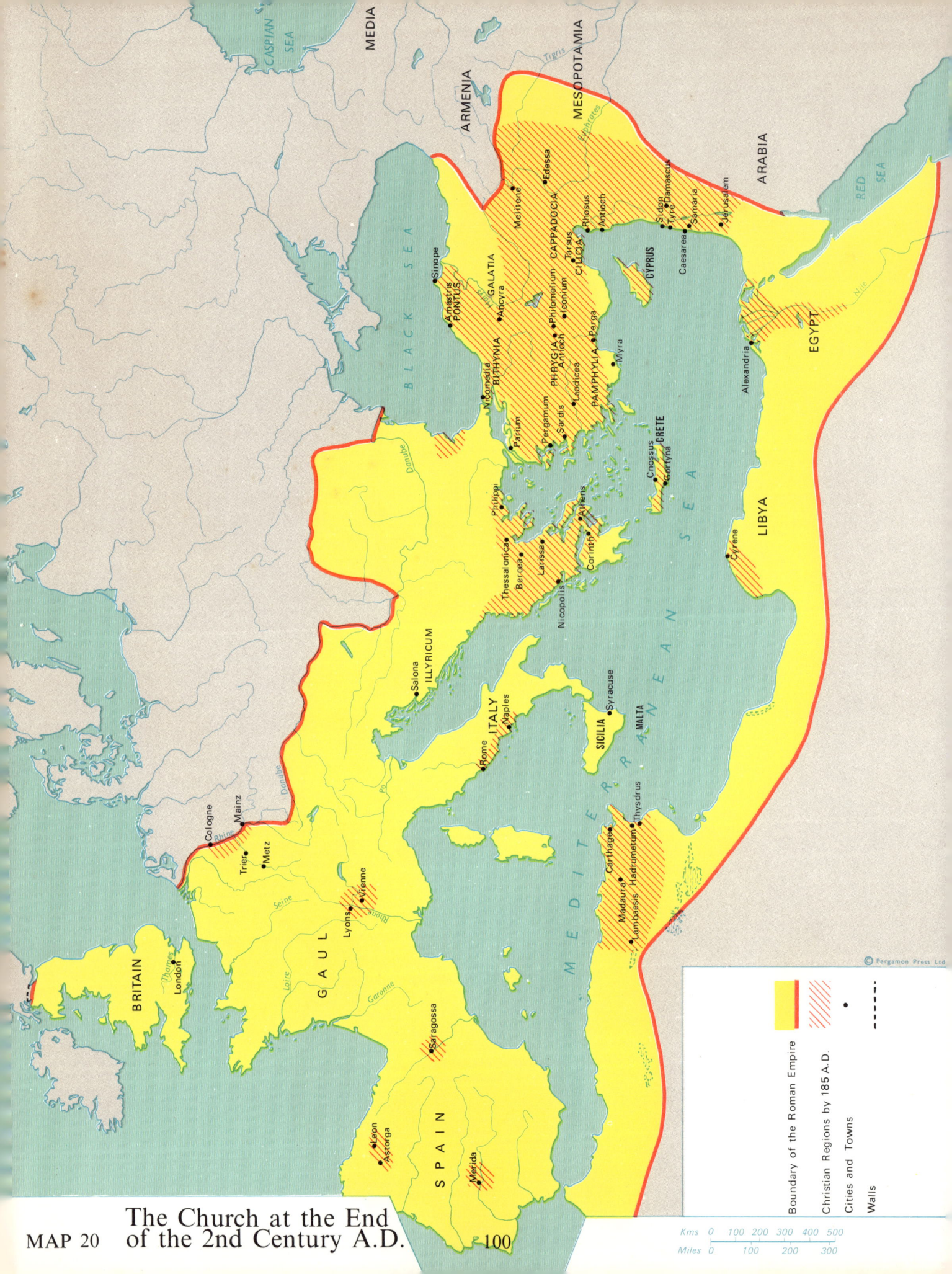

CASPIAN SEA

MEDIA

ARMENIA

MESOPOTAMIA

Tigris

Euphrates

ARABIA

RED SEA

Edessa

Melitene

CAPPADOCIA

Rhosus

Antioch

Sidon

Tyre

Damascus

Samaria

Jerusalem

Caesarea

BLACK SEA

Sinope

Amastris

PONTUS

GALATIA

Ancyra

CILICIA

Tarsus

Philomelium

Iconium

Perga

PAMPHYLIA

Myra

CYPRUS

Nicomedia

BITHYNIA

PHRYGIA

Antioch

Parium

Pergamum

Sardis

Laodicea

EGYPT

Alexandria

Nile

CRETE

Cnossus

Gortyna

LIBYA

Philippi

Athens

Thessalonica

Larissa

Beroea

Corinth

Nicopolis

Cyrene

Danube

Salona

ILLYRICUM

ITALY

Naples

Rome

SICILIA

Syracuse

MALTA

M E D I T E R R A N E A N   S E A

Thysdrus

Carthage

Hadrumetum

Madaura

Lambaesis

Cologne

Mainz

Rhine

Trier

Metz

Vienne

Lyons

Rhône

GAUL

Seine

Loire

Garonne

BRITAIN

Thames

London

Saragossa

SPAIN

León

Astorga

Mérida

100

© Pergamon Press Ltd

The Church at the End
MAP 20   of the 2nd Century A.D.

Kms 0   100 200 300 400 500

Miles 0   100   200   300

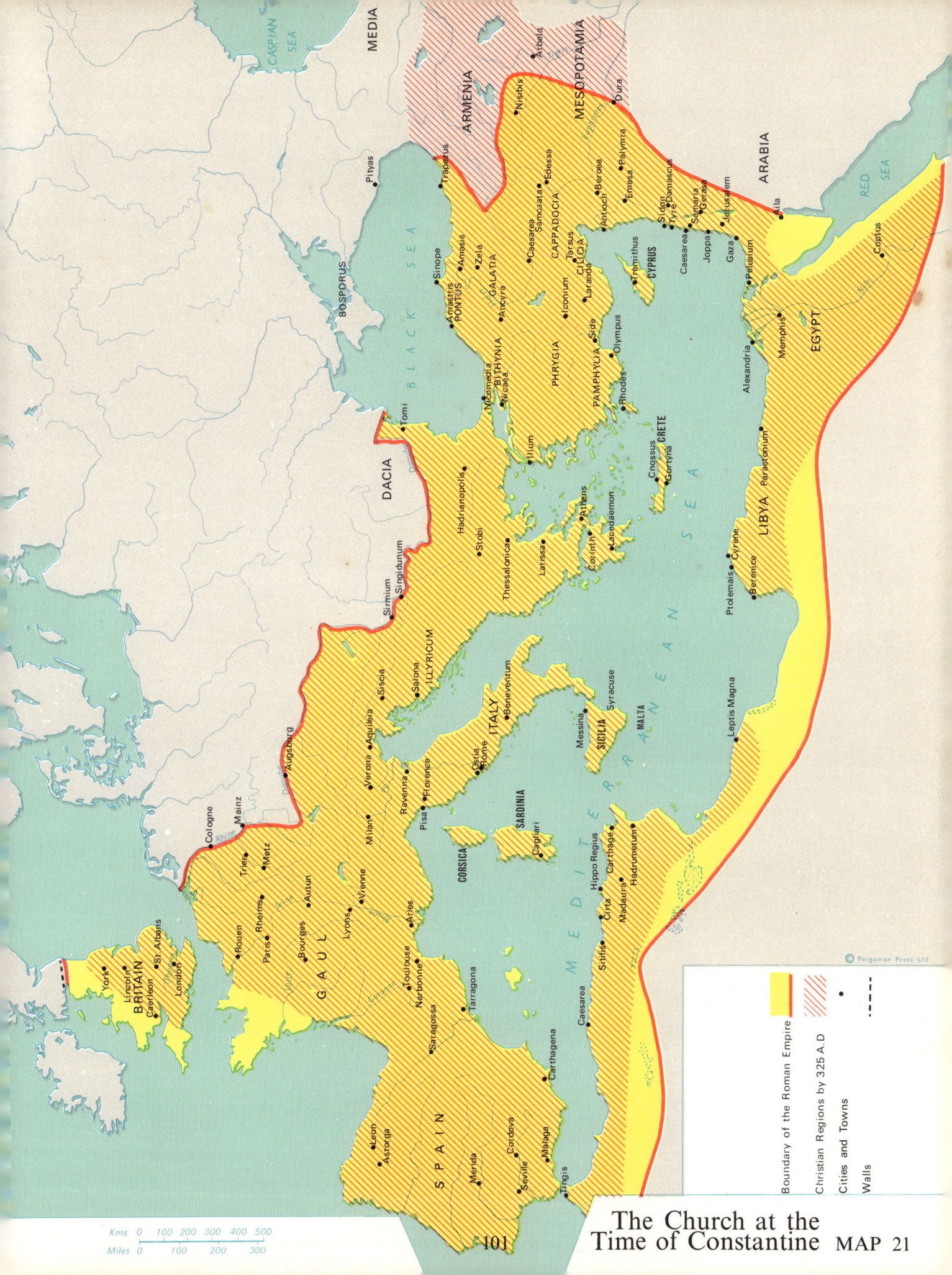

MEDIA

CASPIAN SEA

ARMENIA

MESOPOTAMIA

Arbela

ARABIA

RED SEA

Pityas

Artaxata

Trapezus

Nisibis

Dura

BOSPORUS

BLACK SEA

Amastris
PONTUS
Sinope
Amasia
Zela
Neocaesarea
Caesarea
Samosata
Edessa
Beroea
Palmyra
Antioch
Emesa
Damascus
Sidon
Tyre
Samaria
Gerasa
Jerusalem
Aila

GALATIA
Ancyra
CAPPADOCIA
Tarsus
CILICIA
Laranda
Tremithus
Caesarea
Joppa
Gaza
Pelusium

BITHYNIA
Nicomedia
Nicaea
Iconium
PHRYGIA
Side
Olympus
CYPRUS

Alexandria
Memphis
EGYPT

Ilium
PAMPHYLIA
Rhodes

Tomi

DACIA

Sirmium
Singidunum

Hadrianopolis

Stobi

Thessalonica

Larissa

Athens
Corinth
Lacedaemon
CRETE
Cnossus
Gortyna

Coptus

Paraetonium

LIBYA

Cyrene
Ptolemais
Berenice

MEDITERRANEAN SEA

Sisoia
Salona
ILLYRICUM
Aquileia
Verona
Milan
Ravenna
Pisa
Florence
ITALY
Ostia
Rome
Beneventum

Augsburg

Cologne
Mainz
Trier
Metz
Vienne
Autun
Lyons
Arles

Rhine

SARDINIA
Cagliari

CORSICA

Syracuse
Messina
SICILIA
MALTA

Leptis Magna

GAUL

Rouen
Paris
Rheims
Bourges
Toulouse
Narbonne
Tarragona

Hippo Regius
Carthage
Hadrumetum
Madaura
Cirta
Sitifis
Caesarea

York
Lincoln
Caerleon
St. Albans
London
BRITAIN

Leon
Astorga
Merida
Cordova
Seville
Malaga
Tingis
SPAIN
Saragossa
Carthagena

© Pergamon Press Ltd

		Boundary of the Roman Empire	
		Christian Regions by 325 A.D	
		Cities and Towns	
		Walls	

Kms 0   100 200 300 400 500
Miles 0   100   200   300

101

The Church at the
Time of Constantine MAP 21

Colour explanation

Christians	
Muslims (Sunni and Shiah.)	
Buddhists	
Hindus	
Animists (The primitive religions)	
Confucianists (The popular religion of China)	
Others (In Israel, Jews in Japan,Shintoist)	
Secularism	

(Uninhabited areas left white)

MAP 22   World: Religions   102   © Pergamon Press Ltd

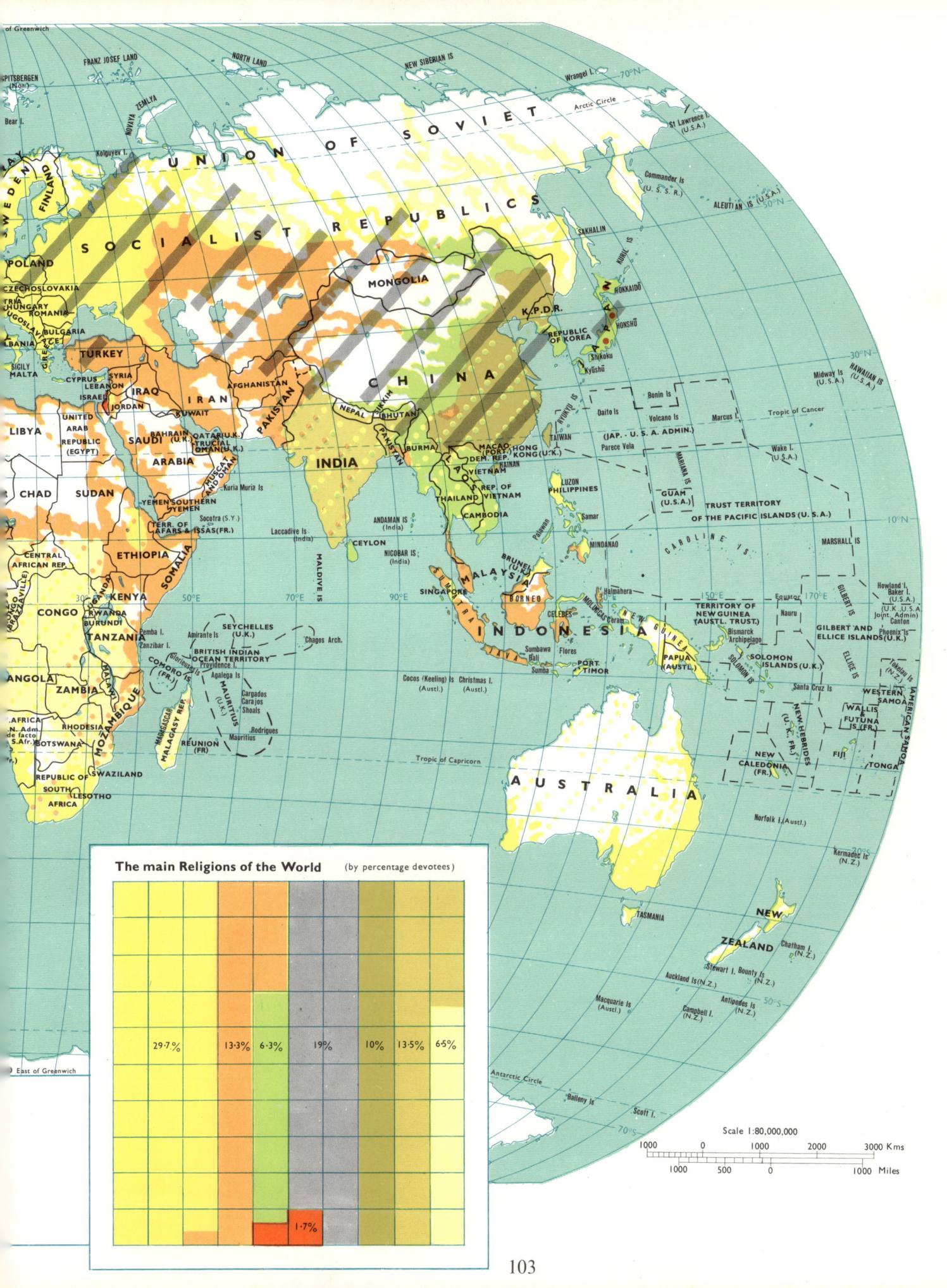

The main Religions of the World (by percentage devotees)

| 29·7% | 13·3% | 6·3% | 19% | 10% | 13·5% | 6·5% |

1·7%

Scale 1:80,000,000

1000   0   1000   2000   3000 Kms

1000   500   0   1000 Miles

103

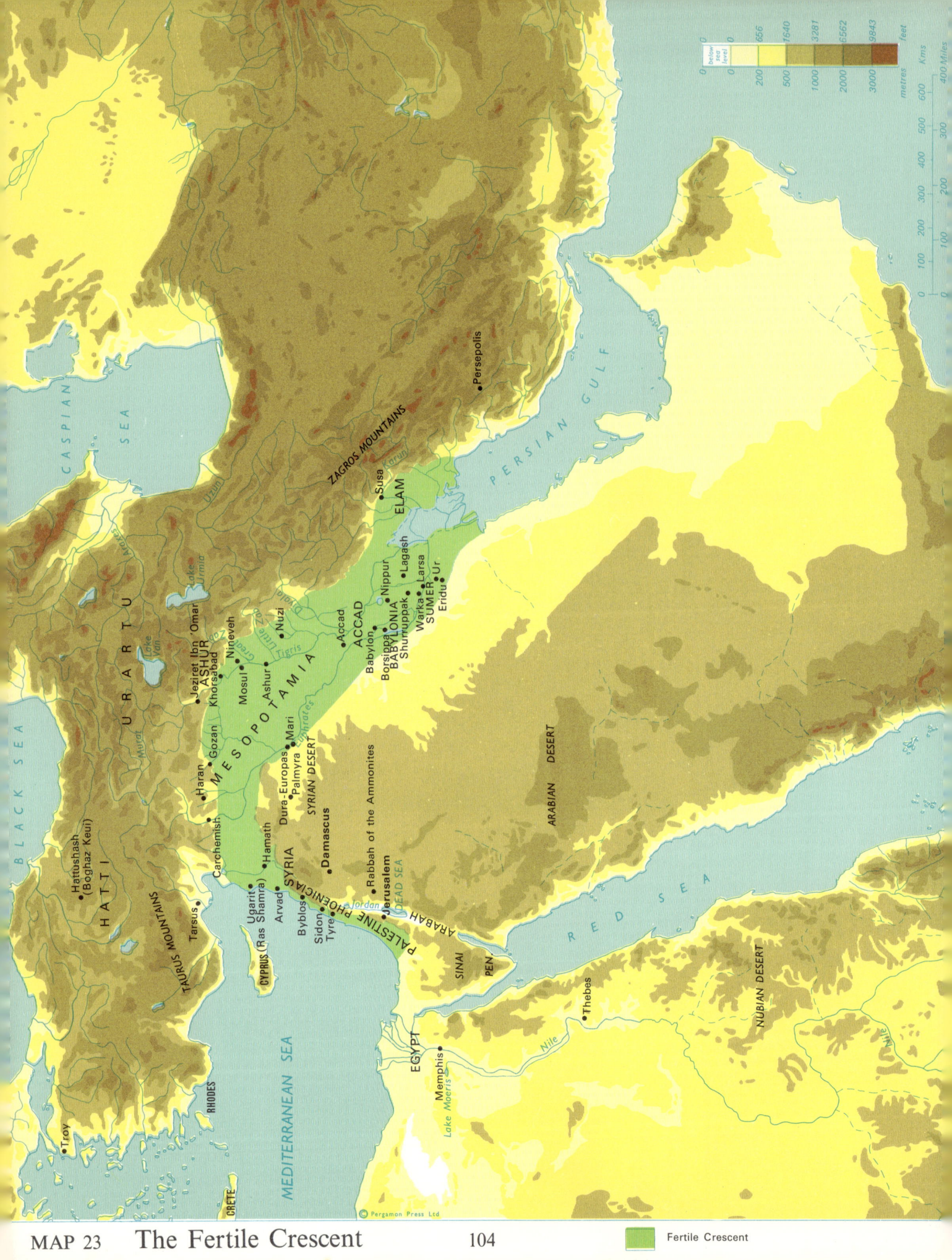

CASPIAN SEA

BLACK SEA

URARTU

Lake Urmia

Lake Van

HATTI

Hattushash (Boghaz Keui)

TAURUS MOUNTAINS

Tarsus

RHODES

CRETE

MEDITERRANEAN SEA

Troy

CYPRUS (Ras Shamra)

Arvad

Byblos

Sidon

Tyre

Jeziret Ibn 'Omar

Khorsabad

Mosul

Nineveh

ASHUR

Ashur

Gozan

Haran

Carchemish

Hamath

SYRIA

Damascus

PHOENICIA

PALESTINE

Jerusalem

Jordan

DEAD SEA

ARABAH

Rabbah of the Ammonites

SYRIAN DESERT

Dura-Europas

Palmyra

Mari

Nuzi

MESOPOTAMIA

Greater Zab

Little Zab

Tigris

Euphrates

Accad

ACCAD

Babylon

Borsippa

BABYLONIA

Nippur

Shuruppak

Lagash

Warka

SUMER

Larsa

Ur

Eridu

ZAGROS MOUNTAINS

Karun

Susa

ELAM

Persepolis

PERSIAN GULF

ARABIAN DESERT

SINAI PEN.

RED SEA

EGYPT

Memphis

Lake Moeris

Thebes

Nile

Nile

NUBIAN DESERT

below sea level
0   656   1640   3281   6562   9843   feet
0   200   500   1000 2000   3000 metres

Kms
400
300
200
100
0

400 Miles
300
200
100
0

© Pergamon Press Ltd

MAP 23   The Fertile Crescent   104   ▮ Fertile Crescent

656 1640 3281 6562 9843 feet

Below sea level
0 200 500 1000 2000 3000 metres

CASPIAN SEA

ZAGROS MOUNTAINS

Susa
ELAM

PERSIAN GULF

Nineveh
Arbela
ASSYRIA
Mardin
Ashur
MITANNI
Harran
Carchemish
Niy
Nippur
Lagash
Larsa
Ur
BABYLONIA
Babylon
Tigris
Euphrates

Tadmor (Palmyra)
SYRIAN DESERT

ARABIAN DESERT

BLACK SEA

HATTI
Arinna
Tyana
TAURUS MTS
Kumani
Milid
Marash
Samal
Aleppo
NAHARIN

Hamath
Arvad
Byblus
Tyre
Megiddo
Taanach
Askalon
Gaza
CYPRUS

LYCIA

Restan
Kadesh
AMOR
Damascus

Jerusalem
Lachish
EDOM
SEIR
SINAI
PEN.

DEAD SEA

RED SEA

Myos Hormos

MEDITERRANEAN SEA

Tharu
Pithom
Sais
Heliopolis (On)
Memphis
Lake Moeris
Arsinoe
Hermapolis
Hermapolis

Abydus
Thebes
Elerthyiapolis
Ombos
Syene

E G Y P T

NUBIAN DESERT

Kummeh
Gem Aton
Soleb
Napata

Nile

Meroe

© Pergamon Press Ltd.

BOUNDARIES
Egyptian Empire
Hittite Empire
Kingdom of Mitanni
Maximum extent of Egyptian Empire

The Egyptian World Empire (c.1500-1200 B.C.)   MAP 24

0 100 200 300 400 500 600 Kms
0 100 200 300 400 Miles

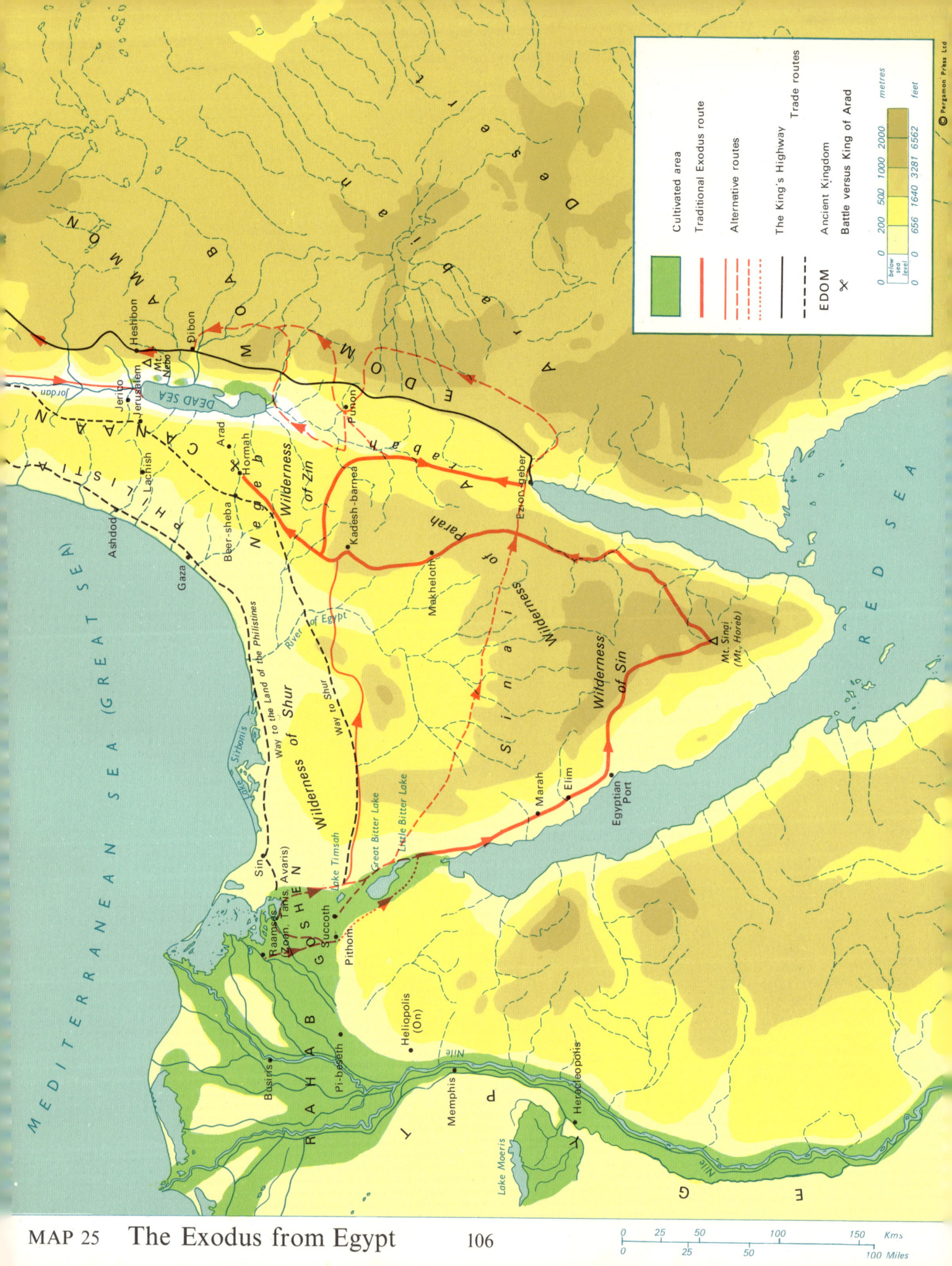

MAP 25   The Exodus from Egypt   106

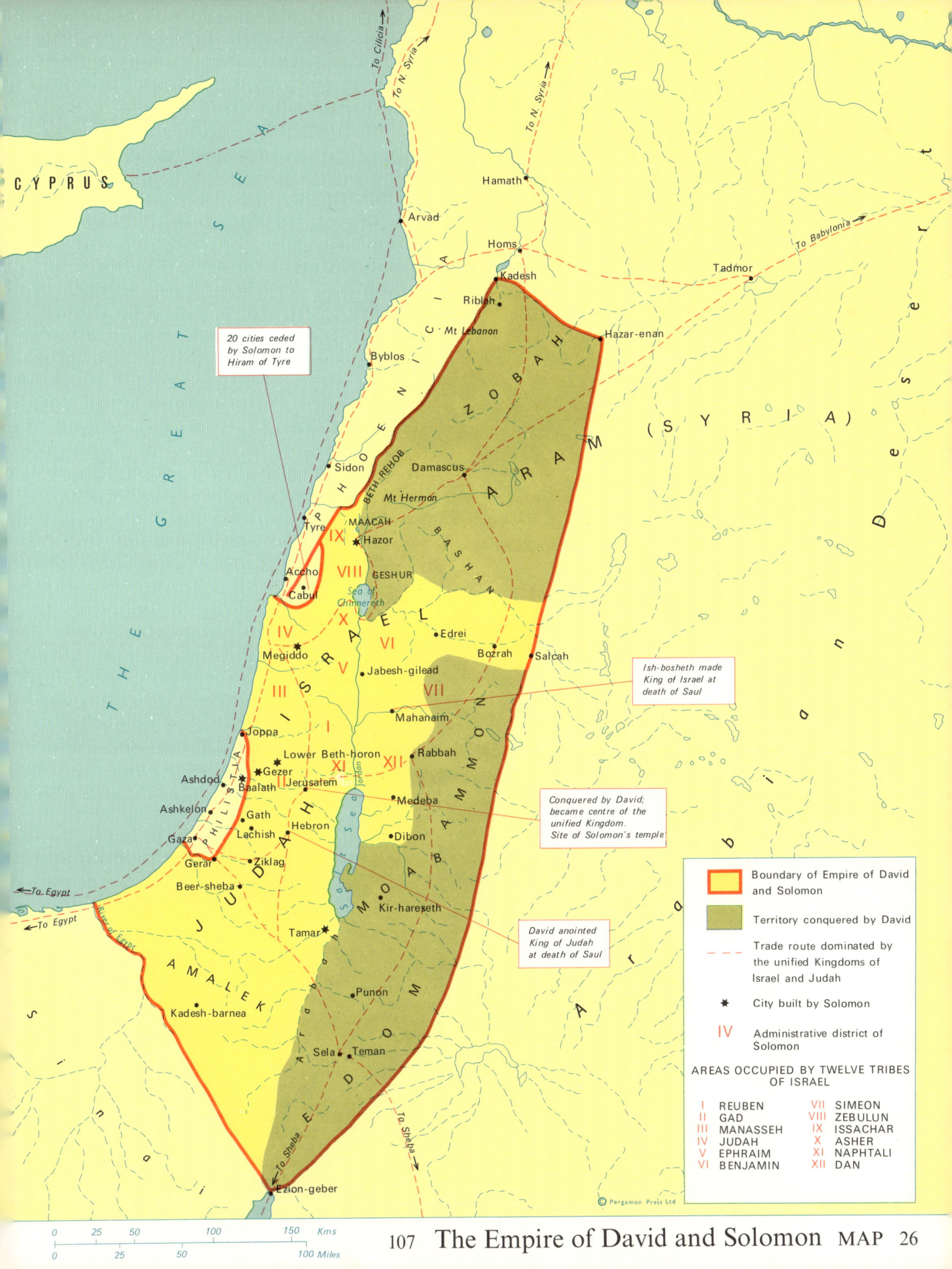

CYPRUS

THE GREAT SEA

To Cilicia →
To N. Syria →
To N. Syria →
To Babylonia →

Hamath

Arvad

Homs

Kadesh
Riblah
Mt Lebanon

Byblos

Hazar-enan

Tadmor

ZOBAH

ARAM (SYRIA)

Sidon

BETH-REHOB

Damascus

Mt Hermon

Tyre   IX   MAACAH
Hazor
Accho   VIII
Cabul   GESHUR
Sea of Chinnereth

BASHAN

X
IV
Megiddo   VI
V   Edrei
Jabesh-gilead   Bozrah   Salcah

ISRAEL

III
VII
I
Mahanaim

AMMON

Joppa
Lower Beth-horon   XI   XII   Rabbah
Ashdod   Gezer
Baalath   Jerusalem
Ashkelon
Gath   Medeba
Gaza   Lachish
Gerar   Hebron   Dibon
Ziklag
Beer-sheba   Kir-hareseth

JUDAH

PHILISTIA

MOAB

Tamar

AMALEK

EDOM

Punon

Kadesh-barnea

Sela   Teman

To Egypt →
To Egypt →
River of Egypt
Arabah
Sea of Sheba
To Sheba

To Sheba

Ezion-geber

Sinai

Desert

Arabia

20 cities ceded by Solomon to Hiram of Tyre

Ish-bosheth made King of Israel at death of Saul

Conquered by David; became centre of the unified Kingdom. Site of Solomon's temple

David anointed King of Judah at death of Saul

Boundary of Empire of David and Solomon

Territory conquered by David

Trade route dominated by the unified Kingdoms of Israel and Judah

★ City built by Solomon

IV   Administrative district of Solomon

AREAS OCCUPIED BY TWELVE TRIBES OF ISRAEL

I	REUBEN	VII	SIMEON
II	GAD	VIII	ZEBULUN
III	MANASSEH	IX	ISSACHAR
IV	JUDAH	X	ASHER
V	EPHRAIM	XI	NAPHTALI
VI	BENJAMIN	XII	DAN

© Pergamon Press Ltd

0 25 50 100 150 Kms
0 25 50 100 Miles

107   The Empire of David and Solomon   MAP 26

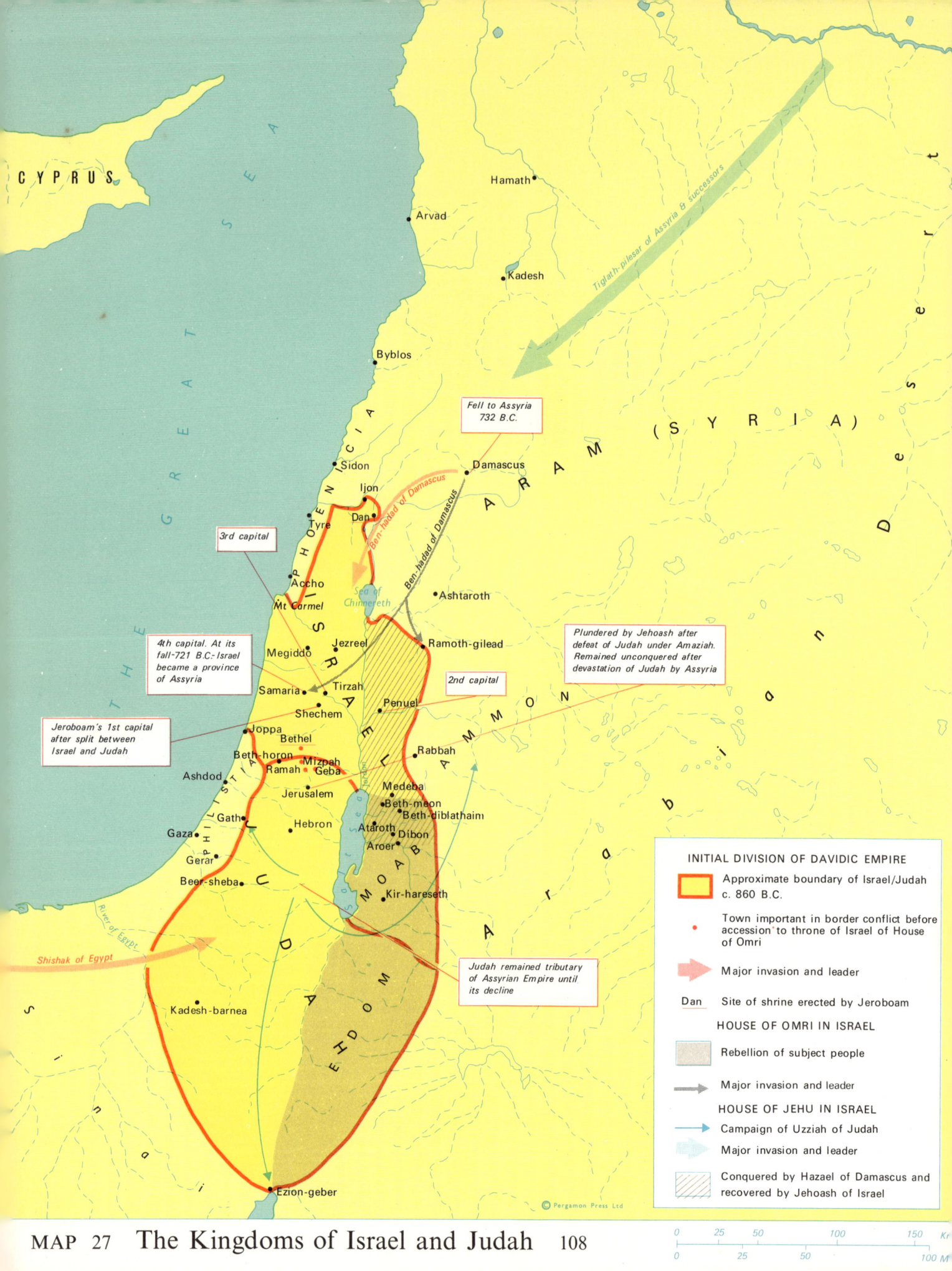

CYPRUS

Hamath

Arvad

Kadesh

Tiglath-pileser of Assyria & successors

Byblos

Fell to Assyria
732 B.C.

Sidon
Ijon
Dan
Tyre

3rd capital

ARAM (SYRIA)

Ben-hadad of Damascus

Damascus

Ben-hadad of Damascus

Accho
Mt Carmel
Sea of
Chinnereth

Ashtaroth

4th capital. At its
fall-721 B.C.-Israel
became a province
of Assyria

Jezreel
Megiddo
Samaria
Tirzah

Ramoth-gilead

Plundered by Jehoash after
defeat of Judah under Amaziah.
Remained unconquered after
devastation of Judah by Assyria

Shechem
Penuel

2nd capital

Jeroboam's 1st capital
after split between
Israel and Judah

Joppa
Bethel
Beth-horon
Ashdod
Ramah Geba
Mizpah

Rabbah

AMMON

Jerusalem

Medeba
Beth-meon
Beth-diblathaim

Gath
Gaza
Hebron
Ataroth
Dibon
Aroer

MOAB

Gerar

Beer-sheba

JUDAH

Kir-hareseth

Judah remained tributary
of Assyrian Empire until
its decline

Shishak of Egypt

River of Egypt

Kadesh-barnea

EDOM

Arabian Desert

Ezion-geber

INITIAL DIVISION OF DAVIDIC EMPIRE

Approximate boundary of Israel/Judah
c. 860 B.C.

Town important in border conflict before
accession to throne of Israel of House
of Omri

Major invasion and leader

Dan   Site of shrine erected by Jeroboam

HOUSE OF OMRI IN ISRAEL

Rebellion of subject people

Major invasion and leader

HOUSE OF JEHU IN ISRAEL

Campaign of Uzziah of Judah

Major invasion and leader

Conquered by Hazael of Damascus and
recovered by Jehoash of Israel

© Pergamon Press Ltd

MAP 27   The Kingdoms of Israel and Judah   108

0   25   50   100   150
0   25   50   100

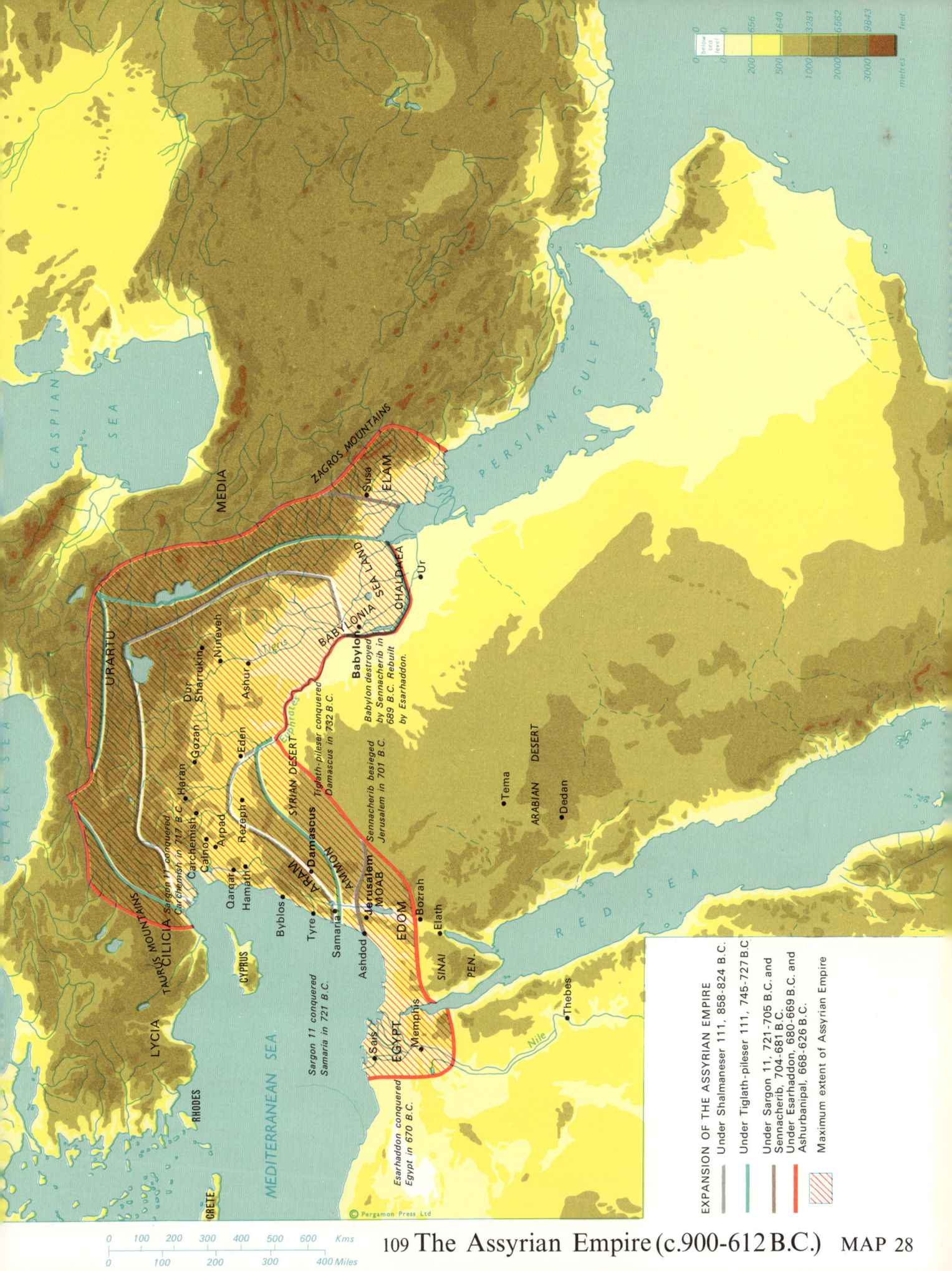

feet
0
656
1640
3281
6562
9843

below sea level
0
200
500
1000
2000
3000
metres

CASPIAN SEA

BLACK SEA

MEDITERRANEAN SEA

RED SEA

PERSIAN GULF

ARABIAN DESERT

SYRIAN DESERT

ZAGROS MOUNTAINS

TAURUS MOUNTAINS

MEDIA

URARTU

ELAM

CHALDAEA

BABYLONIA

SEA LAND

ARAM

AMMON

MOAB

EDOM

EGYPT

SINAI PEN.

CILICIA

LYCIA

CYPRUS

RHODES

CRETE

Susa

Ur

Babylon

Nineveh

Dur Sharrukin

Ashur

Gozan

Harran

Carchemish

Calno

Eden

Arpad

Rezeph

Hamath

Qarqar

Byblos

Tyre

Samaria

Ashdod

Jerusalem

Damascus

Bozrah

Elath

Memphis

Sais

Thebes

Tema

Dedan

Tigris

Euphrates

Nile

Babylon destroyed by Sennacherib in 689 B.C. Rebuilt by Esarhaddon.

Tiglath-pileser conquered Damascus in 732 B.C.

Sennacherib besieged Jerusalem in 701 B.C.

Sargon 11 conquered Carchemish in 717 B.C.

Sargon 11 conquered Samaria in 721 B.C.

Esarhaddon conquered Egypt in 670 B.C.

EXPANSION OF THE ASSYRIAN EMPIRE

Under Shalmaneser 111, 858–824 B.C.

Under Tiglath-pileser 111, 745–727 B.C.

Under Sargon 11, 721–705 B.C. and Sennacherib, 704–681 B.C.

Under Esarhaddon, 680–669 B.C. and Ashurbanipal, 668–626 B.C.

Maximum extent of Assyrian Empire

© Pergamon Press Ltd

0 100 200 300 400 500 600 Kms
0 100 200 300 400 Miles

109 The Assyrian Empire (c.900–612 B.C.)   MAP 28

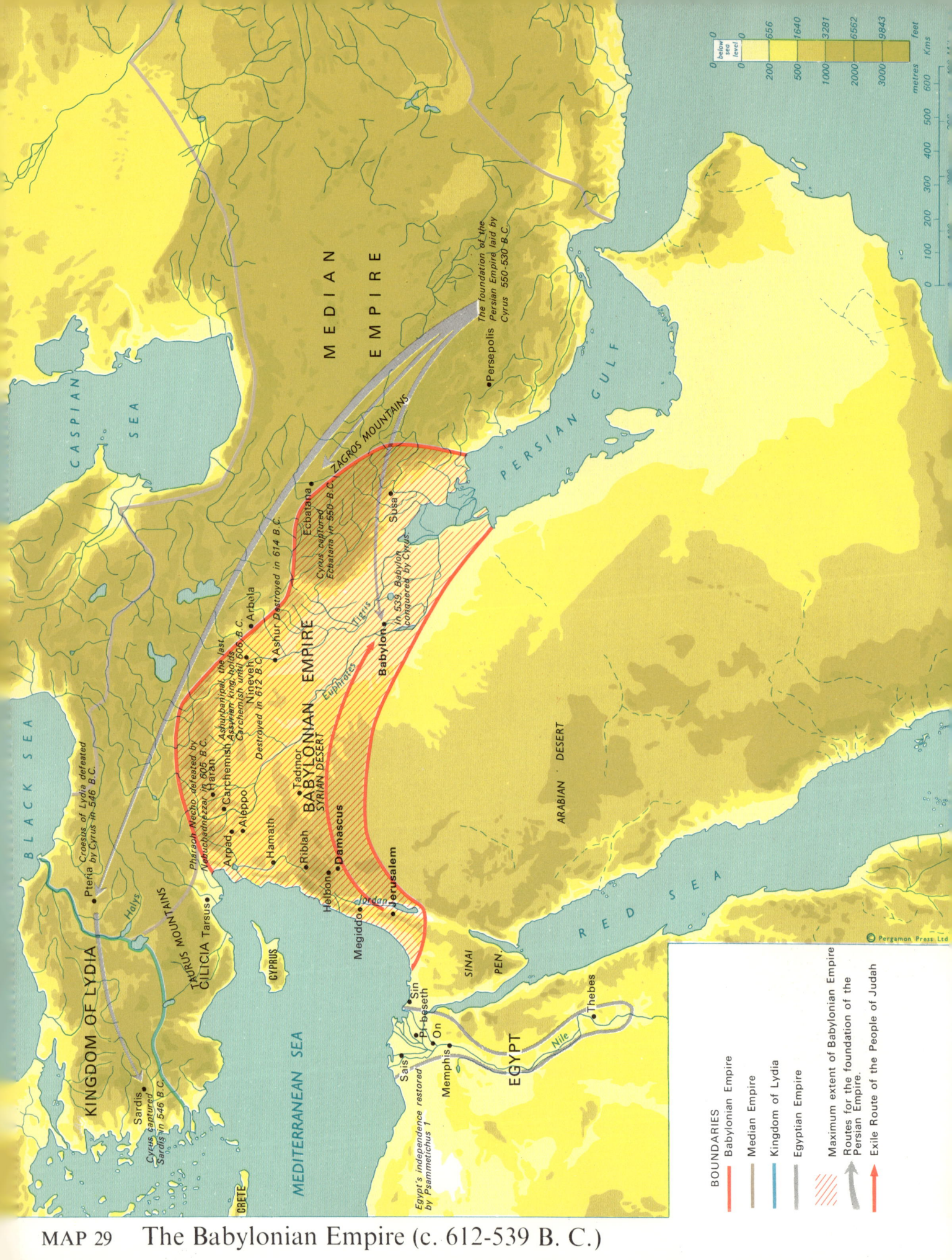

below sea level · 0 · 656 · 1640 · 3281 · 6562 · 9843 feet
below sea level · 0 · 200 · 500 · 1000 · 2000 · 3000 metres

M E D I A N E M P I R E

The foundation of the Persian Empire laid by Cyrus 550-530 B.C.

•Persepolis

CASPIAN SEA

ZAGROS MOUNTAINS

•Ecbatana
Cyrus captured Ecbatana in 550 B.C.

•Susa

•Ashur *Destroyed in 614 B.C.*

•Arbela

•Nineveh *Destroyed in 612 B.C.*

•Carchemish *Ashurbanipal, the last Assyrian king, holds Carchemish until 606 B.C.*

•Harran

Babylon In 539, Babylon conquered by Cyrus
•Babylon

PERSIAN GULF

BLACK SEA

•Pteria *Croesus of Lydia defeated by Cyrus in 546 B.C.*

Halys

TAURUS MOUNTAINS

•Tarsus
CILICIA

CYPRUS

•Arpad
•Aleppo
•Hamath
•Riblah
•Tadmor

Pharaoh Necho defeated by Nebuchadnezzar in 605 B.C.

B A B Y L O N I A N   E M P I R E
SYRIAN DESERT

Euphrates
Tigris

•Damascus

•Helbon
•Jordan
•Jerusalem

•Megiddo

KINGDOM OF LYDIA

•Sardis
Cyrus captured Sardis in 546 B.C.

MEDITERRANEAN SEA

CRETE

ARABIAN DESERT

RED SEA

SINAI PEN.

•Sin
•Pi-beseth
•On
•Sais
•Memphis

Egypt's independence restored by Psammetichus 1

E G Y P T

Nile

•Thebes

© Pergamon Press Ltd

BOUNDARIES
Babylonian Empire
Median Empire
Kingdom of Lydia
Egyptian Empire
Maximum extent of Babylonian Empire
Routes for the foundation of the Persian Empire.
Exile Route of the People of Judah

MAP 29   The Babylonian Empire (c. 612-539 B. C.)

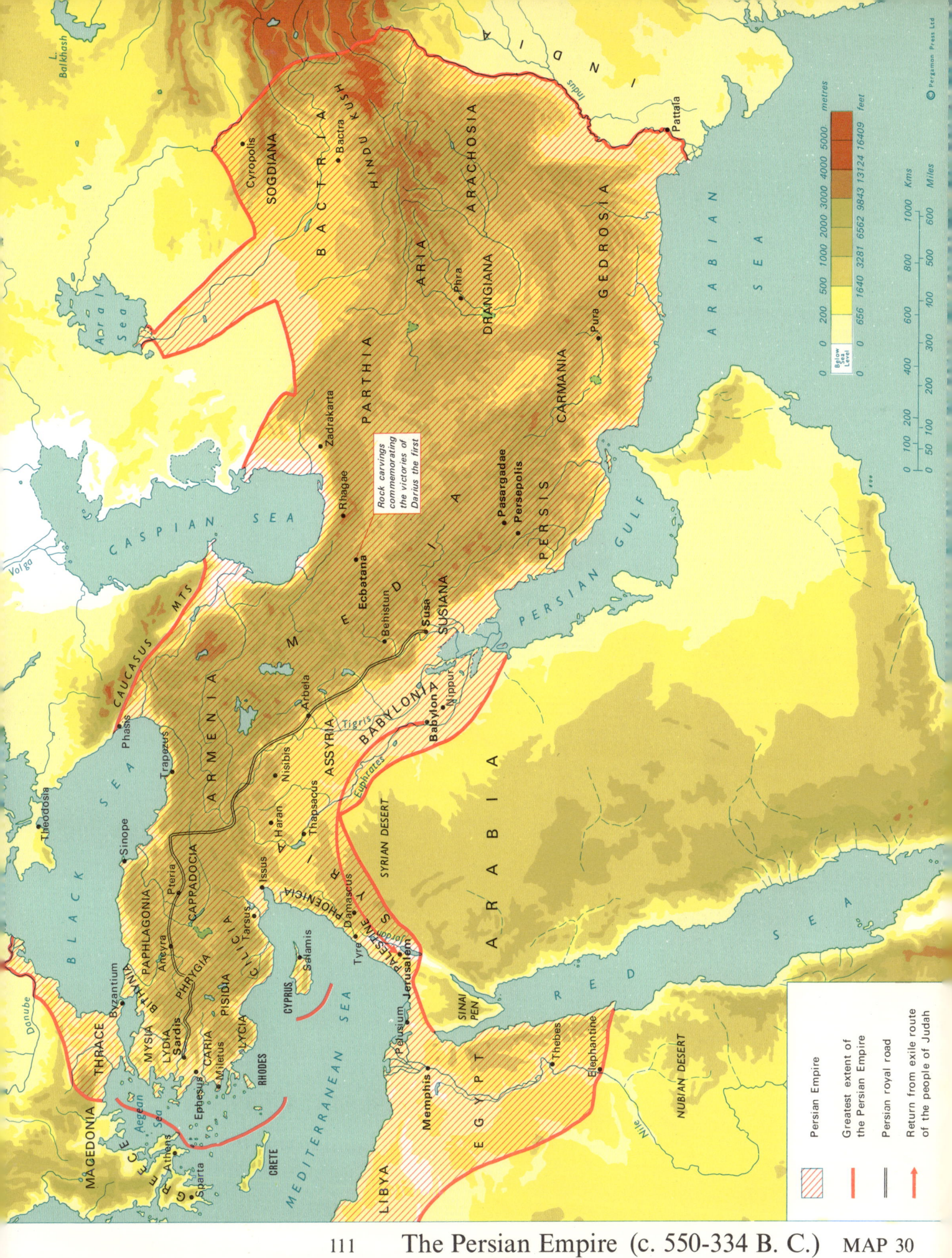

metres feet

below Sea Level		

Persian Empire

Greatest extent of the Persian Empire

Persian royal road

Return from exile route of the people of Judah

111   The Persian Empire (c. 550-334 B. C.)   MAP 30

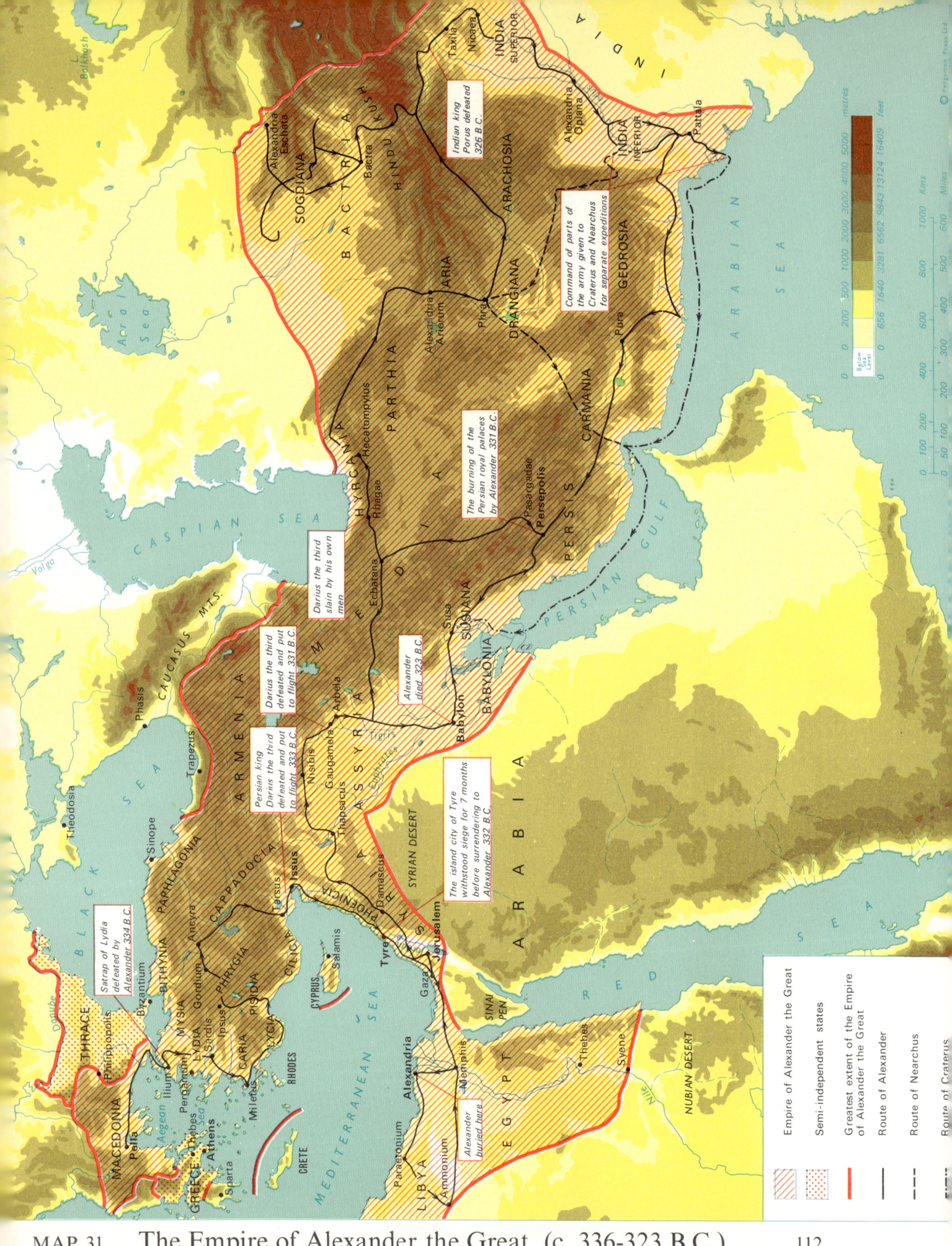

INDIA SUPERIOR

INDIA INFERIOR

Indian king Porus defeated 326 B.C.

Command of parts of the army given to Craterus and Nearchus for separate expeditions

ARABIAN SEA

SOGDIANA

BACTRIA

Alexandria Eschata

Bactra

HINDU KUSH

ARIA

ARACHOSIA

Alexandria Opiana

Taxila

Nicaea

Pattala

GEDROSIA

Alexandria Arionum

DRANGIANA

Phra

Pura

CARMANIA

The burning of the Persian royal palaces by Alexander 331 B.C.

PARTHIA

Hecatompylus

Pasargadae

Persepolis

PERSIS

PERSIAN GULF

Darius the third slain by his own men

Rhagae

Ecbatana

H Y R C A N I A

M E D I A

Susa

SUSIANA

Alexander died, 323 B.C.

CASPIAN SEA

Volga

Aral Sea

L. Balkhash

Darius the third defeated and put to flight 331 B.C.

Persian king Darius the third defeated and put to flight 333 B.C.

Nisibis

Gaugamela

Arbela

Thapsacus

A S S Y R I A

Babylon

BABYLONIA

Tigris

Euphrates

A R A B I A

SYRIAN DESERT

The island city of Tyre withstood siege for 7 months before surrendering to Alexander 332 B.C.

ARMENIA

CAUCASUS MTS.

Phasis

Trapezus

Sinope

BLACK SEA

Theodosia

CAPPADOCIA

PAPHLAGONIA

BITHYNIA

Ancyra

Gordium

PHRYGIA

Tarsus

Issus

CILICIA

Damascus

PHOENICIA

S Y R I A

Jerusalem

Tyre

Gaza

Satrap of Lydia defeated by Alexander 334 B.C.

Byzantium

Philippopolis

THRACE

Danube

MACEDONIA

Pella

Ilium

Pergamum

MYSIA

LYDIA

Sardis

Ipsus

PISIDIA

LYCIA

CARIA

Miletus

RHODES

CRETE

CYPRUS

Salamis

MEDITERRANEAN SEA

Aegean Sea

GREECE

Thebes

Athens

Sparta

Alexandria

Paraetonium

Ammonium

LIBYA

Alexander buried here

E G Y P T

Memphis

SINAI PEN

RED SEA

Thebes

Syene

NUBIAN DESERT

Nile

metres 5000 4000 3000 2000 1000 500 200 0 Below Sea Level

feet 16403 13124 9843 6562 3287 1640 656 0 Below Sea Level

Kms 1000 800 600 400 200 100 0

Miles 600 400 200 100 50 0

Empire of Alexander the Great

Semi-independent states

Greatest extent of the Empire of Alexander the Great

Route of Alexander

Route of Nearchus

Route of Craterus

MAP 31   The Empire of Alexander the Great (c. 336-323 B.C.)   112

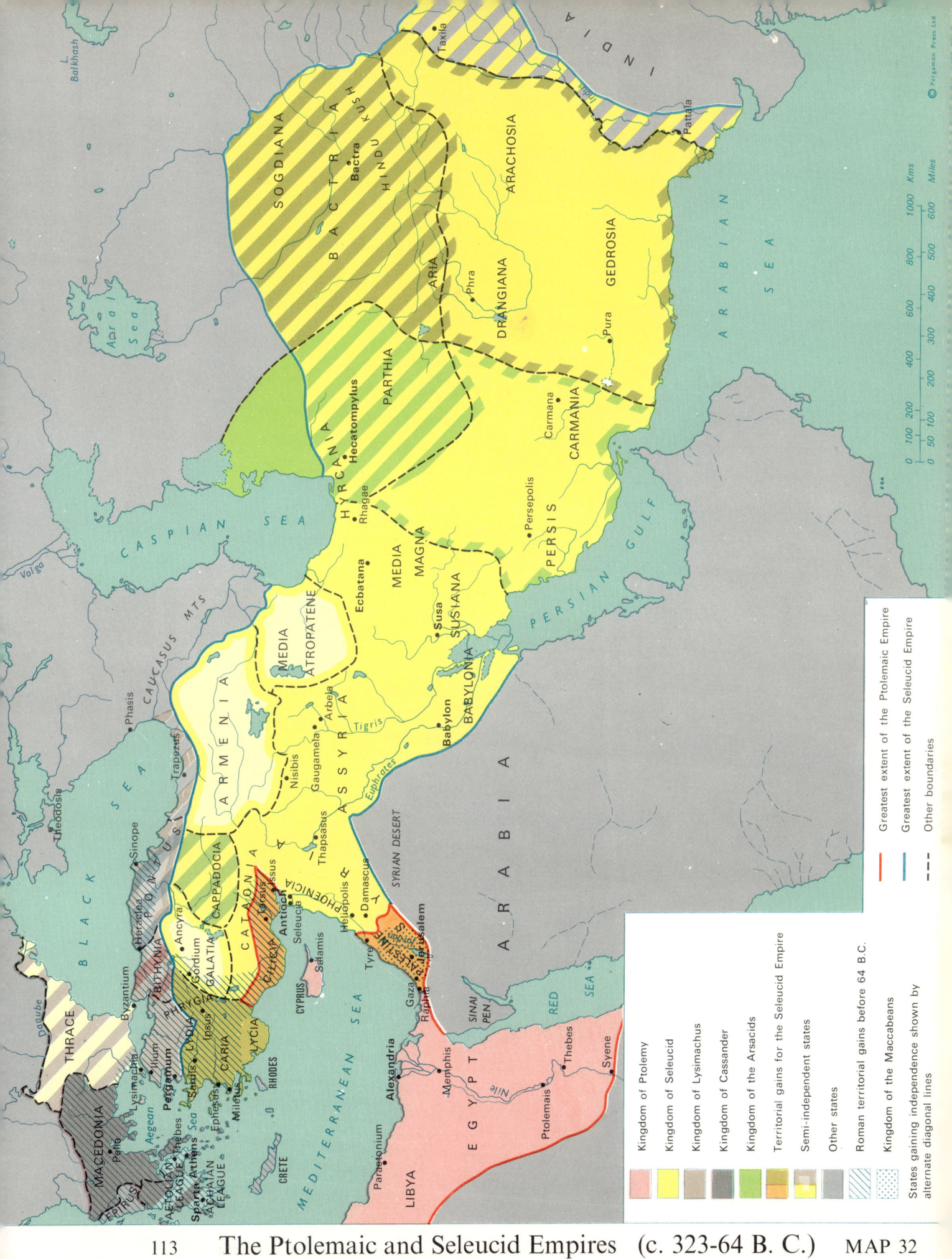

Legend

Kingdom of Ptolemy	Kingdom of Seleucid	Kingdom of Lysimachus	Kingdom of Cassander	Kingdom of the Arsacids	Territorial gains for the Seleucid Empire	Semi-independent states	Other states	Roman territorial gains before 64 B.C.	Kingdom of the Maccabeans

States gaining independence shown by alternate diagonal lines

Greatest extent of the Ptolemaic Empire
Greatest extent of the Seleucid Empire
Other boundaries

The Ptolemaic and Seleucid Empires (c. 323–64 B.C.) MAP 32

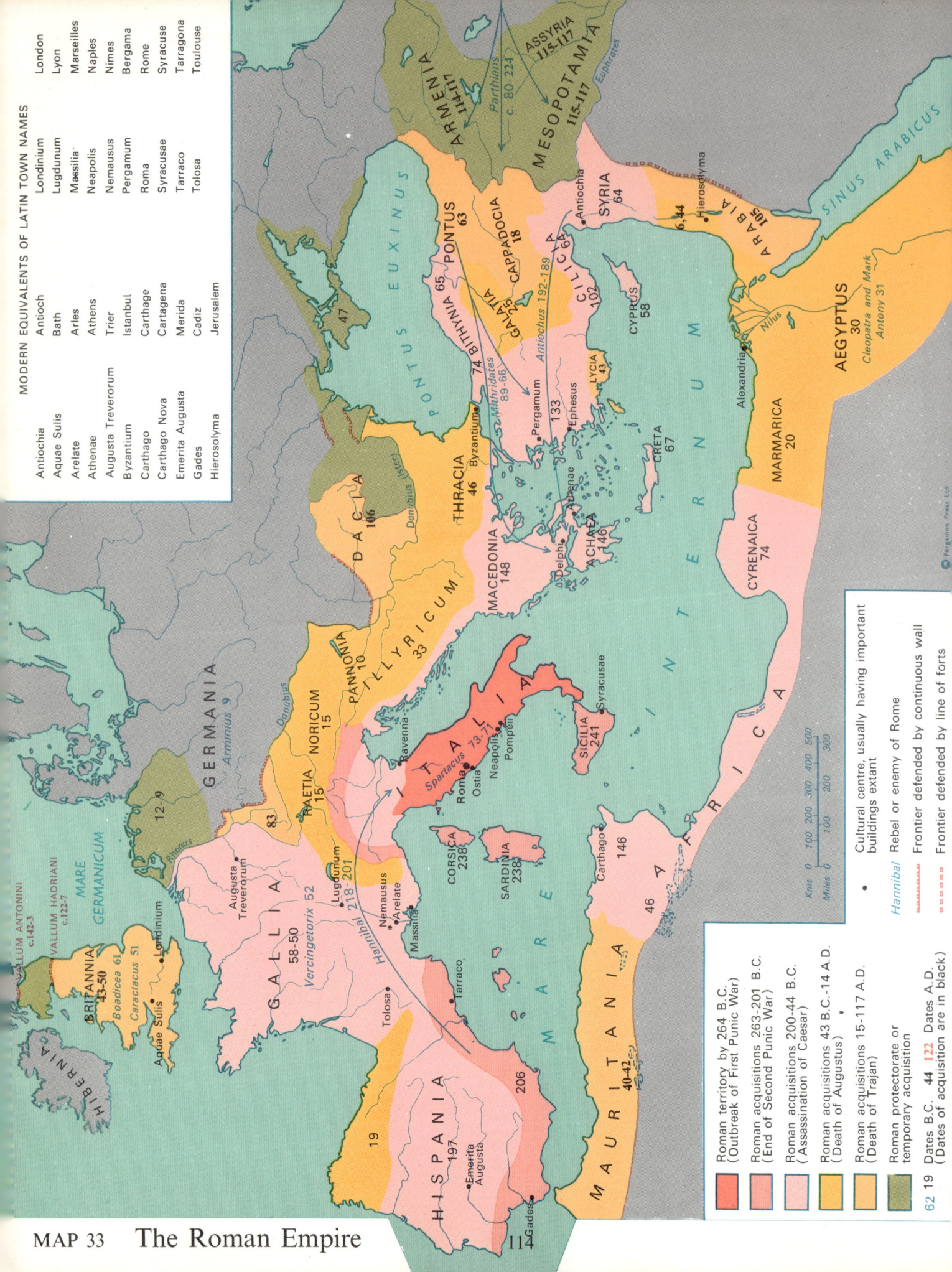

MAP 33   The Roman Empire

MODERN EQUIVALENTS OF LATIN TOWN NAMES

Antiochia	Antioch
Aquae Sulis	Bath
Arelate	Arles
Athenae	Athens
Augusta Treverorum	Trier
Byzantium	Istanbul
Carthago	Carthage
Carthago Nova	Cartagena
Emerita Augusta	Merida
Gades	Cadiz
Hierosolyma	Jerusalem

Londinium	London
Lugdunum	Lyon
Massilia	Marseilles
Neapolis	Naples
Nemausus	Nimes
Pergamum	Bergama
Roma	Rome
Syracusae	Syracuse
Tarraco	Tarragona
Tolosa	Toulouse

Legend:

- Roman territory by 264 B.C. (Outbreak of First Punic War)
- Roman acquisitions 263–201 B.C. (End of Second Punic War)
- Roman acquisitions 200–44 B.C. (Assassination of Caesar)
- Roman acquisitions 43 B.C.–14 A.D. (Death of Augustus)
- Roman acquisitions 15–117 A.D. (Death of Trajan)
- Roman protectorate or temporary acquisition

62 19   Dates B.C.   44 122   Dates A.D.
(Dates of acquisition are in black)

- • Cultural centre, usually having important buildings extant
- *Hannibal* Rebel or enemy of Rome
- Frontier defended by continuous wall
- Frontier defended by line of forts

Kms 0 100 200 300 400 500
Miles 0 100 200 300

Map labels:

HIBERNIA

VALLUM ANTONINI c.142-3
VALLUM HADRIANI c.122-7

MARE GERMANICUM

BRITANNIA 43-50
Boadicea 61
Caractacus 51
Aquae Sulis • Londinium

GERMANIA
Arminius 9
Rhenus
12-9

GALLIA 58-50
Vercingetorix 52
Augusta Treverorum •
Lugdunum • 218-201
Nemausus •
Arelate
Massilia •

HISPANIA 197
Tolosa
Tarraco
Emerita Augusta •
Gades •
19
206
Hannibal

RAETIA 15
NORICUM 15
83
PANNONIA 10
ILLYRICUM 33
DACIA 106
Danubius (Ister)

ITALIA
Ravenna •
Roma • *Spartacus* 73-71
Ostia • Neapolis • Pompeii •
46

CORSICA 238
SARDINIA 238
SICILIA 241
Syracusae •

Carthago • 146

MAURITANIA 40-42

A F R I C A

MARE INTERNUM

THRACIA 46
Byzantium •
MACEDONIA 148
ACHAEA 146
Delphi • Athenae •
CRETA 67

PONTUS EUXINUS

PONTUS 63
BITHYNIA 65
Mithridates 89-66
GALATIA 25
CAPPADOCIA 18
Pergamum • 133
Ephesus •
LYCIA 43
CILICIA 102
Antiochus 192-189
CYPRUS 58

ARMENIA 114-117
Parthians
ASSYRIA 115-117
MESOPOTAMIA 115-117
c. 80-224
Euphrates

SYRIA 64
6,44
Antiochia •
ARABIA 105
Hierosolyma •

AEGYPTUS 30
Cleopatra and Mark Antony 31
Alexandria •
Nilus
MARMARICA 20
CYRENAICA 74

SINUS ARABICUS

Pergamon Press Ltd

114

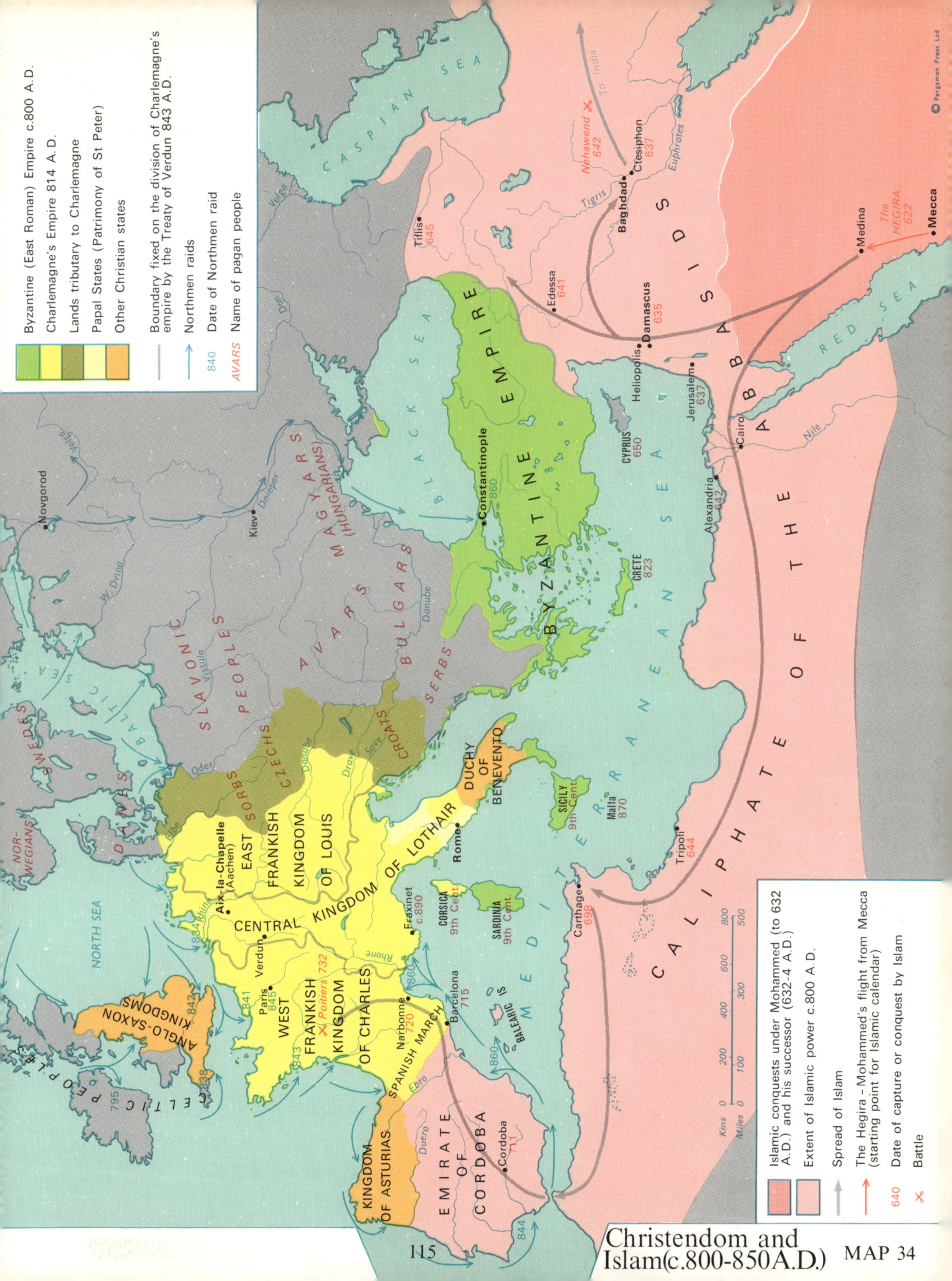

Christendom and Islam (c.800-850 A.D.)   MAP 34

Legend (top left):
- Byzantine (East Roman) Empire c.800 A.D.
- Charlemagne's Empire 814 A.D.
- Lands tributary to Charlemagne
- Papal States (Patrimony of St Peter)
- Other Christian states
- Boundary fixed on the division of Charlemagne's empire by the Treaty of Verdun 843 A.D.
- Northmen raids
- 840 Date of Northmen raid
- AVARS Name of pagan people

Legend (bottom right):
- Islamic conquests under Mohammed (to 632 A.D.) and his successor (632-4 A.D.)
- Extent of Islamic power c.800 A.D.
- Spread of Islam
- The Hegira – Mohammed's flight from Mecca (starting point for Islamic calendar)
- 640 Date of capture or conquest by Islam
- ✕ Battle

Map labels:
CASPIAN SEA, Volga, Don, Dnieper, W. Dvina, Novgorod, Kiev, BLACK SEA, BALTIC SEA, NORTH SEA, Tigris, Euphrates, Nile, RED SEA, MEDITERRANEAN SEA

Nehawend ✕ 642, To India, Ctesiphon 637, Baghdad, The HEGIRA 622, Mecca, Medina, Tiflis 645, Edessa 641, Damascus 635, Heliopolis, Jerusalem 637, CYPRUS 650, Alexandria 642, Cairo, ABBASIDS, CALIPHATE OF THE

BYZANTINE EMPIRE, Constantinople 860, CRETE 823, SICILY 9th Cent., Malta 870, Tripoli 644, Carthage 698, SARDINIA 9th Cent., CORSICA 9th Cent., DUCHY OF BENEVENTO, Rome, Fraxinet c.890

SWEDES, NORWEGIANS, DANES, CELTIC PEOPLES, ANGLO-SAXON KINGDOMS 842, 838, 795, SLAVONIC PEOPLES, MAGYARS (HUNGARIANS), AVARS, BULGARS, SERBS, CROATS, CZECHS, SORBS, Oder, Elbe, Vistula, Danube, Drave, Save

EAST FRANKISH KINGDOM OF LOUIS, CENTRAL KINGDOM OF LOTHAIR, WEST FRANKISH KINGDOM OF CHARLES, Aix-la-Chapelle (Aachen), Verdun 843, Paris 845, 841, ✕ Poitiers 732, Narbonne 720, Barcelona 715, SPANISH MARCH, BALEARIC IS, Rhine, Rhone, 834, 860, 860

EMIRATE OF CORDOBA, Cordoba 711, KINGDOM OF ASTURIAS, Ebro, Duero, 844

Scale: Kms 0 200 400 600 800; Miles 0 100 300 500

© Pergamon Press Ltd

115

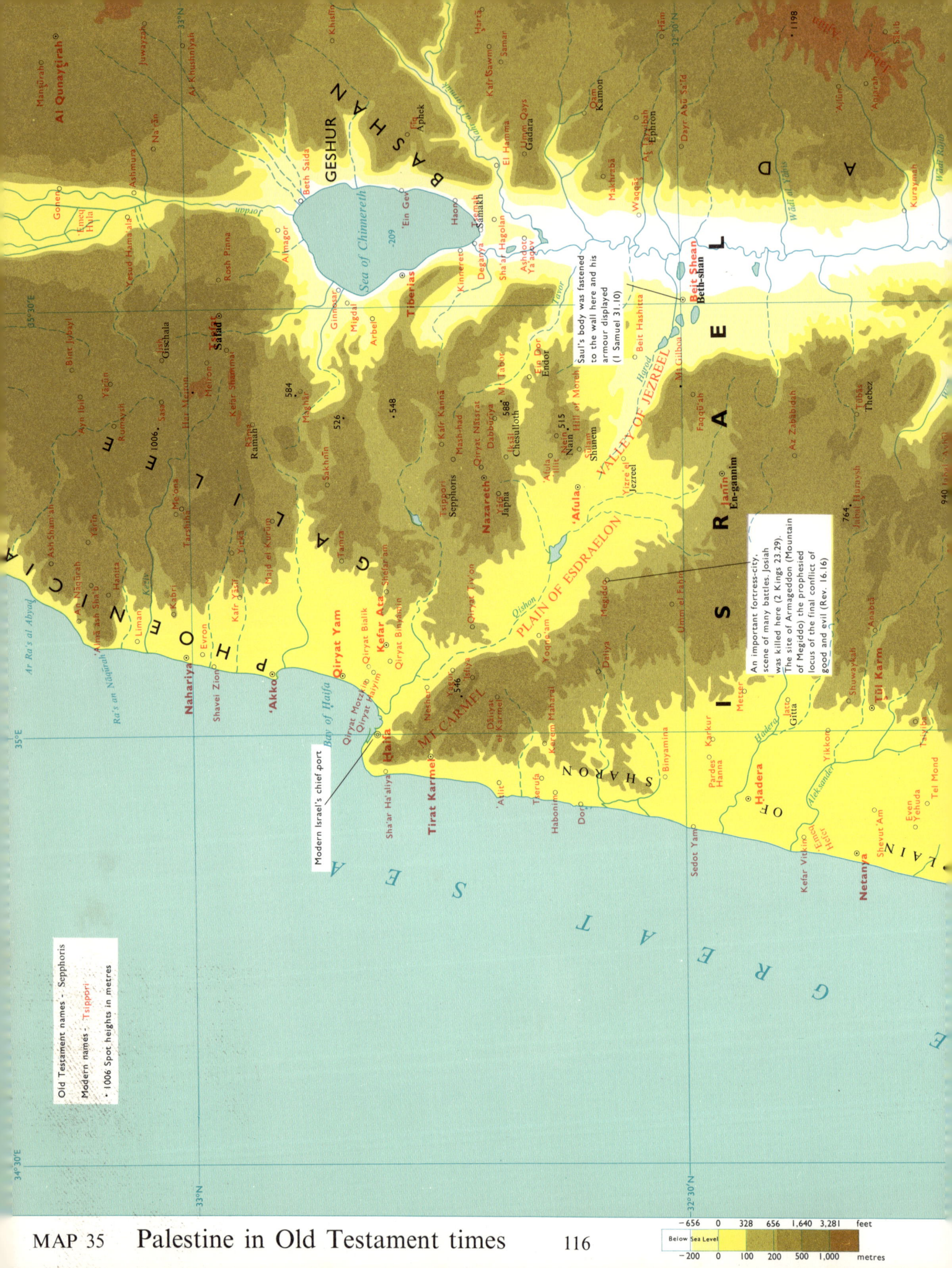

Al Qunayţirah

GESHUR   BASHAN

Beth Saida   Aphek

Sea of Chinnereth   El Hamma   Gadara

-209   Samakh

Tiberias   Haon   Golan   Makhrūbā

Ashdoto Ya'aqov

Safad   Degania   Sha'ar Hagolan   Beit Shean
Beth-shan

584   Saul's body was fastened
to the wall here and his
armour displayed
(1 Samuel 31.10)

526   548   Mt Gilboa

Nazareth   Sepphoris   M. Tabor   End Dor   Endor   Hill of Moreh   588   Shunem   VALLEY OF JEZREEL

515   Nain   Jezreel   En-gannim
Janin   Az Zabadah

PHOENICIA   'Afula   PLAIN OF ESDRAELON   I S R A E L

Nahariya   Qishon   Megiddo   An important fortress-city,
scene of many battles. Josiah
was killed here (2 Kings 23.29).
The site of Armageddon (Mountain
of Megiddo) the prophesied
locus of the final conflict of
good and evil (Rev. 16.16)

'Akko   Qiryat Yam   Kefar Ata   764

546   Tel Karm

Qiryat Motzkin   Hadera   SHARON

Haifa   MT CARMEL

Tirat Karmel   Modern Israel's chief port   Netanya   P L A I N

Sedot Yam

G R E A T   S E A

MAP 35   Palestine in Old Testament times   116

Old Testament names - Sepphoris

Modern names : Tsippori

•1006 Spot heights in metres

-656   0   328   656   1,640   3,281   feet

Below Sea Level

-200   0   100   200   500   1,000   metres

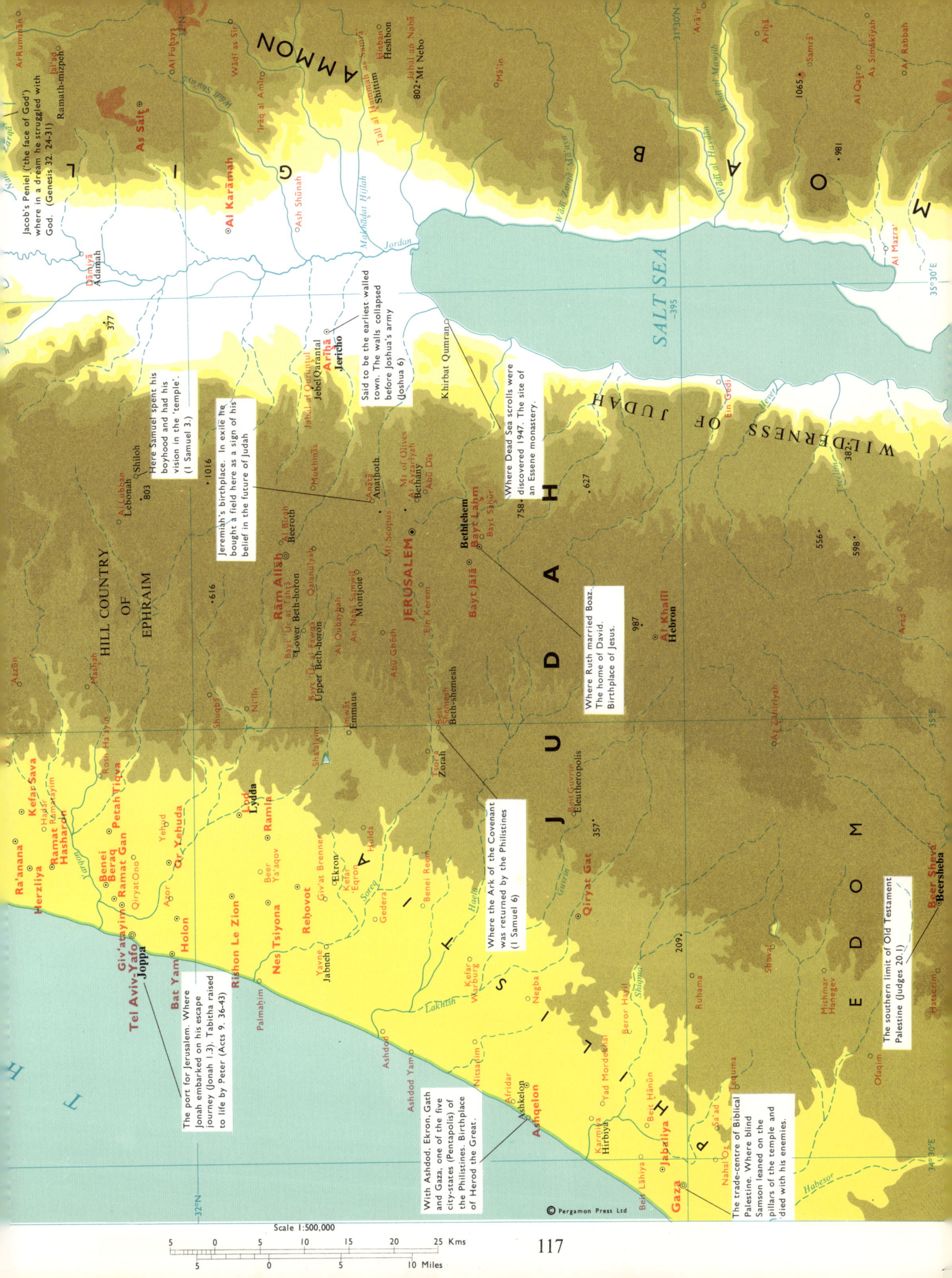

A M M O N

N
O
W
W
A

Jacob's Peniel ('the face of God') where in a dream he struggled with God. (Genesis 32. 24-31)

A'Rummān

Jarāsh

Al Fuḥayṣ

Al Karāmah

Ḥisbān
Heshbon

Wādī as Sir

Wādī Sha'ayb

Ramath-mizpeh

As Salt

'Iraq al Amīr

Ash Shūnah

Ma'īn

Mā'in

Jubail un Naḥā
802 Mt Nebo
Tall al Ḥammā'm as Sauid
Shittim

O
O
B
O
A
M

Wādī al Ḥaidān

Wādī Zarqā Mā'in

Al Qaṣr

As Sinākiyah

1065

186

Al Rabbah

377

Dāmiyā
Adamah

SALT SEA
-395

Jordan

Makhādat Ḥijlah

35°30'E

Al Mazra'

HILL COUNTRY OF EPHRAIM

Al Lubbān
Lebonah

Shiloh
803

Here Samuel spent his boyhood and had his vision in the 'temple'. (1 Samuel 3.)

•1016

Jeremiah's birthplace. In exile he bought a field here as a sign of his belief in the future of Judah

Rām Allāh
Al Bīrah
Beeroth

Qalandiyah

Anata
Anathoth

Mukhmās

An Nabi Samwīl
Montjoie

Mt of Olives
Al 'Azarīyeh
Bethany

Said to be the earliest walled town. The walls collapsed before Joshua's army (Joshua 6)

Jabal Qarantal
Jebel Qarantal
Arīḥā
Jericho

Khirbat Qumran

Where Dead Sea scrolls were discovered 1947. The site of an Essene monastery.

.616

Bayt Ūr al Taḥṭā
Lower Beth-horon

Al Qubaybah

Abū Dīs

Abū Ghōsh

JERUSALEM

Ein Karem

Bayt Ūr al Fawqā
Upper Beth-horon

Shuqbā

Niʿlīn

Bayt 'Anān

Emmaus
'Imwās

Bayt Ṣaḥūr

Bayt Jālā

Bethlehem
Bayt Laḥm

627

W
I
L
D
E
R
N
E
S
S

O
F

J
U
D
A
H

758

Ẓaḥir al Ghar

Ein Gedi

Shaʿfāt

Tor'a

Ṣar'ah
Zorah

Beth-shemesh
'Ein Shemesh

Where the Ark of the Covenant was returned by the Philistines (1 Samuel 6)

Where Ruth married Boaz. The home of David. Birthplace of Jesus.

987
Al Khalīl
Hebron

556

598

382

Arad

Ra'anana
Kefar Sava
Herzliya
Ramat Hasharon
Hijār
Ramat Ramatayim

Rosh Ha'ayin

Azzūn

Maṣḥah

Qiryat Ono

Benei Beraq
Ramat Gan

Or Yehuda

Yaẓūr

Agor

Yarqon

Lod
Lydda

Ramla

Shalqum

Ḥulda

Ḥ

Tel Aviv-Yafo
Joppa
Giv'atayim

Bat Yam

Holon

The port for Jerusalem. Where Jonah embarked on his escape journey (Jonah 1.3). Tabitha raised to life by Peter (Acts 9. 36-43)

Rishon Le Zion

Nes Tsiyona

Rehovot

Giv'at Brenner

Ekron
Kefar
Eqron

Gedera

Beer Ya'aqov

Sorek

I
L
F
I
S
T
I
N
E
S

Beit Guvrin
Eleutheropolis

357

Guvrin

Ḥaela

Qiryat Gat

Lakhīsh

Kefar Warburg

Benei Re'am

209

E
D
O
M

Palmaḥim

Yavne
Jabneh

Ashdod

Ashdod Yam

Nitsanim

Afrīdar

Ashkelon
Ashqelon

With Ashdod, Ekron, Gath and Gaza, one of the five city-states (Pentapolis) of the Philistines. Birthplace of Herod the Great.

Negba

Beit Mordekhai

Yad Mordekhai

Beror Ḥayil

Shuqma

Ruhama

Shovali

Beer Sheva
Beersheba

The southern limit of Old Testament Palestine (Judges 20.1)

Mishmar Hanegev

Aṭ Ẓāhirīyah

31°N

35°E

34°30'E

Beit Lāhiya

Nahal 'Oz

Beit Ḥānūn

Beit Ḥānūn

Sa'ad

Gezuma

Ofaqim

Ḥabesor

Gaza
Jabaliya
Hirbiyah
Karmiya

The trade-centre of Biblical Palestine. Where blind Samson leaned on the pillars of the temple and died with his enemies.

© Pergamon Press Ltd

Scale 1:500,000

5   0   5   10   15   20   25 Kms

5   0   5   10 Miles

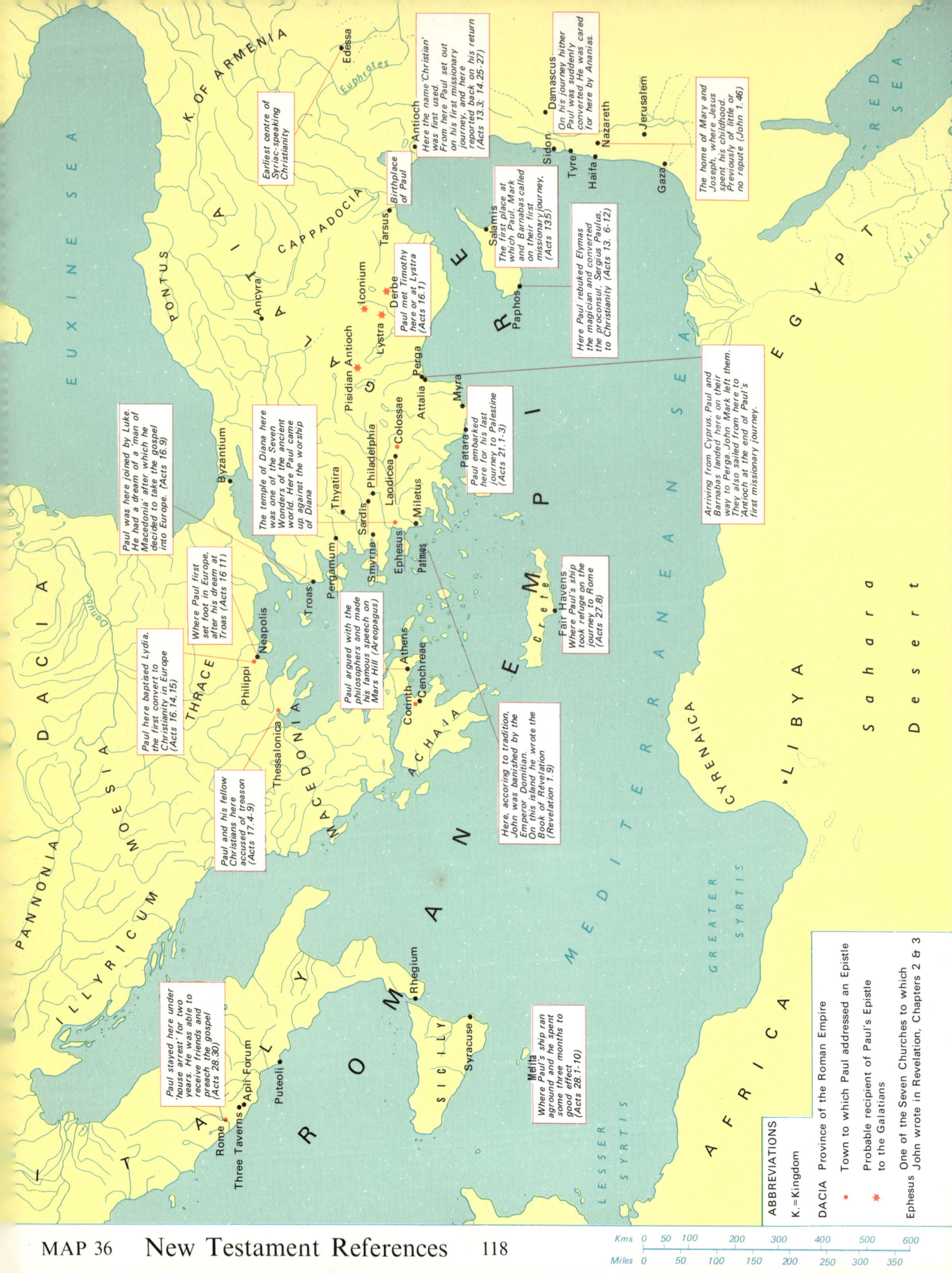

K. OF ARMENIA

Edessa

Euphrates

Earliest centre of Syriac-speaking Christianity

EUXINE SEA

PONTUS

Antioch
Here the name 'Christian' was first used. From here Paul set out on his first missionary journey, and here reported back on his return (Acts 13.3; 14.25-27)

Damascus
On his journey hither Paul was suddenly converted. He was cared for here by Ananias.

Sidon

Tyre

Haifa

Nazareth
The home of Mary and Joseph, where Jesus spent his childhood. Previously of little or no repute (John 1.46)

Jerusalem

Gaza

RED SEA

CAPPADOCIA

Birthplace of Paul

Tarsus

Derbe
Paul met Timothy here or at Lystra (Acts 16.1)

Iconium

Lystra

Salamis
The first place at which Paul Mark and Barnabas called on their first missionary journey. (Acts 13.5)

Ancyra

Pisidian Antioch

GALATIA

Perga

Paphos
Here Paul rebuked Elymas the magician and converted the proconsul, Sergius Paulus, to Christianity (Acts 13. 6-12)

Myra

CYPRUS

Attalia

Patara
Paul embarked here for his last journey to Palestine (Acts 21.1-3)

Arriving from Cyprus, Paul and Barnabas landed here on their way to Perga. John Mark left them. They also sailed from here to Antioch at the end of Paul's first missionary journey.

EGYPT

Nile

Paul was here joined by Luke. He had a dream of a 'man of Macedonia' after which he decided to take the gospel into Europe. (Acts 16.9)

Byzantium

The temple of Diana here was one of the Seven Wonders of the ancient world. Here Paul came up against the worship of Diana

Thyatira

Sardis

Philadelphia

Laodicea

Colossae

Pergamum

Miletus

Smyrna

Ephesus

Patmos

DACIA

Where Paul first set foot in Europe, after his dream at Troas (Acts 16.11)

Troas

MYSIA

THRACE

Neapolis

Paul here baptised Lydia, the first convert to Christianity in Europe (Acts 16.14,15)

Philippi

Paul argued with the philosophers and made his famous speech on Mars Hill (Areopagus)

Athens

Corinth

Cenchreae

MOESIA

Danube

PANNONIA

Paul and his fellow Christians here accused of treason (Acts 17.4-9)

Thessalonica

MACEDONIA

ACHAIA

Here, according to tradition, John was banished by the Emperor Domitian. On this island he wrote the Book of Revelation (Revelation 1.9)

Crete

Fair Havens
Where Paul's ship took refuge on the journey to Rome (Acts 27.8)

MEDITERRANEAN SEA

ILLYRICUM

ITALY

ROMAN

Paul stayed here under 'house arrest' for two years. He was able to receive friends and preach the gospel (Acts 28.30)

Rome

Three Taverns

Appii Forum

Puteoli

Rhegium

SICILY

Syracuse

Melita
Where Paul's ship ran aground and he spent some three months to good effect (Acts 28.1-10)

LIBYA

Sahara Desert

CYRENAICA

GREATER SYRTIS

LESSER SYRTIS

AFRICA

ABBREVIATIONS

K.=Kingdom

DACIA   Province of the Roman Empire

•   Town to which Paul addressed an Epistle

✳   Probable recipient of Paul's Epistle to the Galatians

Ephesus   One of the Seven Churches to which John wrote in Revelation, Chapters 2 & 3

MAP 36   New Testament References   118

Kms 0   50   100   200   300   400   500   600
Miles 0   50   100   150   200   250   300   350

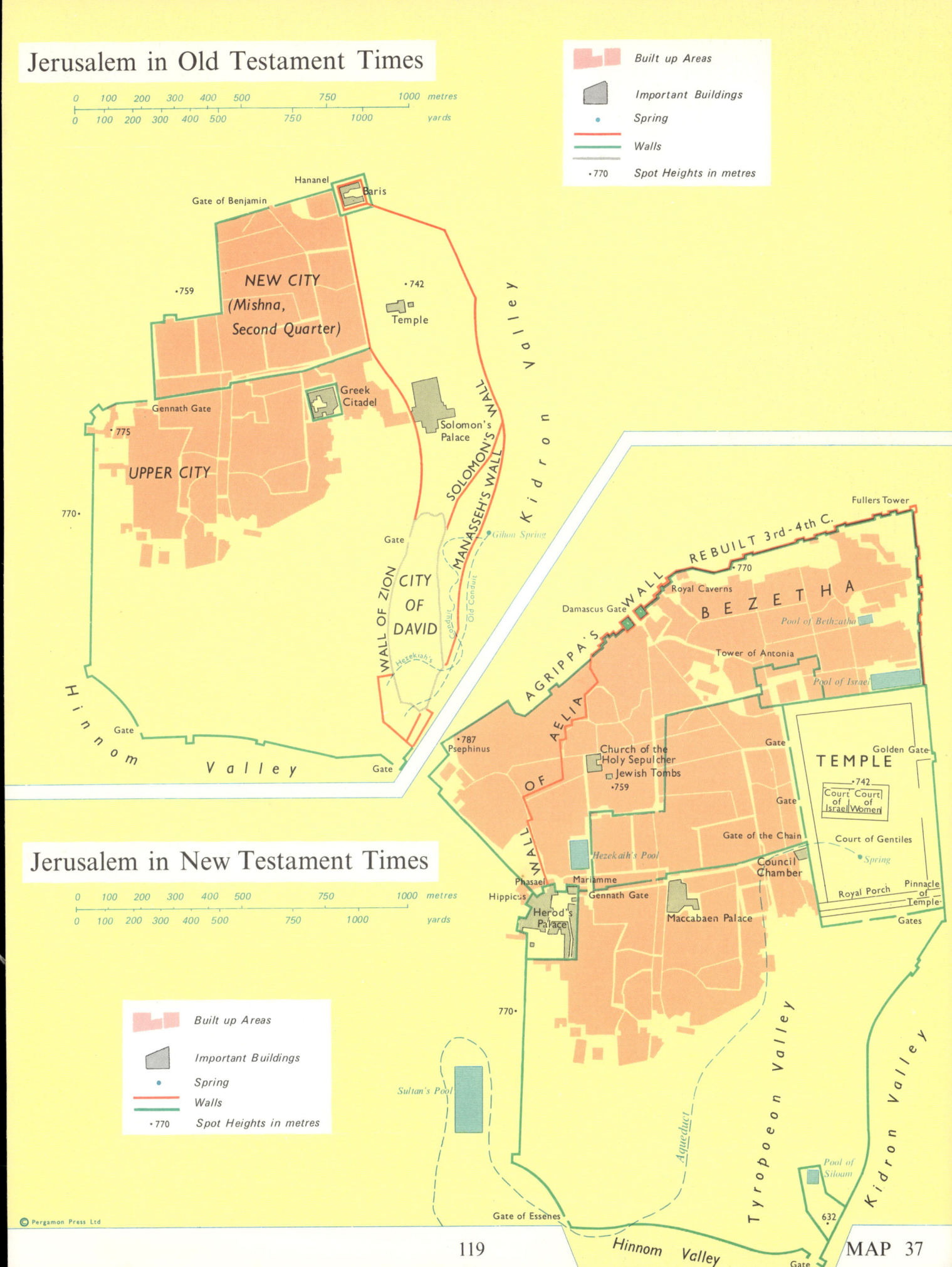

Jerusalem in Old Testament Times

Built up Areas
Important Buildings
• Spring
Walls
•770 Spot Heights in metres

Hananel
Gate of Benjamin
Baris

NEW CITY
(Mishna,
Second Quarter)

•759

•742
Temple

Gennath Gate

Greek
Citadel

•775

UPPER CITY

Solomon's
Palace

770•

SOLOMON'S WALL

MANASSEH'S WALL

Kidron Valley

Gate
Gihon Spring

WALL OF ZION

CITY
OF
DAVID

Old Conduit
conduit
Hezekiah's

Hinnom
Valley

Gate

Gate

Jerusalem in New Testament Times

Fullers Tower

AGRIPPA'S WALL

REBUILT 3rd-4th C.

•770

Royal Caverns

BEZETHA

Pool of Bethzatha

Damascus Gate

Tower of Antonia

Pool of Israel

WALL OF AELIA

•787
Psephinus

Church of the
Holy Sepulcher
Jewish Tombs
•759

Gate

Gate

TEMPLE

•742

Golden Gate

Court
of
Israel

Court
of
Women

Court of Gentiles

Gate of the Chain

Hezekaih's Pool

Council
Chamber

• Spring

Phasael
Hippicus

Mariamme

Gennath Gate

Royal Porch

Pinnacle
of
Temple

Herod's
Palace

Maccabaen Palace

Gates

770•

Built up Areas
Important Buildings
• Spring
Walls
•770 Spot Heights in metres

Sultan's Pool

Aqueduct

Tyropoeon Valley

Pool of
Siloam

Kidron Valley

Gate of Essenes

Hinnom Valley

632•

Gate

MAP 37

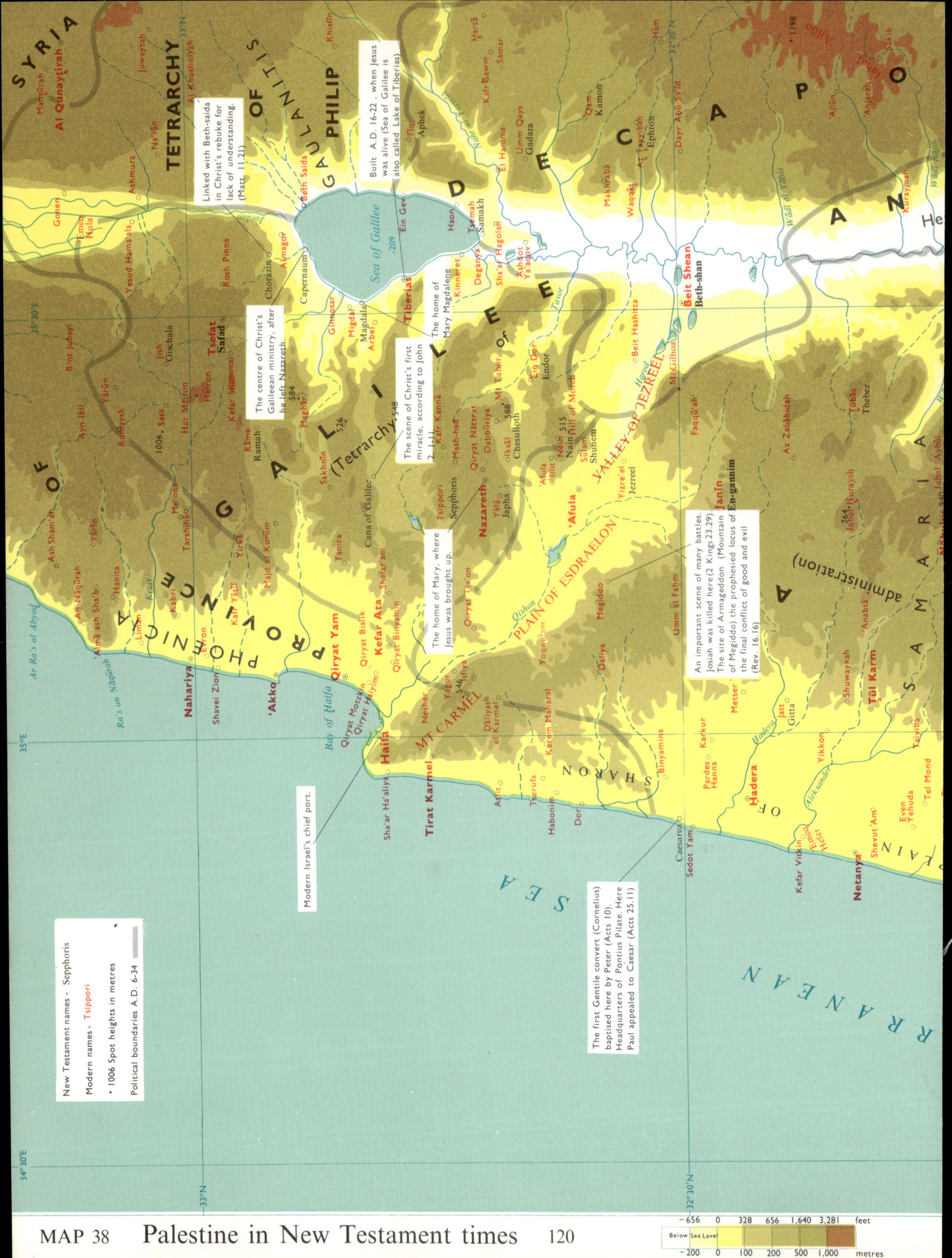

SYRIA

Mangûrah
Al Qunayṭirah

TETRARCHY

OF GAULANITIS

Na'rân

Juwayzah

Al Khushnīyah

Ḥisfīn

Khisfīn

Linked with Beth-saida in Christ's rebuke for lack of understanding. (Matt. 11.21)

Built A.D. 16-22, when Jesus was alive (Sea of Galilee is also called Lake of Tiberias)

PHILIP

Beth Saida

GALILEE

Gohen
Emeq Ḥula

Ashmura

Yesud Hamaʻala

Tel Hai

Na'rân

Jordan

Chorazin

Aïmagor

Capernaum

Sea of Galilee
-209

Ein Gev

Ḥaon

Aphek

Kafr Ṣawm

Umm Qays

Gadara

DECAPOLIS

Fïq

El Hamma
Tsemaḥ
Samakh

Ḥartā

Samar

Ḥām

Ajlûn

1 198

The centre of Christ's Galilean ministry, after he left Nazareth.

Tiberias

The home of Mary Magdalene

Deganya

Sha'a Hagolan

Ashdot Ya'aqov

Beit Shean
Beit-shan

Dayr Abū Saïd

Ephron

Anjarah

He

B'ni Jubayl

Jish

Gischala

Tsefat
Safad

Mefron

Kefar Shammai

Rāma
Ramah

584

Magdala
Arbel

Migdal

Gimosar

526

Kinneret

The scene of Christ's first miracle, according to John 2.1-11.

Kafr Kanna

548

Mash-had
Qiryat Naṣrat Dabbûriya

'Ilksāl

588
Mt Tabor of

Chesulloth

Ein Dor

Endor

Na'ūra

Nain Hill of Moreh

515

Shunem

Tavor

Mt Gilboa

Beit Hashitta

Ḥarod

VALLEY OF JEZREEL

Manaṣrah

Kamont

Qam

As Ṭayyibah

Tûbās

Thebez

(Tetrarchy)

The home of Mary, where Jesus was brought up.

Cana of Galilee

Tamra

Sakhnîn

Shefar'am

Tsippori

Sepphoris

Nazareth

Yāfa
Japha

Qiryat Tiv'on

'Afula
'Ilit

'Afula

Yizre'el
Jezreel

Qishon

Megiddo

PLAIN OF ESDRAELON

Yoqne'am

Umm el Faḥm

An important scene of many battles. Josiah was killed here (2 Kings 23.29). The site of Armageddon (Mountain of Megiddo) the prophesied locus of the final conflict of good and evil (Rev. 16.16)

Janïn

En-gannim

Faqqû'ah

764
Jabal Juraysh

'Anabtā

Az Zabābidah

SAMARIA

Ṭūl Karm

(administration)

OF

PHOENICIA

PROVINCE

SYRIA

Ar Ra's al Abyaḍ

Ash Sham'ah

An Nāqūrah

Ayn Ibil

Ṭarūn

Rumayṣh

1006, Sasa

Ḥār Meiron

Me'ona

Ḥanita

Kabri

Majd el Kurūm

Kefar Yasif

Qiryat Bialik

Qiryat Motzkin

Qiryat Ḥayîm

Qiryat Yam

Kefar Ata

Naharîya

Shavei Zion

'Akko

Nesher

Yagur

546
Shfiya

Daliyat el Karmel

Modern Israel's chief port.

Haifa

Bay of Haifa

MT CARMEL

Tirat Karmel

'Atlit

Sha'ar Ha'aliya

546

Ḥaritīyat

el Karmel

Tserufa

Habonim

Dor

SHARON

Daliya

Kefar Maharal

Karkur

Pardes
Hanna

Binyamina

Metser

Jatt

Gitta

Ḥadera

Hadera

SEA

Caesarea

Sedot Yam

OF

PLAIN

Kefar Vitkin

Emeq
Ḥefer

Yikkon

Aleksander

Ḥadera

Shuwaykah

Ṭaiyîba

'Atara

Tel Mond

Even
Yehuda

Shevut Am

Netanya

The first Gentile convert (Cornelius) baptised here by Peter (Acts 10). Headquarters of Pontius Pilate. Here Paul appealed to Caesar (Acts 25.11)

MEDITERRANEAN

SEA

New Testament names – Sepphoris

Modern names – Tsippori

• 1006 Spot heights in metres

Political boundaries A.D. 6-34

MAP 38   Palestine in New Testament times   120

-656	0	328	656	1,640	3,281		feet
Below Sea Level							
-200	0	100	200	500	1,000		metres

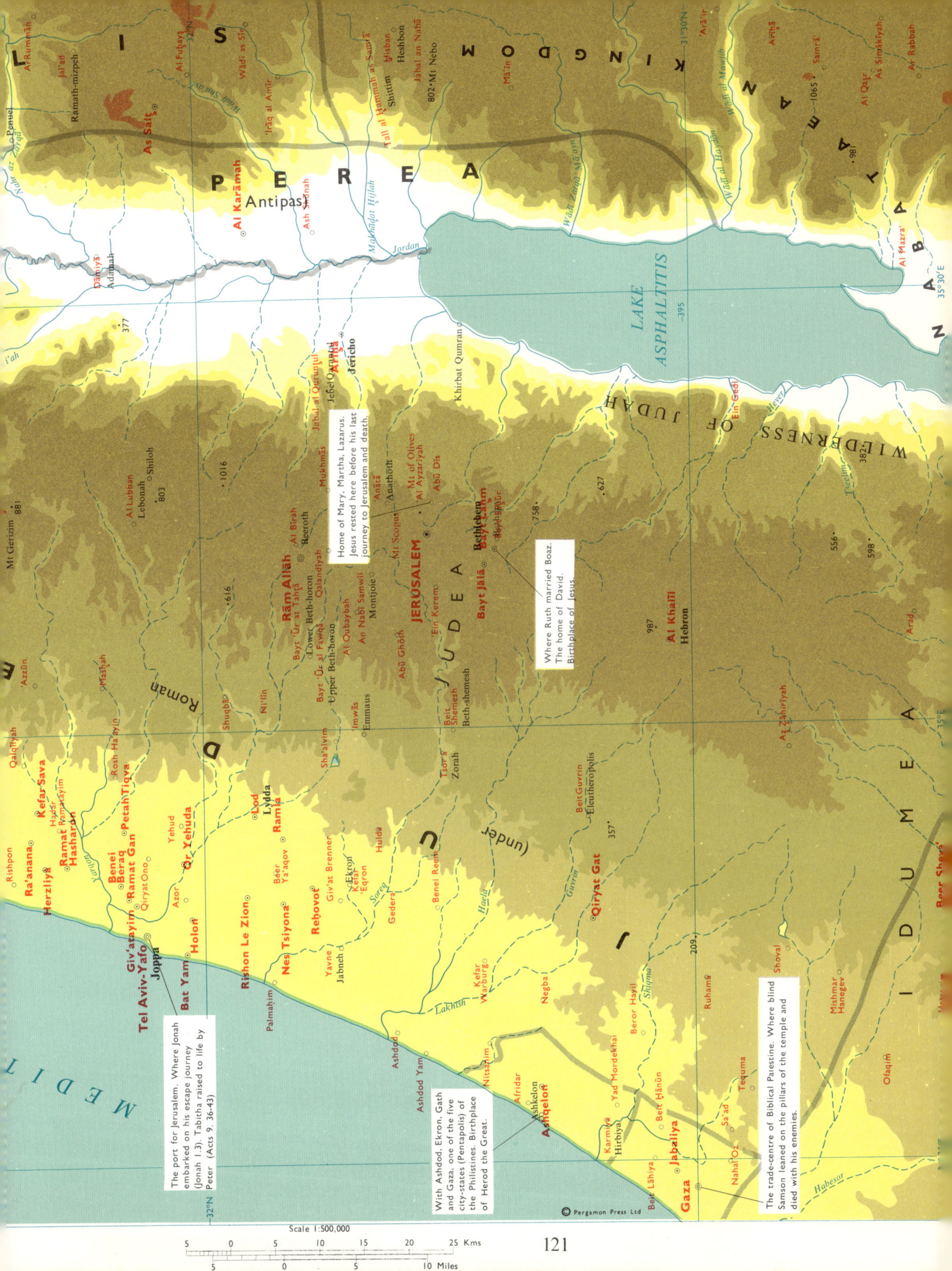

LIS
PEREA
M KINGDOM
TAMA
NABA

Al Fuhays
Jal'ad
Al Kumran
Ramath-mizpeh
Nahr az Zarqa
Penuel
'Iraq al Amir
Wādī ash Shu'ib
Wādī al Amīr
Jabal an Nabī
Hisbān Hesbhon
Tall al Ḥammām as Samrā'
Mā'in
Shittim
802 Mt Nebo
Jabal an Nabī
'Arā'ir
Al Qaṣr
Aṣ Ṣimākīyah
Ar Rabbah
'Aṭārūṣ
1065

As Salṭ
Antipas
Al Karāmah
Ash Jūnah
Mukhādat Ḥijlah
35°30'E

Dāmiya
Adamah
Jordan

LAKE ASPHALTITIS
-395

Al Mazra'
Aṣ Ṣafī

377

Jebel Qarantul
Jabal al Qaruntul
Jericho

Khirbat Qumran

WILDERNESS OF JUDAH
382
Ḥever
Tseelim
'Ein Gedi

1016

Al Lubban
Lebonah
Shiloh
803

Mukhmās
Home of Mary, Martha, Lazarus.
Jesus rested here before his last
journey to Jerusalem and death.
Anāṭā Anathoth
Mt of Olives
'Al Ayzarīyah
Abū Dīs

627

Mt Gerizim
881

616

Rām Allāh
Al Bīrah
Bayt 'Ur at Taḥtā
Beeroth
Qalandiyah
Al Qubaybah
An Nabī Samwīl
Montjoie
Mt Scopus
JERUSALEM
'Ein Kerem
Abū Ghōsh

556
758

Bethlehem
Bayt Jālā
Bayt Saḥūr
Where Ruth married Boaz.
The home of David.
Birthplace of Jesus.

987
Al Khalīl
Hebron
598

JUDEA

Bayt 'Ur al Fawqā
Upper Beth-horon
Sha'alvim
Imwās
Emmaus
Beit
Shemesh
Beth-shemesh

E
Mataḥ
'Azzūn
Shuqbā
Ni'lin

D Roman
A

Az Zāhirīyah

Tsor'a
Zorah

(under)

Arad

Qalqīlyah
Rosh Ha'ayin
Kefar Sava
Petah Tiqva
Ramat
Hasharon
Hadar
Ramatayim
Masḥah

Lod
Lydda
Ramla

Hulda

(under)

Beit Guvrin
Eleutheropolis
357

Beror Ḥayil
Shiqma

Ruhama

Rishon
Rishpon
Ra'anana
Herzliya
Benei Beraq
Ramat Gan
Giv'atayim
Yehud
Qiryat Ono
Azor
Or Yehuda
Bat Yam
Holon

Tel Aviv-Yafo
Joppa

Rishon Le Zion
Be'er Ya'aqov
Nes Tsiyona
Rehovot
Givat Brenner
Ekron
Qeṭah
Eqron
Yavne
Jabneh
Gedera
Benei Reem
Soreq
Shuqbā

Kefar
Warburg
Negba
Qiryat Gat

209

Sa'ad
Shoval

Mishmar
Hanegev

The port for Jerusalem. Where Jonah
embarked on his escape journey
(Jonah 1.3). Tabitha raised to life by
Peter (Acts 9. 36-43).

MEDIT
32°N

Palmaḥim
Yavne
Lakhish
Ashdod
Ashdod
Yam

Nitsanim
Afridar
Ashkelon
Ashqelon

With Ashdod, Ekron, Gath
and Gaza, one of the five
city-states (Pentapolis) of
the Philistines. Birthplace
of Herod the Great.

Yad Mordekhai
Nahal 'Oz

Karmia
Hirbiya
Beit Ḥānūn
Jabaliya
Bet Lāhiya
Gaza
Nahal 'Oz
Sa'ad
Tequma
Ofaqim

IDUMEA

Be'er Sheva

The trade-centre of Biblical Palestine. Where blind
Samson leaned on the pillars of the temple and
died with his enemies.

Huhesor

© Pergamon Press Ltd

Scale 1:500,000

5   0   5   10   15   20   25 Kms

5   0   5   10 Miles

121

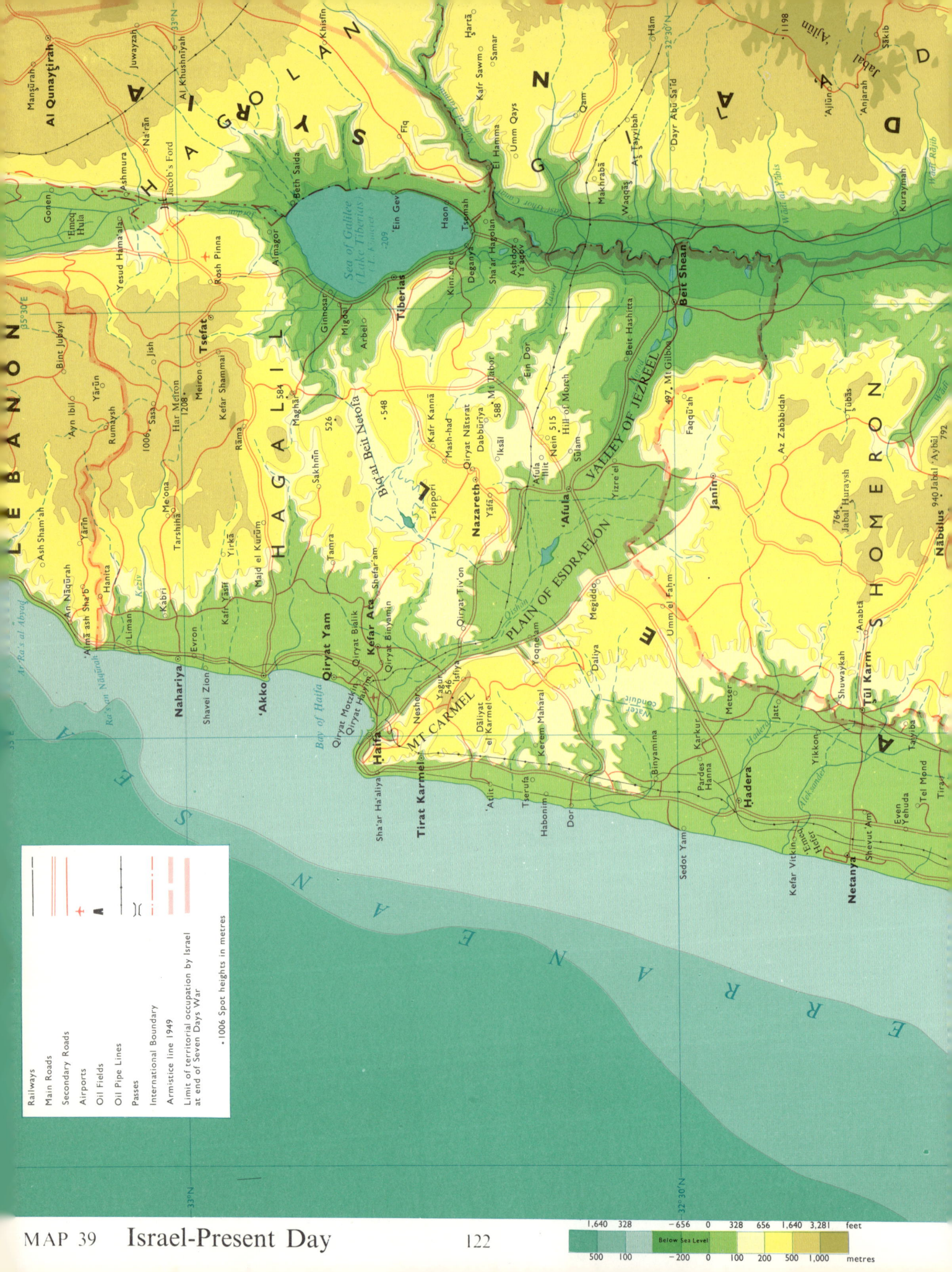

J O L A N

S Y R I A

J O R D A N

N

Na'rān Ashmura Jacob's Ford

Beth Saida

Gonen

Elmeq Hula

Yesud Hama'ala

Rosh Pinna

Almagor

Fiq

Umm Qays Qam El Hamma

At Ṭayyibah

Dayr Abū Sa'īd

'Anjarah

LEBANON

Bint Jubayl

Ayn Ibil Yārūn Rumaysh

Me'ona Sasa Har Meron 1208

Meiron Kefar Shammai

Tsefat

Ginnosar Migdal Arbelo

Sea of Galilee (Lake Tiberias)

'Ein Gev Haon Tsemah

Sha'ar Hagolan

Ein Gev -209

Deganya Kinneret

Ashdot Ya'aqov

Makhrabā Waqqāṣ

Beit Shean

West Ghor Canal

H A G A L I L

584 Maghar 526 Rāma Sakhnin Tamra

Biq'at Beit Netofa 548

Mash-had Qiryat Natsrat 588 Iksāl Nein 515 Hill of Moreh

Kafr Kannā Dabbūrīya Mt Tabor

Ein Dor Sūlam

VALLEY OF JEZREEL 497, Mt Gilboa

Faqqū'ah

Az Zabābidah

Kurraymah

Wādī al-Yābis

N Ā B L U S

S H O M E R O N

Tūbās

Jabal 'Aybāl 940 792

Nābulus

Nazareth Yāfa Afula Illit Yizre'el

'Afula Yoqneam Megiddo

PLAIN OF ESDRAELON

Jānin

Ummel Fahm

Tūl Karm Anabtā

Anjarah

An Nāqūrah

'Almā ash Sha'b

Hanita Liman Kabri Kfar Yasif

Evron Shavei Zion

Naharīya

'Akko

Qiryat Yam Kefar Ata Shefar'am Qiryat Binyamin

Qiryat Motzkin Qiryat Hayim Qiryat Bialik

Haifa Nesher Yagur 546 Isfiya

Bay of Haifa

MT CARMEL

Tirat Karmel Dāliyat el Karmel Kerem Maharal Daliya Dālīyat

Qiryat Tiv'on

Water Conduit

Metser Jatt Shuwaykah

Karkur Pardes Hanna

Ḥadera

Tel Mond

'Afīt Tserufa Habonim Dor Binyamina

Sedot Yam

Emeq Ḥefer Shevut 'Am Yikkon Even Yehuda

Kefar Vitkin

Netanya

Ṭayyiba

Nahal Alexander

Beersheba

M E D I T E R R A N E A N   S E A

MAP 39   Israel–Present Day   122

1,640	328		−656	0	328	656	1,640	3,281	feet
		Below Sea Level							
500	100		−200	0	100	200	500	1,000	metres

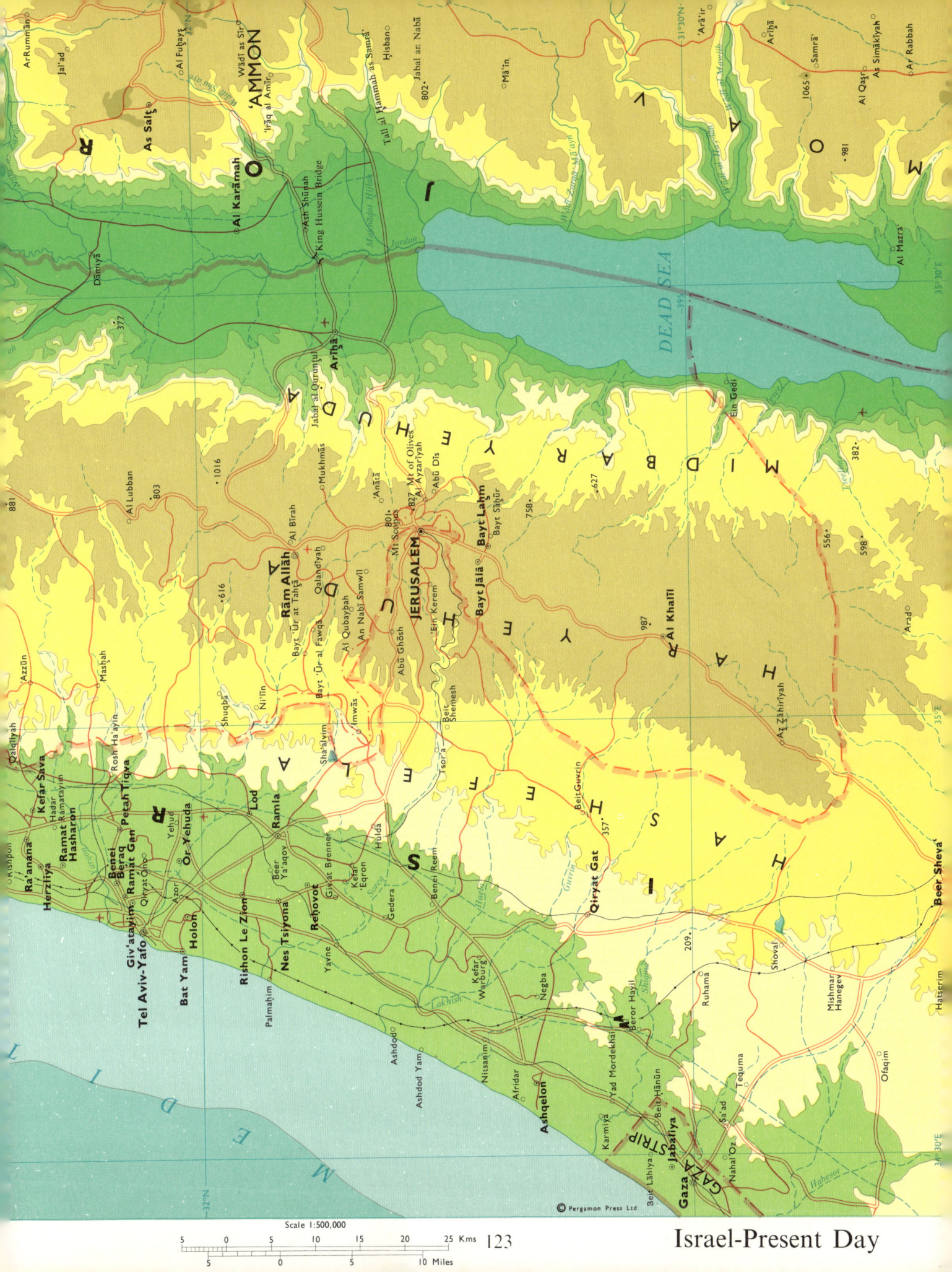

Scale 1:500,000

5   0   5   10   15   20   25 Kms

5   0   5   10 Miles

123

Israel–Present Day

© Pergamon Press Ltd

QUEEN ELIZABETH ISLANDS
BANKS I.
VICTORIA ISLAND
DEVON I.
ELLESMERE ISLAND
BAFFIN ISLAND

49th State 1959
UNITED STATES (ALASKA)

Arctic Circle

Kodiak I.

ALEUTIAN ISLANDS (U.S.A.)

50°N

Queen Charlotte Islands

Vancouver I.

C A N A D A

1945

GREENLAND (Denmark)

Peripheral settlements only

The Hag
Internati
Court o
Justice

ICELAND 1946

Faeroe Is (Denmark)
Shetland Is (U.K.)
Orkney Is

London IMCO

UNITED DENM
1955 1945
IRELAND KINGDOM
1948 BELGIUM
NETHERLANDS

(Westminster) First meeting of UNO

Paris UNESCO

FRANCE
SWITZERLA

U N I T E D
1945
S T A T E S

San Francisco
Agreement on organisation and membership of UNO

Dumbarton Oaks
First discussions of UNO principles

Lake Success
First H.Q. of UNO

Montreal ICAO

Berne UPU

Vienna UNIDO IAEA

Rome FAO

PORTUGAL 1955 SPAIN 1955
Azores (Port.)

GIBRALTAR (U.K.)

SARDI

M E X I C O
1945

Washington D.C.
WORLD BANK
FUND
IDA
IFC

Geneva
UNCTAD
GATT
ILO
WHO
ITU
WMO

Madeira (Port.)

MOROCCO 1956

ALGERIA 1962

SPANISH SAHARA

BERMUDA (U.K.)

New York City
UNITAR
UNICEF
UNRWA
UNHCR
Present H.Q. of UNO

Canary Islands (Sp.)

MAURITANIA 1961

MALI 1960

Tropic of Cancer

HAWAIIAN IS (U.S.A.)
50th State 1959

30°N

Johnston I. (U.S.A.)

BAHAMAS 1945
CUBA
CAYMAN IS (U.K.)
TURKS & CAICOS IS
JAMAICA 1962
HAITI
DOMINICAN REP. 1945

(U.K.)

ANTIGUA
GUADELOUPE (FR.)
DOMINICA
MARTINIQUE (FR.)
ST LUCIA
BARBADOS 1966
GRENADA

Cape Verde Is (Port.)

SENEGAL 1960
GAMBIA 1965
PORT. GUINEA

UPPER VOLTA 1960

GUINEA 1958

TOGO 1960
DAHOMEY 1960

IVORY COAST 1960

GHANA 1957

10°N

GUATEMALA 1945
HONDURAS 1945
EL SALVADOR 1945
NICARAGUA 1945

BRITISH HONDURAS

PUERTO RICO (U.S.A.)

ST VINCENT

SIERRA LEONE 1961

Clipperton I. (Fr.)

COSTA RICA 1945

PANAMA 1947

VENEZUELA 1945

TRINIDAD & TOBAGO 1962

Revilla Gigedo Is (Mexico)

Cocos I. (Costa Rica)

Malpelo I. (Col.)

NETH. VER. GUIANA

Palmyra I. (U.S.A.)

Christmas I. (U.K.)

Equator

COLOMBIA 1945

Galapagos Is (Ecuador)

St Peter & St Paul Rocks (Braz.)

EQUATOR 1968 GUI
São Tomé & Principe Is (Port.)
Annobón (Sp.)

CA (to

Equator

130°W

110°W

Jarvis I. (U.S.A.)

LINE ISLANDS (U.K.)

ECUADOR 1945

70°W

50°W

10°W

P E R U
1945

B R A Z I L
1945

Rocas I. Fernando de Noronha I. (Braz.)

Marquesas Is

FRENCH
TUAMOTU ARCH.
POLYNESIA
Society Is

Cook Is

Tubuai Is

BOLIVIA 1945

Ascension I. (U.K.)

St Helena (U.K.)

COOK IS (N.Z.)

PITCAIRN (U.K.)
Pitcairn I.

Tropic of Capricorn

Desventurados Is (Chile)

PARAGUAY 1945

Trindade (Braz.)

WAL (Rep

T

Easter I. (Chile)

URUGUAY 1945

Tristan da Cunha Group (U.K.)

A R G E N T I N A
1945

C H I L E
1945

Juan Fernández Is (Chile)

Gough (U.K.)

30°S

Chiloé I. (Chile)

FALKLAND IS (U.K.)

South Georgia (U.K.)

Bouvet I. (Nor.)

Tierra del Fuego

50°S

South Sandwich Is (U.K.)

South Shetland Is

South Orkney Is

All territorial claims suspended in 1961 and

70°S

ANTARCTIC PENINSULA

Antarctic Circle

West of Greenwich QUEEN MA

	Founder member showing area in 1945	⊙	Centres involved in early development of UN
	New member, showing area on admission	⊙	Agency Headquarters
	U.N. Trust Territory	▲	Dispute involving UNO
	Dependencies or Overseas Provinces	———	International Boundaries

MAP 40   United Nations Organization   124

MAJOR NON-MEMBER STATES 1968

Switzerland
China (Mainland)
Germany (East & West)
Korea (North & South)
Muscat & Oman
Vietnam(North & South)

Scale 1:80,000,000

1000   0   1000   2000   3000 Kms

1000   500   0   1000 Miles

Landmarks in the Development

MAP 41 of the World Council of Churches

© Pergamon Press Ltd

Meeting places of the International Missionary Council Assemblies or the D.W.M.E. (Division of World Mission and Evangelism)

oikoumene

The World Council of Churches symbol is based on the Christian image of the Church as a ship afloat on the sea of the world. The symbol carries the word **oikumene** which describes the whole inhabited earth and its circular form represents the wholeness of the Church's mission to the entire world.

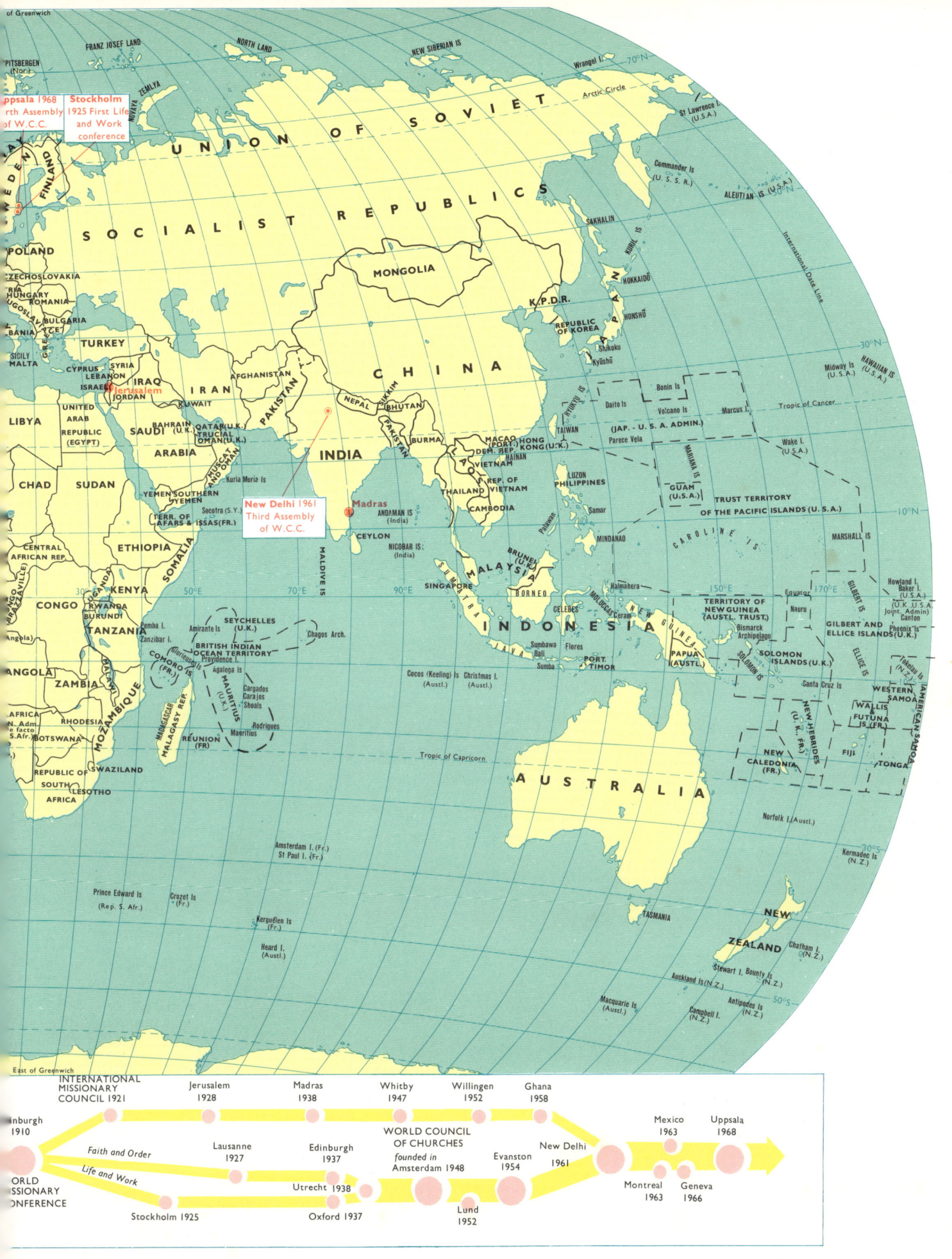

UNION OF SOVIET

SOCIALIST REPUBLICS